# Managing ESL Programs in Rural and Small Urban Schools

Barney Bérubé

TESOL Teachers of English to Speakers of Other Languages, Inc.

Typeset in Janson Text, with Berkeley display
by Capitol Communications Systems, Inc., Crofton, Maryland USA
Printed by Pantagraph Printing, Bloomington, Illinois USA
Indexed by Couglin Indexing Services, Inc., Annapolis, Maryland USA

Teachers of English to Speakers of Other Languages, Inc.
700 South Washington Street, Suite 200
Alexandria, Virginia 22314 USA
Tel. 703-836-0774 • Fax 703-836-7864 • E-mail tesol@tesol.org •
http://www.tesol.org/

Director of Communications and Marketing: Helen Kornblum
Managing Editor: Marilyn Kupetz
Copy Editor: Marcella Fecteau Weiner
Cover Design: Charles Akins

ISBN 0-939791-91-9
Library of Congress Catalogue No. 00-134901

*Pour Kyra et Chantal*

# Contents

# Preface

Overseeing English as a second language (ESL) instruction can be a lonely profession. Those who provide ESL services in U.S. rural and small urban communities are often quick to amplify sentiments of their insularity. *Managing ESL Programs in Rural and Small Urban Schools* was written in part to comfort that audience. The phrase *ESL program manager* is used liberally in this volume not so much as a titular position as a day-to-day reality.

Who is this ESL manager? At the outset, it is likely to be the school district's person assigned to all or some of the following eight responsibilities:

1. developing ESL policy for the district
2. implementing ESL policy and practices for the district
3. developing ESL curriculum
4. developing ESL assessments
5. serving as the parent liaison for the ESL program
6. coordinating ESL activity in collaboration with regular content-area teachers, guidance counselors, and other staff as needed
7. supervising a small ESL staff, if there is any
8. teaching ESL to a few students of limited English proficiency at the K–12 level

There may be other tasks as well. Overall, however, the ESL manager's goal is to guide colleagues as they guide children whose first or native language is not English toward an equitable, quality education conducted in their new language.

The ESL manager may, in fact, not be credentialed in the ESL field. Perhaps the ESL manager is the lead manager for other non-ESL functions districtwide, such as curriculum or special services. The ESL manager could be, perhaps by default, a principal who oversees an ESL teacher or tutor in one or more buildings as may occur in small urban schools that enroll fewer than 10,000 students. In short, the ESL manager includes those who find any of the above eight descriptors as applying to them. Whether it be for the ESL novice or the seasoned manager, this book is an educator's guide to helping rural and small urban schools deliver quality ESL programs tailored to the needs of the small number of limited English proficient (LEP) students enrolled across any combination of grade levels.

*Managing ESL Programs in Rural and Small Urban Schools* might not have had to be written until now. Harking back to my earlier years in ESL training and program development for scores of rural schools, the changes of the past 20 years have been astonishing. For example, between the last two decennial U.S. Census years (1980–1990), the United States experienced an increase of more than a half million students of limited English proficiency enrolling in its schools. Today, more than 5% of school-age youth in the United States are LEP. Those demographic reality checks appear in the book's first chapter.

In the 1970s, ESL program quality issues were hardly challenged. Then came the *Casteñada v. Pickard* court decision of 1981, which ruled that schools must be held accountable for programs grounded in sound research. So, too, came added security for LEP students through strengthened instructional policy when, in 1991, the U.S. Supreme Court commissioned the Office for Civil Rights to craft an enforcement policy for schools that enroll such students—a benefit particularly enjoyed today by LEP students living in rural communities. These and other case law and statutory initiatives are discussed in chapter 2.

In the 1970s and 1980s, the standard for curriculum for LEP students (if there was any) was of a scope and sequence design and rarely applied to LEP students, who had their own isolated program. Besides, there was virtually no national attention given to standards for all children until the early 1990s with the advent of the National Education Goals and Goals 2000. Now it befalls the ESL program manager to assume leadership with colleagues to ensure that children can equitably access a sound education conducted in their new language.

Enter the millennium. With federal pressure and funds to support standards, every state now has standards-driven curriculum for ESL instruction (described in chapter 4) within those standards. The ESL standards developed by TESOL (1997) enhanced the debate and current practice.

Unlike in the early 1970s, when ESL program accountability was a marginal issue for rural schools, licensures and professional development for ESL exist in nearly every state today. These are discussed in detail in chapter 5. Student and program assessments were once largely psychometric in design and more accountable to short-term student performance than to improved instruction; now, authentic assessment cultures pervade the ESL rural landscapes as they do in urban areas.

As suggested in chapter 9, resources abound today for everyone connected to the ESL profession, whether in rural or urban communities. That was, of course, not the case a mere decade ago, particularly regarding the newer technologies now available to us. Those are some of the immediate realities of the changing resources in the United States that make *Managing ESL Programs in Rural and Small Urban Schools* a particularly relevant guide for the next decade. Telephone numbers and Web site addresses appear generously in this chapter and throughout the text.

The volume concludes with a glossary and a list of acronyms commonly used in the ESL profession. The glossary provides detailed definitions of terms often used in the ESL field. The list of acronyms enables the reader to have a quick reference to unfamiliar terms.

It was not only the many years of work in rural schools that inspired me to write this book but also the many professional colleagues whose expertise, support, and friendship made my presence in the ESL profession so much richer. For example, I have enjoyed generous consultative support in advising schools on civil rights protections for students, thanks to Boston Regional Office for Civil Rights former director Marc Brenman. Luis Catarineau, a longtime friend at the U.S. Department of Education who works with state education agencies, has guided me through many years of Title VII of the Improving America's Schools Act (IASA) on many, many occasions. Jane Yedlin and Bob Parker, Brown University's experts in the ESL field, are household names across Maine for their insights into best practice and so, too, are Carolyn Vincent and Susan Reichman, whose guidance in the assessment arena has perfected the accountability of countless programs across the state.

Many valued colleagues at the Maine Department of Education have contributed their wisdom, skills, and knowledge, which I have applied liberally throughout the book. They include Pamela Gatcomb, John Kierstead, Mona Baker, Dennis Kunces, Kathryn Manning, Horace "Brud" Maxcy, Heidi McGinley, Susan Parks, and the late Leigh Phillips.

Several of Maine's ESL teachers, the tried and true practitioners in our rural schools, deeply inspired the crafting of this book. Among them: Gil Albert of Fort Kent, Linda Ward of Kennebunk, Elizabeth Bartlett of Brunswick,

Charlotte Jones of Sanford, Pat Mayo of Hampden, Sandi Crites of Turner, Robin Fleck of Auburn, Nancy Kelly of Augusta, Ruth Taylor of South Portland, Grayce Studley of Nobleboro, and Grace Valenzuela and Val Hart of Peak's Island.

For the initial technical processing of the manuscript, I am deeply indebted to Sandy St. Michael, whose patience and understanding never wavered. Thanks are very much in order for Kathleen Graves, the chair of TESOL's Publications Committee; members of the Publications Committee and outside reviewers who found it worthy to publish; and Marilyn Kupetz, TESOL's managing editor. And although I thought I had crafted an untouchable manuscript, I wish to especially acknowledge my copy editor, Marcella Weiner. The meticulous and professional attention Marcella has given to the details of the manuscript is evident from the introductory pages to the last reference entry. Every reader of this book will benefit from her skills, knowledge, and unwavering attention to accuracy.

From Mt. Ararat High School at Topsham, Maine, home to one of Maine's preeminent ESL teachers, Peggy Callahan provided comments and editing of the manuscript that greatly enhanced the presentation of the text.

Enter the gentle guru, the understanding Goliath for ESL in Maine: Donald L. Bouchard. Don has collaborated with me on ESL projects too numerous to list, including university training events, curriculum and materials development, ongoing technical assistance, and, indeed, advisement on this book for which I am honored to have him present the foreword. More than all of this, Don is my valued friend.

Barney Bérubé
Augusta, Maine

# Foreword

The population of school-age students in the United States for whom English is their new language, as well as foreign-born students requiring English as second language (ESL) services, has traditionally congregated in the larger urban areas. As the demographics outlined in chapter 1 of this volume suggest, this no longer appears to be the case. The ESL population at the K–12 level has rippled into the smaller school districts, including small urban schools, in every state, and this is a trend that will likely continue into the foreseeable future. As a result, many educators are experiencing the academic and sociocultural challenges of working for the first time with students for whom English is a developing other language. They are being confronted with the challenge of providing services to a population of students for whom they have little or no familiarity, both in terms of delivering these services equitably and in terms of providing methodology based on sound research. In this context, *Managing ESL Programs in Rural and Small Urban Schools* is extremely relevant. As an ESL professional working with Maine's rural schools for several years, Dr. Bérubé is well poised, in this volume, to provide the theoretical and practical information found in its chapters. He presents an abundance of data to substantiate the rationale for, as well as the statutory requirements of, providing a quality ESL program for one or more students of limited English proficiency in rural schools. This volume accurately describes how a program of services can fit into the standards movement, regardless of locale, along with the personnel needed to adequately staff delivery of such services. Most importantly, perhaps, this volume contains a plethora of suggestions for instruction, student assessment, program evaluation, parent and community involvement, and multimedia resources for the education of the second language population in low-density communities. One caveat with regard to this text: Chapter 2 provides a critically important regulatory rationale for the focus of this volume; it is consequently dense with background statutory information. The reader will find this chapter, on the one hand, to be an excellent reference in defending the legality of certain ESL practices and policies. On the other hand, this chapter is probably the only one in the text that may rest in isolation from the others because it is not dependent on following the kind of topical sequence the other chapters appear to require.

This volume is for both the educator being introduced to the population of LEP students for the first time and the ESL professional who wishes to have a resource for advising colleagues about relevant, state-of-the-art practice. The reference to an *ESL manager* is used for the first time in this guide. This reflects Dr. Bérubé's accurate prefatory description of educators in low-density ESL populated areas whose varied responsibilities are both administrative and classroom based.

A quality ESL program is predicated on a state-of-the art pedagogical appr ach and a comprehensive administrative plan. *Managing ESL Programs in Rural and Small Urban Schools* blends best practices in language acquisition, methodology, and assessment with a thorough grounding in implementing these practices in a rural landscape. The importance of comprehending the components of program delivery in classroom, school, and community settings cannot be underestimated. Dr. Bérubé is to be commended for having assembled the ingredients in this eminently practical and timely guide for the ESL educator in rural and small urban schools.

Donald L. Bouchard
Literacy Education/ESL
University of Southern Maine

# Chapter 1
# Pressing the Numbers

*It is easier to live with the plurality between persons than within them.*
—Sandel, 1996, p. 349

## The Changing Faces of Our Towns

**W**elcome to the joys and challenges of teaching students whose primary or home language is other than English. In our continuously shrinking planet, those students are indeed among the universe's 91% who speak one among more than 200 of the world's non-English languages. Language minority students, those who speak a language other than English (and who are growing in number in the United States), enrich their communities and classrooms with their diverse cultural heritages. Many of these students enter U.S. schools with little or no English proficiency. The need to better understand this population is compelling as schools seek to determine appropriate and effective methods for including these students within challenging instructional environments. A reasonable first step may be to have an awareness and appreciation of the impact that rural and small urban schools are now experiencing as suggested by the demographics.

U.S. Census data reveal that the growth in student enrollments is greatest among minorities (U.S. Department of Commerce, 1990). For example, the student population of Asian/Pacific Islanders grew by 70%, the Latino school population was up by 54%, followed by Native Americans at 29% and African Americans at 13%. The least population growth occurred among

1

Whites at 5%. Indeed, rural and small urban communities in the United States will need to plan on school settings more reflective of their colors and languages. U.S. Census projections suggest that at least one third of the U.S. population will be speakers of English as a second language (ESL) by the time the results of the 2000 U.S. Census appear. Nearly one half of those non-English speakers will be limited in their comfort with the English language.

Although there is some controversy about the actual number of K–12 students who are not fluent in English, one finding is certain: There is a 3–10% annual growth rate of those student enrollments. U.S. Census data for 1980–1990 indicate that decade's growth of 518,329 such students. State departments of education, by contrast, report an 8-year (1989–1997) growth rate of 1,421,622 students nationally (Macías, 1998b)—more than double that of 1980–1990. In addition, in 1993, those state education departments reported that 7% of the children in U.S. schools were not fluent in English. In 1980, the U.S. Department of Education reported that there were 1,752,000 K–12 students not fluent in English. Seventeen years later, that number rose to 3,452,073. The National Clearinghouse for Bilingual Education (1999) projects that this number will rise to 4,148,997 in 2000—an increase of 13.4% from 1990.

Table 1.1 describes the results of a national mail survey conducted by Development Associates, Inc., of Virginia of 745 school districts of non-English-fluent student enrollments by grade. That descriptive study demonstrates a trend that the ESL program manager would be advised to examine closely: The highest increase in number as well as in percentage of students in the United States is of those who are not fluent in English, and these students are enrolled at the earliest grades (60% from K–5). In short, these students will be in our schools for the proverbial long haul without an anticipated decrease in their numbers.

# Defining Limited English Proficiency

What is the measure for defining limited proficiency with the English language for students whose native (or heritage or primary) language is not English? Measures used by the U.S. Census as well as state and federal departments of education for defining limited English proficiency are inconsistent. In its long-form questionnaire, the U.S. Census simply asked respondents to answer a multiple-choice question that revealed how well children ages 5–17 speak English (U.S. Department of Commerce, 1990). State and federal education

**Table 1.1**   Number of Non-English-Fluent Students
in the United States

| Grade Level | Number of Non-English-Fluent Students | Total Students in the United States | Total Percentage of Non-English-Fluent Students |
|---|---|---|---|
| Kindergarten | 277,914 | 3,305,619 | 8.4% |
| 1st Grade | 279,257 | 3,554,274 | 7.9% |
| 2nd Grade | 246,979 | 3,359,193 | 7.4% |
| 3rd Grade | 221,936 | 3,333,285 | 6.7% |
| 4th Grade | 197,211 | 3,312,443 | 6.0% |
| 5th Grade | 177,412 | 3,268,381 | 5.4% |
| 6th Grade | 150,421 | 3,238,095 | 4.6% |
| 7th Grade | 134,907 | 3,108,120 | 4.6% |
| 8th Grade | 125,849 | 3,019,826 | 4.2% |
| 9th Grade | 159,208 | 3,310,290 | 4.8% |
| 10th Grade | 137,101 | 2,913,951 | 4.7% |
| 11th Grade | 103,337 | 2,642,554 | 3.9% |
| 12th Grade | 75,423 | 2,390,329 | 3.2% |
| Ungraded | 16,469 | —— | —— |
| Total | 2,303,424 | 40,756,360 | 5.5% |

*Note.* From *Descriptive Study of Services to Limited English Proficient Students: Volume 1, Summary of Findings and Conclusions*, (p. 7), by H. L. Fleischman and P. J. Hopstock, 1993, Arlington, VA: Development Associates, Inc. Adapted with permission.

agencies and most schools use the term limited English proficient (LEP). A definition of limited English proficiency appears in most education legislation and, notably, in the Improving America's Schools Act (IASA) of 1994:

Limited English proficiency and limited English proficient. The terms "limited English proficiency" and "limited English proficient," when used with reference to an individual, mean an individual—

(A) who—(i) was not born in the United States or whose native language is a language other than English and comes from an environment where a language other than English is dominant; or (ii) is a Native American or Alaska Native or who is a native resident of the outlying areas and comes from an environment where a language other than English has had a significant impact on such individual's level of English language proficiency; or (iii) is migratory and whose native language is other than English and comes from an environment where a language other than English is dominant; and

(B) who has sufficient difficulty speaking, reading, writing, or understanding the English language and whose difficulties may deny such individual the opportunity to learn successfully in classrooms where the language of instruction is English or to participate fully in our society. (§ 7501(8)(A)–(B))

A general consensus from ESL professionals is that an LEP student is one who comes from a non-English language background and whose language skills limit his or her ability to function successfully in an all-English classroom. What remain at issue are the following questions:

- What means of English communication (speaking, listening, reading, and writing) and specific skills within those modes need to be considered in determining LEP status?
- What levels of English language skills are sufficient for one not to be described as LEP?
- Are there some students who should always be considered LEP because they sustain a low level of English proficiency (i.e., they are unlikely to score above a certain level on a standardized achievement test)?

The designation of limited English proficiency incorporates a range of common references used to describe students as they move toward ultimate fluency in English. These references include non-English proficient (NEP), limited English-speaking ability (LESA), transitionally English proficient (TEP), and fully English proficient (FEP).

In some communities, students who enter school speaking a language other than English are simply called ESL students instead of LEP students. Some argue that the "limited" in *limited English proficient* implies that these students have a deficit; therefore, educators and administrators in the ESL profession have opted for the more neutral terms such as *English language learners* or *potentially English proficient* or even *language minority student* (which does not by itself suggest a level of English proficiency). For those who argue that second languages are acquired not learned, *English language learner* does not fit. Furthermore, anglophone children are, in fact, English language learners as they endure 13 years of English learning before graduation. *Potentially English proficient* has a welcoming ring to it but has never won sufficient acceptance as the better reference. The "potential" in this label does in effect point to a student's temporary language limitation or deficit. The other label, *language minority students*, is an umbrella from which LEP students are drawn. So, what is the better reference?

*Limited English proficient* remains the clinically universal reference for now. The meaning of limited English proficiency is clear, though some persist in noting that the label is an unneeded barrier confronting language minority students. Collier (1995a), a scholar from George Mason University, says that the children are not limited; rather, they are not tooled in the standard language (English) used in schools. The learner's heritage language is complex and obviously has a comprehensive grammar and vocabulary system. For this writer, limited English proficiency, the clearer phrase, is used in this volume for convenience of its current universality if not for its connotative accuracy and shortcomings.

Ascertaining limited English proficiency with reliable measures is beyond the scope of this discussion because practices vary widely. Securing statistical data that might compare LEP populations across communities would appear to be a largely limited exercise. For example, state departments of education nationwide operationalized the limited English proficiency determination through a variety of methods as shown in Table 1.2. More recent data are released annually by the U.S. Department of Education. During the 1996–1997 school year, 49 states reported at least one language proficiency test as their measure of limited English proficiency. The Language Assessment Scales, the IDEA Language Proficiency Test, and the Language Assessment Battery were most commonly reported across as the language proficiency instruments they used (Macías, 1998a). (See Table 7.2 in chapter 7.) Hence, the range of subjective strategies used in determining limited English proficiency across the United States forces one to remain cautious about the numbers.

## Staffing Our Schools for Changing Demographics and Changing Needs

For most teachers in the United States, their university training regimen at the undergraduate level did not include issues of cultural diversity, especially for those teachers working in rural education environments. According to the 1990 U.S. Census, one out of every six teachers in the United States is at least

**Table 1.2**   Methods Reported by State Departments of Education for Identifying Limited English Proficient Students (1996–1997)

| Rank | Method | Number of States Reporting This Method |
|:---:|---|:---:|
| 1 | Home Language Survey | 46 |
| 2 | Language Proficiency Test | 45 |
| 3 | Parent Information | 38 |
| 4 | Teacher Observations; Student Records | 40 |
| 5 | Achievement Test | 36 |
| 6 | Teacher Interview | 31 |
| 7 | Referral | 34 |
| 8 | Student Grades | 34 |
| 9 | Informal Assessment | 34 |
| 10 | Criterion Referenced Test | 20 |

*Note.* From *Summary Report of the Survey of the States' Limited English Proficient Students and Available Educational Programs and Services, 1996–97* (Table A-6), by R. Macías, 1998, Washington, DC: National Clearinghouse for Bilingual Education. Reprinted with permission.

a 25-year veteran of the teaching profession whose classroom preparation may be reasonably described as more fitting to the bygone era of the 1960s suburbia. Data released by Stowe (1993) provide compelling cause for educators and prospective teachers to rethink their roles with regard to the consumers of knowledge they serve or will serve:

- At least 93% of first-year teachers are Caucasian.
- A mere 14% of new teachers will seek work in culturally diverse schools.
- The average classroom experience for teachers is 17 years.

Table 1.3 describes minority profiles according to the positions of influence that each one (i.e., superintendents, board members, elected officials, and teachers) wields in setting local education policy. The data suggest that the demographics of empowerment do not align well with the reality of the students served. Particularly evident is the gap between race-minority students and their representation in the education profession.

Teacher preparation must take into account the high likelihood that educators, wherever they may locate, will encounter students struggling to acquire English as their second or third language. And the data suggest clearly that U.S. teachers are not ready for that challenge: Less than one third of U.S. teachers serving LEP students had any training in teaching LEP students (Crawford, 1997). The national shortage of trained teachers is acute, with as many as 175,000 such positions vacant. See chapter 5 for further detail on critical ESL staffing needs.

Table 1.3   Minority Groups in Education

|  | *Percent of Teachers 1996* | *Percent of Principals in Public Schools 1987–1988* | *Percent of Students 1998* |
|---|---|---|---|
| Caucasian | 90.7% | 84.2% | 64.8% |
| African American | 7.3% | 10.1% | 16.8% |
| Latino | 4% | 4.1% | 13.5% |
| Asian/Pacific Islander | 1% | 0.8% | 3.7% |
| American Indian/ Alaskan Native | 1% | 0.8% | 1.1% |

*Note.* The source for the data in column 1 is the *Status of the American Public School Teacher 1995–96: Highlights* (National Education Association, 1997). The data in column 2 are adapted from *Public and Private School Principals in the United States: A Statistical Profile, 1987–88 to 1993–94* (Ch. 2), by the National Center for Education Statistics, 1997, Washington, DC: U.S. Department of Education, retrieved July 18, 2000, from the World Wide Web: http://www.nces.ed.gov/pubs/ppsp/97455-2.html. The data in column 3 are adapted from *The Condition of Education 1998* (Supplemental Table 43-1), by the National Center for Education Statistics, 1998, Washington, DC: U.S. Department of Education, retrieved July 18, 2000, from the World Wide Web: http://www.nces.ed.gov/pubs/condition98.

# Reconciling Low-Incidence Enrollments With High-Need Enrollees

What threshold shall be used to define low incidence? Table 1.4 lists 14 states and the U.S. capital that may be loosely described as those whose schools are low incidence with regard to LEP student enrollments for K–12. Hence, about one third of the states report having enrolled fewer than 5,000 LEP students during the 1993–1994 school year, which I, somewhat arbitrarily, will refer to as low-incidence statewide enrollments. Only 3 years later all but 3 of those states (and 1 U.S. territory) experienced significant increases in their LEP student enrollments. In fact, as many as 6 of the 18 states and territories experienced increases in 1996–1997 that no longer characterize them as low-incidence states, having crossed the threshold of 5,000 LEP students.

The U.S. Department of Education, in its zeal to address smaller LEP student populations, is exploring a somewhat arbitrary 10,000 count of all students enrolled that may distinguish them from the larger urban schools. These numbers, however arbitrarily selected, serve to point to the impact that rural and small urban schools across the United States are experiencing with increasing LEP enrollments. The 18 states and territories described in Table 1.4 offer examples of this challenge. Of course, virtually every state and U.S. territory have communities whose schools enroll very few LEP students because they are rural and isolated from large urban areas.

There are at least 77 U.S. cities whose populations have more than 200,000 LEP people. These are popularly referred to as high-incidence LEP communities. The schools in these metropolitan communities receive higher public visibility as well as more funds in comparison to the rest of schools in the United States. Thirty-five counties in eight states enroll more than half of the LEP students in the United States. Each of those counties enrolled at least 10,000 LEP students, according to the 1990 U.S. Census (U.S. Department of Commerce, 1990). These small urban communities accounted for 1,327,716 of the 2,388,243 LEP students in the United States.

Although 56% of LEP students in the United States are enrolled in ostensibly high-incidence (i.e., urban) communities, that also means that the lower incidence LEP enrollments account for the other 44% of LEP youth in the United States. Typically, those rural schools will enroll from as few as 1 to as many as 500 LEP students districtwide in ESL programs (rather than bilingual education programs). In fact, the Office of Bilingual Education and Minority Languages Affairs (1995) reports that since 1993, approximately 28,000 public schools enrolled at least 1 LEP student. Figure 1.1 illustrates

## Table 1.4 Public School Limited English Proficient (LEP) Student Enrollments in Select Low-Incidence States and Territories, 1993–1997

|  | *1993–1994* | *1994–1995* | *1995–1996* | *1996–1997* |
|---|---|---|---|---|
| Alabama | 3,214 | 3,502 | 4,550 | 5,565 |
| Arkansas | 4,000 | 4,405 | 4,405 | 5,282 |
| Delaware | 1,470 | 1,684 | 1,640 | 1,928 |
| District of Columbia | 4,449 | 5,151 | 5,193 | 4,911 |
| Kentucky | 2,108 | 2,061 | 2,653 | 3,194 |
| Maine | 1,763 | 2,332 | 2,360 | 2,386 |
| Mississippi | 1,910 | 1,310 | 1,356 | 1,594 |
| Missouri | 4,382 | 5,110 | 5,660 | 6,514 |
| Nebraska | 3,543 | 3,865 | 4,869 | 6,250 |
| New Hampshire | 1,070 | 1,084 | 867 | 1,590 |
| So. Carolina | 1,965 | 1,826 | 2,353 | 3,702 |
| So. Dakota | 3,848 | 4,630 | 5,514 | 6,515 |
| Tennessee | 3,450 | 4,002 | 5,180 | 7,223 |
| Vermont | 848 | 869 | 740 | 750 |
| Wyoming | 1,938 | 1,791 | 1,814 | 1,850 |
| **U.S. Territories** | | | | |
| Palau* | 2,143 | 2,175 | —— | 2,756 |
| Virgin Islands | 4,749 | 4,584 | 1,883 | 1,264 |
| Guam | —— | —— | 7,910 | 4,765 |

*This island's student enrollment is 95% limited English proficient.

Note. From *Summary Report of the Survey of the States' Limited English Proficient Students and Available Educational Programs and Services, 1994–95; 1996–97*, by R. Macías, 1996 & 1998, Washington, DC: National Clearinghouse for Bilingual Education. Reprinted with permission.

how rural ESL programs are continuing to grow. Furthermore, nearly one third of small rural towns in the United States enroll LEP students. Although bilingual education programs appear to receive the most press attention because of their high LEP student population, it is ESL instruction that is increasingly commonplace across the United States. The National Center for

Education Statistics (1996) reported that from 1988 to 1994, schools providing bilingual education (see chapter 3) declined about 20% as the percentage of schools providing ESL increased by 10%. With so much press attention given to federally supported programs of bilingual education, the reality is that 36% of the states reported that none of their schools received IASA Title VII funds (Macías, 1998a). In short, all schools from the 18 states and territories listed in Table 1.4 without support under Title VII were very much supported by local or state funds in the quest to provide supplemental instruction to their LEP students.

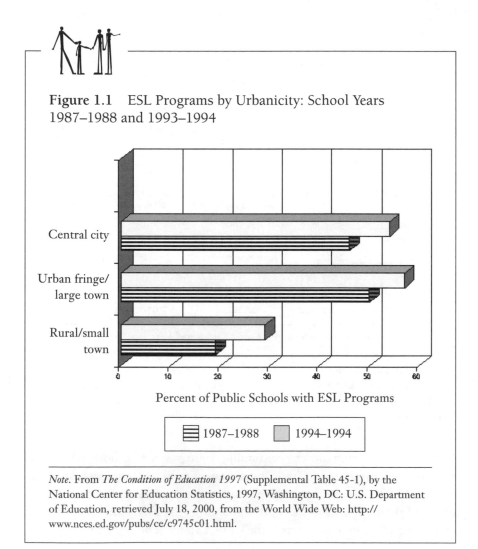

**Figure 1.1**   ESL Programs by Urbanicity: School Years 1987–1988 and 1993–1994

Percent of Public Schools with ESL Programs

▤ 1987–1988    ▧ 1994–1994

*Note.* From *The Condition of Education 1997* (Supplemental Table 45-1), by the National Center for Education Statistics, 1997, Washington, DC: U.S. Department of Education, retrieved July 18, 2000, from the World Wide Web: http://www.nces.ed.gov/pubs/ce/c9745c01.html.

The data presented in Figure 1.1 and Table 1.5 would suggest that the issues presented in educating LEP students in rural and small urban communities are indeed compelling. The challenges are, in many respects, greater than what high-incidence urban schools may argue in at least these respects:

- Growth in numbers is accelerating for rural and small urban schools at a rate greater than in larger urban schools.
- Rural schools are more likely to lack qualified, experienced ESL teachers and to find that costs for teacher training are prohibitive, given their distances from universities.
- Rural schools are less likely to have formal policy for effectively accommodating their LEP students.
- Rural and small urban schools that are characteristically more homogenous are less likely to incorporate pedagogical approaches that are more reflective of the diversity experienced in larger school systems.
- There are few if any nationally well-known ESL program models transferable to rural or small urban schools that would help gauge accountability.

**Table 1.5**  Percentages of Public Schools Enrolling Limited English Proficient (LEP) Students With Corresponding Programs by Urbanicity, 1993–1994

| | | *Percent Providing:* | | |
| *Urbanicity* | *Percent With LEP Students* | *Bilingual Education* | *ESL* | *Bilingual Education or ESL* |
|---|---|---|---|---|
| Total | 46.3% | 17.8% | 42.7% | 44.3% |
| Central city | 61.4% | 29.2% | 54.0% | 56.0% |
| Urban fringe/ large town | 60.7% | 16.9% | 57.6% | 58.9% |
| Rural/small town | 31.1% | 12.8% | 29.0% | 30.6% |

*Note.* Adapted from *The Condition of Education 1997* (Supplemental Table 45-1), by the National Center for Education Statistics, 1997, Washington, DC: U.S. Department of Education, retrieved July 18, 2000, from the World Wide Web: http://www.nces.ed.gov/pubs/ce/c9745c01.html.

- Through family mobility from cities into smaller communities, rural and small urban schools are rapidly receiving more students who come from larger schools where they have enjoyed comprehensive bilingual education programs and strongly grounded ESL support services.
- There appears to be no unified political power base emerging nationally among rural schools that enroll 1,000 or fewer students or among small urban schools that have characteristics found in rural schools.
- Expectations of rural community ESL teachers are lower than the expectations characteristic of teachers in urban schools. For example, rural schools are more likely to hire a classroom ESL education technician than a bona fide ESL teacher that an urban school would employ.
- Rural schools cannot readily access federal discretionary funding support (such as IASA Title VII funding) that larger districts commonly receive.

Rural schools cannot continue the practices of their past, when diversity was a concept attributed almost exclusively to the cities. Shortcomings of the past, such as a sink-or-swim attitude or expectations of students' quick exit from language support programs, must be corrected. High dropout rates and lower expectations of rural schools' LEP enrollees, too, are matters of the past. ESL practitioners in rural communities, in concert with all school personnel, must work to build equity in curriculum, testing, and teaching styles that are conducive to holistic, integrative learning.

## Summative Guidance for the ESL Program Manager

Establishing an ESL program in a rural or small urban school system is, on the one hand, a daunting task. School systems that have never enrolled such students or that have rarely encountered arrivals of such students are decreasing in numbers exponentially. As the data from this chapter suggests, the ESL manager or would-be manager must look toward a new and continually evolving era in rural school demographics. Although the students in most rural and small urban schools still do not quite look like the rest of the United States, their colors and languages will continue to change and grow.

On the other hand, there are a good many enviable features in undertaking ESL management in rural schools. ESL managers in rural and small urban schools, unlike their larger urban counterparts, are generally more closely connected to their communities and parents (see chapter 6). As a result, they are well positioned to nurture their LEP students as a positive part of the community. The ratio of ESL teacher to LEP student is generally low in rural and small urban schools, with a full-time load of 20 students to one teacher a common scenario.

Subsequent chapters in this book will help the ESL manager navigate his or her profession by providing the steps needed to craft and implement an appropriate language support program—one that is responsive to the growing and more complex demands of the United States' bucolic and diverse villages. This chapter's demographic presentation of the United States' linguistically diverse population transitions to the several chapters that follow chapter 3 in addressing strategies for an ESL manager's proactive and comprehensive response to students' varied needs.

## Suggested Resources on the Web

For demographics on LEP students nationally and state by state:
*National Clearinghouse for Bilingual Education (NCBE)* (http://www.ncbe.gwu.edu)

For data on language use in families across the United States:
*U.S. Census Bureau: Language Use* (http://www.census.gov /population/www/socdemo/lang_use.html)

For on-line ethnic and linguistic minority data across the United States:
*Numbers & Needs* (http://www.asu.edu/educ/cber/n_n/)

# Chapter 2
# Statutory Requirements

*LEP students are faced with educational problems confronting minority students generally, in addition to special problems related to the need to master a second language. Moreover, the research indicates that it is not uncommon for one set of problems to compound the other.*

—Office for Civil Rights, 1991, p. 2

J ust what services are schools required to provide for children of limited English proficiency? And why should it matter to the ESL manager? The answer is simple: For at least 3 decades, our courts and Congress have established significant protections for language minority students. In effect, there is ongoing, improved clarification about the implementation of instructional practices that ensure equitable access for all students of limited English proficiency in publicly supported programs and practices.

The following chronology of milestones describes those protections in response to the opening questions posed above. The ESL manager may find that referencing some of these court decisions, though decidedly dull reading, will serve as a richly resourceful alliance in the pursuit of advocacy for LEP students.

What about state statutes and the LEP student? It is not within the purview of this volume to describe the widely varied provisions of state laws protective of LEP students. The ESL manager is advised to visit the state education agencies listed on each state government's Web site to access this information. It is instructive to note that a survey of state education departments conducted in 1999 (McKnight & Antunez) revealed that 43 states and the District of Columbia do have legislation that affects instructional practices for LEP students. Seven states do not have legislative provisions that target LEP students. These states include Alabama, Hawaii, Louisiana, Mississippi, New Mexico, Tennessee, and West Virginia.

## 1964: The End of Legal Discrimination

The era for equal opportunity among minorities predates the past 30 years. In 1964, the first Civil Rights Act was passed. This law remains at the very core of virtually all interpretations of subsequent legal challenges. Title VI of the Civil Rights Act of 1964 declared the following law for all people:

> No person in the United States shall, on the ground of race, color, or national origin, be excluded from participation in, be denied the benefits of, or be subjected to discrimination under any program or activity receiving Federal financial assistance. (§ 2000d)

Under Title VI, an applicant for or recipient of federal funds may not select facilities that exclude federally protected groups from programs to which Title VI applies. Such discrimination grounded on race, color, or national origin is illegal. Defeating or substantially impairing the accomplishment of Title VI's objectives or its accompanying regulations is also illegal under the act.

At the time of the Civil Rights Act, Congress acted to ensure that all public schools would comply with this act, not just those receiving federal funds. With regard to ESL, this statute recognizes the state's role in ensuring equal educational opportunity for language minority students. The statute also stresses that an educational agency's failure to appropriately rectify an LEP student's English competency is a denial of equal educational opportunity on the basis of national origin.

Almost all public schools in the United States receive federal financial assistance, and all such schools are covered by Title VI of the Civil Rights Act. Thus, the Civil Rights Act began a new era in educating all children inclusively. Children of limited English proficiency were included under the broad language used in Title VI of that act:

> (1) A recipient under any program to which this part applies may not, directly or through contractual or other arrangements, on ground of race, color, or national origin:

(ii) Provide any service, financial aid, or other benefit to an individual which is different, or is provided in a different manner from that provided to others under the program. (34 C.F.R. § 100.3(b)(1)(ii))

In essence, all schools, according to this law, must provide services to LEP students that are comparable to those provided to their English dominant peers. If a public school receives federal financial assistance, then it is bound by provisions of Title VI of the Civil Rights Act. Students whose limited English proficiency is founded on their national origin must not be denied the educational services they need to enable them to benefit from the school's educational program.

## Implications for the ESL Manager

Because of the provisions of Title VI of the Civil Rights Act, schools must

- treat LEP students in the same way as their non-LEP peers in accommodating them in school buildings and classrooms (see Questions 9 and 12 at the end of this chapter);
- provide a schedule of instruction that is consistent with that of non-LEP students (see Question 15 at the end of this chapter)
- provide supplemental language support for LEP children in English-only classrooms, which would include an English language intervention such as ESL (see Questions 8 and 17 at the end of this chapter)

# 1970: Regulation of Schools

On May 25, 1970, the Office for Civil Rights (OCR), based in the former U.S. Department of Health, Education and Welfare, issued an official memorandum (known as the May 25th Memorandum) to clarify the responsibility of school districts to provide equal educational opportunities to LEP students. The memorandum issued the following major directives that related to compliance with Title VI among school districts enrolling 5% or more language minority populations:

(1) Where inability to speak and understand the English language excludes national origin-minority group children from effective participation in the educational program offered by a school district, the district must take affirmative steps to rectify the language deficiency in order to open its instructional program to these students.

(2) School districts must not assign national origin-minority group students to classes for the mentally retarded on the basis of criteria which essentially measure or evaluate English language skills; nor may school districts deny national origin-minority group children access to college preparatory courses on a basis directly related to the failure of the school system to inculcate English language skills.

(3) Any ability grouping or tracking system employed by the school system to deal with the special language skill needs of national origin-minority group children must be designed to meet such language skill needs as soon as possible and must not operate as an educational dead-end or permanent track.

(4) School districts have the responsibility to adequately notify national origin-minority group parents of school activities which are called to the attention of other parents. Such notice in order to be adequate may have to be provided in a language other than English. (Pottinger, 1970, pp. 1–2)

By that memorandum, other issues were included in the regulatory directive. In short, the OCR would seek to determine (a) whether a district has identified all its LEP students who need assistance; (b) whether the identified LEP students needing such assistance were in fact being provided with such assistance; and (c) in the event that a district's program of assistance is not working, whether the district has taken steps to modify its approach or approaches.

In the fall of 1985, the OCR distributed a memo further clarifying the memorandum issued on May 25, 1970. It stated that "Title VI rights are individual rights. Thus, local education agencies (LEAs) must heed the May 25th Memorandum even if they have only a *single* limited English proficient (LEP) student" (Smith, 1985). This memo has ostensibly become a powerful tool for parents in rural schools pressing for equitable access for their LEP children.

## Implications for the ESL Manager

The May 25th Memorandum of the OCR continues to be among those documents frequently cited as a corollary to Title VI of the Civil Rights Act and has guided case law after 1970. The ESL program manager is advised to follow closely the four directives listed previously in crafting ESL interventions even if there is an LEP student population at less than 5% of the school's total enrollment. The rationale for that advisement is suggested by the increase in legal protection for LEP students since 1970.

# 1974: The Landmark Supreme Court Decision

In the 1970s, as activists for equity in education, parents won one of the greatest U.S. Supreme Court decisions since *Brown v. Board of Education* in 1954. In 1974, parents of Chinese descent argued that basic skills in English were the very foundation of what the public schools of San Francisco teach. The Supreme Court, in its unanimous decision in *Lau v. Nichols* of 1974, agreed with them. In this decision, the Court declared that the San Francisco schools were making a mockery of public education when they imposed a requirement that, before children can effectively participate in the educational program, they must already have acquired those basic skills. The Court further said that those who do not understand English are certain to find their classroom experiences wholly incomprehensible and nonmeaningful. Finally, the Court noted the obvious: "that the Chinese-speaking minority receive fewer benefits than the English-speaking majority from the respondents' school system which denies them a meaningful opportunity to participate in the educational program—all earmarks of the discrimination banned by the regulations" (*Lau v. Nichols*, 1974, p. 565).

In part, the Court's opinion stated that

- equality of educational opportunity is not achieved by merely providing all students with "the same facilities, textbooks, teachers, and curriculum; for students who do not understand English are effectively foreclosed from any meaningful education" (p. 566)
- the OCR has the authority to establish regulations for Title VI enforcement that, among other things, prohibit "discrimination . . . which has the effect even though no purposeful design is present" (p. 563)

Congress, too, provided LEP students with powerfully new protections during the same year as the *Lau* decision. It passed and President Gerald Ford signed the Equal Educational Opportunities Act (EEOA) of 1974, which established the following as law:

> No state shall deny equal educational opportunity to an individual on account of his or her race, color, sex, or national origin, by—
>
> (f) the failure of an educational agency to take appropriate action to overcome language barriers that impede equal participation by its students in its instructional programs. (§ 1703)

*Implications for the ESL Manager*

Because of the *Lau* decision, the OCR has considerable authority in regulating how schools must design "meaningful" instructional programs responsive to the English language acquisition and academic needs of LEP students. In instances where there are a significant number of LEP students at the same grade level who speak the same heritage language, instruction may need to be provided in that language.

# 1975: Procedures Provided to the Office for Civil Rights

When the EEOA required schools to "rectify appropriately a limited English proficient student's English opportunities," a point of contention arose between language minority parents and school districts as to how best define the term "appropriate action" for equal educational opportunity (Equal Educational Opportunities Act, 1974, § 1703(f)). As a result, the OCR formulated the *Lau* remedies that became the standard by which the OCR determined compliance with Title VI of the Civil Rights Act. The *Lau* remedies, created in 1975, specified approved approaches, methods, and detailed procedures for (a) identifying and evaluating the English language skills of language minority students, (b) determining appropriate instructional treatments, (c) deciding when LEP children were ready for mainstream classrooms, and (d) determining the professional standards to be met by teachers of language minority children.

The *Lau* remedies went beyond the *Lau* ruling by specifying that schools should instruct elementary students through their strongest language until they could participate effectively in English-only classrooms. The remedies prescribed ESL instruction for all students for whom English was not the strongest language. Finally, any school district that wished to rely exclusively on ESL would be obliged to demonstrate that its programs were as effective as the bilingual programs described in the *Lau* remedies.

Although the *Lau* remedies were criticized as being poorly written and were never promulgated as formal regulations, they quickly evolved into the de facto standards that the OCR staff applied for determining a school's compliance with Title VI under the *Lau* decision.

## Implications for the ESL Manager

As a result of the *Lau* decision, the EEOA, and the enforcement procedures provided to the OCR, schools must craft and implement equal educational opportunities policy, referred popularly as a *Lau* plan. The discussion in chapter 3 is devoted entirely to this process. See also Question 11 at the end of this chapter.

# 1978: Clarification on Duration of Language Support

In the 1978 court case *Cintron v. Brentwood Union Free School District*, the Federal District Court for the Eastern District of New York found that the school district failed to accommodate students whose English language proficiency hindered their understanding of mainstream English instruction. Treating the U.S. Department of Health, Education and Welfare's *Lau* remedies as guidelines, the district court ordered the Brentwood school district to implement a plan of transitional bilingual education. The court rejected the alternative proposal that the school district presented because it substituted tutoring on a pullout basis for full-time bilingual education. In that same year, the case of *Rios v. Read* in the same federal district court as *Cintron* found that the school district's transitional bilingual program was inadequate with regard to its teachers' knowledge of bilingual teaching methods, language assessment, program placement procedures, native language curriculum materials, and native language instruction. The court wrote, "While the district's goal of teaching Hispanic children the English language is certainly proper, it cannot be allowed to compromise a student's right to meaningful education before proficiency in English is obtained" (*Rios v. Read*, 1978, p. 57).

## Implications for the ESL Manager

As a result of the decisions in *Cintron* as well as in *Rios*, school districts may not prematurely exit an LEP student from a supplemental English language support program. See chapter 8 for a detailed discussion on how much time it will likely take for an LEP student to acquire English sufficient to compete with non-LEP peers in English-only classrooms.

# 1981: Program Quality Matters;
# No LEP Student Exclusions

In a far-reaching case, the U.S. Court of Appeals in *Casteñada v. Pickard* (1981) formulated the following three-part test to measure compliance with the EEOA requirement of "appropriate action":

1.　Theory: The court's responsibility, insofar as educational theory was concerned, was only to ascertain that a school system was pursuing a program informed by an educational theory recognized as sound by some experts in the field or, at least, deemed a legitimate experimental strategy.

2.　Practice: The court's second inquiry questioned whether the programs and practices actually used by a school system were reasonably calculated to implement effectively the educational theory adopted by the school. On the one hand, a school system was taking appropriate action to remedy language barriers if it adopted a promising theory. On the other hand, the system then failed if it did not follow through with the practices, resources, and personnel necessary to transform that theory into reality.

3.　Results: The court determined that if a school's program, although premised on a legitimate educational theory and implemented through the use of adequate techniques, failed to produce results indicating that the language barriers confronting students were being overcome, that program may, at that point, no longer constitute appropriate action as far as that school was concerned.

LEP students entering school face daunting tasks not encountered by students who are already proficient in English. Because the number of hours in any school day is limited, students who enter school already proficient in English may devote some of the time that LEP children will spend acquiring English to other subjects. The court ruled that if no remedial action were taken to overcome the academic deficits that LEP students may incur during a period of intensive language training, then the language barrier might pose a lingering and indirect impediment to those students' equal participation in the regular instructional program. The discussion in *Casteñada* permitted schools to determine how limited English-speaking students pursue their language acquisition challenges so long as the schools designed programs that were reasonably calculated to enable those students to attain parity of participation in the standard instructional program within a reasonable length of time after they enter school.

The U.S. Supreme Court case of *Plyler v. Doe*, another significant milestone that occurred in 1981, established that schools are required to provide full access for any student to instructional programs, regardless of his or her immigration status. Students attending school whose families may be undocumented (i.e., illegal) immigrants could not be excluded from provisions of Title VI of the Civil Rights Act. By that ruling, schools would not become enforcers of immigration law within school boundaries.

## Implications for the ESL Manager

As a result of the *Casteñada* decision, school districts must implement an ESL/bilingual education program or other pedagogically sound intervention for their LEP student enrollees. This inevitably requires that the ESL manager and key staff secure the knowledge base for carrying out such a program (see chapter 5). The relationship of sound theory to practice must manifest itself in program evaluation (see chapter 8).

As a result of the *Plyler* decision, school districts may not use identification tools that have the effect of ascertaining immigration status of children, such as proof of citizenship, Social Security numbers, or other tools that could use immigration status to establish children's eligibility for participation in school programs and activities. See also Questions 14 and 18 at the end of this chapter.

# 1988: Acceleration of Civil Rights Compliance

In March 1988, Congress passed and President Bush signed the Civil Rights Restoration Act. This law amended previous civil rights laws by clarifying the definition of "program or activity" to ensure that discrimination is prohibited throughout an entire institution or agency if any part of the institution or agency receives federal assistance. The act covers state and local agencies, school systems, and corporations and other private groups. If any agency or institution were found to be in violation of civil rights law and that institution were to refuse to comply with the law, all of the federal funding for that institution would be in jeopardy of being withdrawn.

*Implications for the ESL Manager*

As a result of the Civil Rights Restoration Act, school districts must comply with all civil rights laws. Their failure to do so places them in jeopardy of losing all federal funds they receive—not just the federally funded program that is out of compliance. See also Questions 13 and 16 at the end of this chapter.

# 1991: Expansion of Criteria for Adequacy of Instruction

Commissioned by the Supreme Court in October 1991, the OCR issued the Office for Civil Rights Enforcement Policy of 1991, an enforcement policy update on the treatment of language minority students who are LEP. The policy addresses components within the compliance points of (a) adequacy of program and (b) need for a formal program. Under the heading of adequacy of program, the policy update lists staffing requirements, exit criteria, and access to programs (e.g., gifted and talented programs). Pertaining to staffing requirements, the policy update states that "a recipient may not in effect relegate LEP students to second-class status by indefinitely allowing teachers without formal qualifications to teach them while requiring teachers of non-LEP students to need formal qualifications" (Office for Civil Rights, 1991, p. 4).

If a district chooses to provide ESL services, the district "should have ascertained that teachers who use those methods have been adequately trained in them. This training can take the form of an in-service training, formal college coursework, or a combination of the two" (p. 4).

The district is also obliged to have the ESL teacher evaluated by someone "familiar with the methods being used" (p. 4). The policy update continues to point out the following:

> Recipients frequently assert that their teachers are unqualified because qualified teachers are not available. If a recipient has shown that it has unsuccessfully tried to hire qualified teachers, it must provide adequate training to teachers already on staff to comply with the Title VI regulation. (See *Casteñada*, 648 F.2d at 1013.) Such training must take place as soon as possible. For example, recipients sometimes require teachers to work toward obtaining a credential as a condition of employment in a program for limited English proficient students. This requirement is not, in itself, sufficient to meet the recipient's obligations under the Title VI regulation. To ensure that LEP students have access to the school's pro-

grams while teachers are completing their formal training, the recipient must ensure that those teachers receive sufficient interim training to enable them to function adequately in the classroom, as well as any assistance from bilingual aides that may be necessary to carry out the recipient's interim program. (p. 6)

The OCR policy update draws heavily from the *Casteñada* case (1981) in outlining certain criteria for meaningful participation of LEP students in the overall program. Some factors it examines in determining whether formerly LEP students are able to participate meaningfully in the regular educational program include

- whether they are able to keep up with their non-LEP peers in the regular educational program
- whether they are able to participate successfully in essentially all aspects of the school's curriculum without the use of simplified English materials
- whether their retention-in-grade and dropout rates are similar to those of their non-LEP peers

Program exit criteria should be based on objective standards, such as standardized test scores, and the district should be able to explain why it has decided that students meeting those standards will be able to participate meaningfully in the regular classroom. In addition, students should not be exited from the structured language program unless they can read, write, and comprehend English well enough to participate meaningfully in the school district's regular educational program.

Regarding special education programs, the enforcement policy update does not claim to be able to address the numerous issues related to assessment and placement of LEP students in special education programs found in Title VI and section 504 of the Rehabilitation Act of 1973. However, it does state that schools cannot have policies of "no double services"; that is, "refusing to provide both alternative language services and special education to children who need them" (Office for Civil Rights, 1991, pp. 7–8).

Similarly, if LEP students meet the eligibility requirements for IASA Title I-A (Disadvantaged Youth) or IASA Title I-C (Migratory Youth) services, they may certainly take advantage of those services along with ESL or bilingual services. In addition, a school district may not use Title I-A or Title I-C (also known as Migrant Education) funds to supplant educational services that it is required to provide to LEP children under federal or state law.

Further, LEP students cannot be "categorically excluded from gifted/

talented or other specialized programs" (Office for Civil Rights, 1991, p. 8). There may be occasions where "educational justifications" are made for excluding an LEP student from a specialized program. Those justifications would include (a) that time for the program would unduly hinder a student's participation in an alternative language program and (b) that the specialized program itself requires proficiency in English language skills for meaningful participation. "Evaluation and testing procedures used for gifted/talented and other special programs must not screen out LEP students solely because of their English language proficiency; the tests must not prevent him/her from qualifying for a program for which they would otherwise be qualified" (p. 9).

## Implications for the ESL Manager

As a result of the Office for Civil Rights Enforcement Policy of 1991, school districts must evaluate their programs periodically so that school programs can be modified to ensure student success. Their programs' success is measured by achievement of program goals. In addition, personnel in all school districts that enroll LEP students should have a working knowledge of the legal provisions for the protection of the rights of LEP students. These guidelines and requirements in the Enforcement Policy of 1991 protect LEP students. In doing so, they provide substantial assistance to school districts as they establish effective programs for their students who are in the process of acquiring English as their second language.

# Other Case Law

The laws and regulations detailed in this chapter are the most commonly cited in protecting the civil rights of LEP students. A considerable number of litigants defending the needs of language minority students have been successful in district courts nationwide. Short of appeals of reversal to the U.S. Supreme Court, the rulings noted below may be invoked for a wide range of issues affecting services to LEP students.

## On Setting Equitable Standards

### Aspira v. Board of Education, 394 F. Supp. 1161 (E.D. N.Y. 1975)

As a result of the plaintiffs' motion to hold the New York Board of Education in contempt of an order to provide bilingual education to LEP students, the trial judge was called on to determine whether the board's assessment of the students' abilities to speak English was adequate. The court found that the board's assessment was not adequate because children were determined to be proficient in English even if their scores on a test of English language ability were lower than those achieved by 90% of monolingual English-speaking children. As a result, the board of education was instructed to raise its minimum score.

## On Mandating Assessment and Supplemental Instruction but Limiting Curriculum Design (Three Decisions)

### Gomez v. Illinois State Board of Education, 811 F.2d 1030 (7th Cir. 1987)

The Seventh Circuit issued a finding that the EEOA requires state, as well as local, educational agencies to ensure that the needs of LEP children are met. The ruling notably extended to testing for English language proficiency and provision of compensatory instruction for LEP students.

### Guadalupe Organization v. Tempe Elementary School District No. 3, 587 F.2d 1022 (9th Cir. 1978)

Plaintiffs representing Yaqui and Hispanic children enrolled in the Tempe (Arizona) school district sought an order requiring bilingual-bicultural education in Grades K–12. The plaintiffs conceded that the district's program of ESL instruction was effective in teaching English. However, the plaintiffs alleged that they were entitled to bicultural curriculum pursuant to Title VI, the EEOA, and the Fourteenth Amendment, regardless of the student's ability to speak English. The court found no such entitlement and denied the requested relief.

### Heavy Runner v. Bremner, 522 F. Supp. 162 (D. Mont. 1981)

The district court reiterated the holding of *Guadalupe* that there is no constitutional right to bilingual-bicultural education. However, the court found that Title VI and the EEOA require the state to ensure that an Indian student's language deficiencies are addressed. In addition, the court found that the language of Title VI and the EEOA mandates remedial assistance to students with English language deficiencies.

## On Holding State Education Agencies Accountable

*Idaho Migrant Council v. Board of Education, 647 F.2d 69 (9th Cir. 1981)*

The appeals court held that a state department of education is required under Title VI and the EEOA to ensure that needs of students with limited English proficiency are addressed. The OCR will often establish the extent to which a state education agency may also be at fault when a school district in its state is found to be out of compliance.

## On Providing Sufficient Resources and Training

*Keyes v. School District No. 1 Denver, Colorado, 521 F.2d 465 (10th Cir. 1975), cert. denied, 423 U.S. 1066 (1976), on remand, 576 F. Supp. 1503 (D. Colo. 1983)*

In a manner similar to that of the trial court judge in *United States v. State of Texas (San Felipe/del Rio)*, 342 F. Supp. 24 (E.D. Tex. 1971), the trial court judge supervising the desegregation of the Denver public schools, relying on the same expert as the judge in Texas, ordered implementation of a bilingual education plan as part of his desegregation decree. The Tenth Circuit reversed. The court of appeals held that the Fourteenth Amendment did not require an education tailored to the unique cultural and developmental needs of minority students. In addition, the court ruled that the district court's plan could not be upheld under Title VI because the district was already providing services to LEP students. The court stated that, even if those services were shown to be inadequate, the district court's plan went beyond what could be ordered to remedy such a Title VI violation. The court also held that an exemption of schools housing bilingual programs from the desegregation requirements imposed on other schools was inconsistent with the district's obligation to desegregate.

Using an analysis delineated in *Casteñada v. Pickard* (1981), the court found that Denver had designed a program based on a sound educational theory (transitional bilingual education) but that its resources were inadequate (e.g., teachers were not properly trained). The district had failed to address the needs of students who spoke and understood the other language and English equally. In addition, there was convincing evidence of failure to achieve equal educational opportunity because of the number of Hispanic dropouts and the leveled (rudimentary) English textbook substitutes designed for secondary LEP students.

## On Accommodating Variants of English

*Martin Luther King Junior Elementary School Children v. Ann Arbor School District, 473 F. Supp. 1371 (E.D. Mich. 1979)*

The plaintiffs alleged denial of equal educational opportunity because of the Ann Arbor (Michigan) school district's failure to take into account their home language, which was Black English. The court found a violation of section 1703(f) of the EEOA. The school district was required to submit a plan to help teachers recognize the home language of the students and to use that knowledge in their attempts to teach reading skills and standard English.

## On Premature Exiting of LEP Students From ESL/Bilingual Education Services

*Rios v. Read, 480 F. Supp. 14 (E.D. N.Y. 1978)*

The district court found that the school district's inadequate bilingual program violated Title VI, the EEOA, the Civil Rights Act, and the Bilingual Education Act of 1965. The court used the *Lau* remedies as the standard for determining compliance with Title VI. The court stated that the statutory obligation is to take affirmative action for language-deficient students by establishing an ESL and bilingual program and to keep the students in such a program until they have attained sufficient proficiency to be instructed with English-speaking students of comparable intelligence. The school district was required to identify children by objective, validated tests conducted by competent personnel and to establish procedures for monitoring the program. Students could exit the program only after validated tests had indicated the appropriate level of English proficiency.

## On Implementing Bilingual Education for Low-Incidence LEP Populations

*Serna v. Portales Municipal Schools, 351 F. Supp. 1279 (D. N.M. 1972), affirmed, 499 F.2d 1147 (10th Cir. 1974)*

The district court found the Portales (New Mexico) school district in violation of Title VI and the U.S. Constitution because of the district's failures to adequately address the educational needs of Hispanic students. The district court found the district's proposed limited expansion of its bilingual-bicultural education program inadequate and substituted a more complete bilingual-bicultural program.

Relying on *Lau*, the court of appeals affirmed the district court's judgment solely on Title VI grounds. The court stated that the plaintiffs were entitled to bilingual education under Title VI and that the district court could properly fashion a bilingual-bicultural program that would ensure that Spanish-surnamed children receive a meaningful education. The Portales school district's failure to provide alternative language services would only violate Title VI when large numbers of LEP students were involved.

## Summative Guidance for the ESL Program Manager

Among the more contentious issues facing ESL managers are administrative procedures that are perceived to be in conflict with statute or case law precedent. Complaints on issues of equity are most often filed with regional offices of the OCR across the United States. Those offices respond to complaints by reviewing schools' programs and practices to determine if they are in compliance with the law. The regional offices of the OCR further require those schools to provide a plan of action that will bring them into compliance. Anyone may file a complaint with the OCR. The locations of the regional offices can be found at the OCR's Web site, which is listed at the end of this chapter.

Short of providing the manager with a pandect of law, this chapter offered a chronology of the major statutes and court decisions protective of the rights of LEP students. This should afford the manager the knowledge base needed in pressing for the kind of instructional environment LEP students are clearly entitled to. No one—neither the ESL manager nor a subordinate—should experience reprisal or recrimination on challenging an administrative practice or decision that may be in conflict with the law. Indeed, that, too, is protected under statute.

The following frequently asked questions may offer the ESL manager advisement in coping with tenuous areas of ESL program implementation. The scenarios come from actual circumstances presented to this writer from rural schools. Advisement in providing reasonable responses to these questions was solicited from the OCR, other federal agencies, and colleagues in Maine's state education agency. Invoking LEP student protections is not intended to confront the policy makers—only to inform judgment.

1. A non-English-speaking student just moved into town and is living with a friend. Is our school required to provide services?

   From a federal posture, the OCR would be concerned that every LEP child needing services be provided the special language services necessary for the student to benefit from an education conducted in English. The OCR does not address the concerns of exchange students or those who reside in the United States on temporary visa in regard to problems connected to their visa status. However, recipients of federal financial assistance cannot discriminate against any person in the United States on the basis of national origin.

2. Does the OCR monitor migrant student programs?

   No, the OCR does not have jurisdiction over migrants as a group. However, migrants whose national origin is other than the United States are within the OCR's jurisdiction. In addition, many migrants are racial minorities and are thus within the jurisdiction of the OCR. See also *Idaho Migrant Council v. Board of Education* (1981), which is discussed earlier in this chapter.

3. Does the OCR investigate complaints stemming from curricular materials—notably those that appear biased against minorities or those that are replete with ethnic stereotypes?

   The OCR does not judge the content of curricular materials in its investigations. Therefore, issues of stereotype are not within its judgmental purview except where the effect is discriminatory. However, the OCR would take notice of the quality and quantity of instructional materials that are significantly less adequate than those materials that fluent English proficient students have when the difference appears to result in less adequate services. For example, the OCR would ask if the school district is claiming to run a special language services program without any instructional materials. See *Guadalupe v. Tempe* (1978), which is discussed earlier in this chapter.

4. A student has reported that she is not allowed to speak French on school grounds. Is this permissible?

   No, this is a violation of Title VI of the Civil Rights Act. Rules that stipulate "speak only English" are grounds for complaint to the OCR. Within certain classes, for specified instructional purposes,

English-only rules could be implemented for that portion of the class where the use of English only would be the sole method of achieving the educational objective. Such usage should be carefully scrutinized. The courts have said that English-only rules are primarily an issue of safety where the students speaking a language other than English might subject themselves or other students to a hazardous situation (e.g., students spotting for one another in gymnastics). There should not be a blanket English-only rule.

5.   There appear to be inequities and injustices happening toward minorities in my school district. Because my job may be at stake, it is best that I not "make waves." Who, then, can complain against an alleged illegality to the OCR?

Anyone may complain to the OCR about an alleged violation of a student's civil rights. In many instances, the principal or you (the ESL manager) are in the best position to voice your concerns or file a complaint because you are the most knowledgeable about the specific situation. Even if you do not complain, the OCR would undoubtedly solicit testimony from you if ever it investigated a complaint or performed a routine compliance review. An important clause is in the law. You have protected behavior in your role as an advocate for the civil rights of any student. Retaliation or harassment is illegal, as stated in the Civil Rights Act of 1964:

> No recipient or other person shall intimidate, threaten, coerce, or discriminate against any individual for the purpose of interfering with any right or privilege secured by section 601 of the Act or this part, or because he has made a complaint, testified, assisted, or participated in any manner in an investigation proceeding or hearing under this part. The identity of complainants shall be kept confidential except to the extent necessary to carry out the purposes of this part, including the conduct of any investigation, hearing, or judicial proceedings arising thereunder. (34 C.F.R. Part 100 § 100.7)

6.   How does the IASA Title I program affect LEP students?

LEP students are one of the target student populations that the IASA Title I law, enacted in 1994, is designed to serve. LEP students are entitled to educational services on the same basis as all other students served by Title I. They must be included in all schoolwide and targeted assistance programs, and their parents must be included in the development, monitoring, and implementation of any school-wide or targeted assistance plan. The plan must be translated into any language that a significant minority of the parents speaks. Further, LEP students are required to meet the same high content and performance standards required of all Title I students. They must be included in all assessments given to the other Title I students. Several components of the law specifically include LEP students. These components include content standards, annual progress, assessment, development of local education agency plans, schoolwide programs, selection of LEP students for participation in targeted assistance schools, school improvement, and parental involvement.

7. Can IASA Title I funds be used to provide services required by other state or federal legislation?

The law enacted in 1994 states that a school participating in a schoolwide program shall use IASA Title I funds only to supplement the funds that would be made available from nonfederal sources for the school, including funds needed to provide services that are required by law for children with disabilities and children with limited English proficiency. Provisions under both schoolwide and targeted assistance programs require that Title I funds supplement rather than supplant funds for services that are required by other laws (e.g., through interpretations of Title VI of the Civil Rights Act, the EEOA, and state bilingual laws). However, Title I funds may be used to coordinate and supplement the services provided for with other funds required by law. Thus, for example, schools may use Title I funds to provide additional language-related services for LEP students, including paying the salaries of staff to provide such additional services to LEP students.

8. Our vocational education school says that certain children cannot be accepted at a center because they are not sufficiently competent in English, which could pose a safety hazard for them. Is this an illegal denial of access?

Yes. Steps must be taken to open all vocational programs to language minority children. Participation that is restricted by reason of limited English proficiency due to national origin may be a violation of Title VI of the Civil Rights Act and of the federal Vocational

Education Programs Guidelines for Eliminating Discrimination and Denial of Services on the Basis of Race, Color, National Origin, Sex and Handicap.

There are court decisions focusing on employment contexts that address issues of English-only rules imposed in the workplace for purposes of safety. However, in an educational context, LEP students should receive instruction (e.g., demonstrations) in good safety practices and in the key safety vocabulary necessary. This safety instructional component is part of many vocational English as a second language (VESL) curricula. It might behoove the vocational education instructor to learn some key safety vocabulary in the minority language to ensure that classroom safety is maintained. The important guideline is for the district to ensure that the LEP students have the necessary skills to benefit from a vocational education conducted in English.

9.  The ESL resource room is located across town. May we assess our LEP children a small fee to cover the cost of transportation?

All students attending public schools are entitled to free public education. Every person within the age limitations prescribed by state statutes must be provided an opportunity to receive the benefits of a free public education. Language minority children cannot be singled out to pay for services directly relating to their instructional needs. Costs must be borne by the school district to the same extent that the district bears costs for all children. If other children are not assessed special transportation costs, then LEP children should not be assessed those costs either. (See also chapter 4.)

10.  Is a postsecondary vocational institution required to send out its recruitment notices in the parents' native language if there is a community of language minority persons within its service area?

If the service area of a recipient of federal funding "contains a community of national origin-minority persons with limited English language skills, public notification materials must be disseminated to that community in its language and must state that recipients will take steps to assure that the lack of English language skills will not be a barrier to admission and participation in vocational education programs" (Vocational Education Programs Guidelines, 1979, p.

17167). Use of multimedia recruitment notices in the parents' native language would also be appropriate.

11.  What is the legal basis for a *Lau* plan and special language services (e.g., ESL, bilingual)?

     A *Lau* plan (see chapter 3) or its equivalent policy, which ensures that LEP students receive equitable access to the total educational program, gets its name from the landmark 1974 U.S. Supreme Court decision, *Lau v. Nichols*. The Supreme Court stated that school systems must take action to see that LEP students are able to benefit from an education in English. The Court did not prescribe a specific program. It stated that teaching English to LEP children is one choice; giving instruction in the students' native language is another. There may be other choices as well.

12.  The only space available for ESL tutoring is backstage (no windows) or the boiler room. Is this space arrangement, given our severe space limitations, legal?

     The burden of proof of acceptability of physical space is on the school district. A helpful rule is to consider this space as it compares to that used by nonminority children. If all children, regardless of national origin, must utilize this space, then it is probable that such space is not a denial of equal education access. Further, the EEOA states that "a school district which fails to take appropriate action to overcome language barriers that impede equal participation by its students in its instructional program is denying equal educational opportunity to language minority students" (Equal Educational Opportunities Act, 1974, § 1703(f)). Any instructional space that isolates or segregates LEP students from the mainstream of hallway traffic would also trigger a concern for the OCR under EEOA. A more enticing environment, such as a regular classroom, may promote equal participation under this scenario. (See also chapter 4.)

13.  What can happen to our district if we do not comply with federal guidelines for services to LEP children? When we are on-site audited, will the OCR be looking at our ESL program as well?

     The federal government encourages all states to set their own priorities and program designs that serve children of limited English proficiency. However, the burden of proof that those programs are effective is on the school district (see *Casteñada v. Pickard* [1981], which is described in detail earlier in this chapter). Such programs may be challenged by a would-be complainant to the OCR, which will follow through on any complaint. In the event of an audit by the OCR, the OCR would examine ESL programs for their appropriateness and adequacy. If the OCR finds that the school district has discriminated against LEP children, it will attempt to bring the district into compliance with the federal law through voluntary negotiations. The district will be asked to correct the problem or problems found and to sign a corrective action plan. If this fails, the OCR may issue a noncompliance letter that puts the district on notice that corrective action must be taken. If the district does not take corrective action, the OCR can take the district to an administrative enforcement hearing where its federal funding could be terminated. Section 557 of the Civil Rights Restoration Act (March 1988) extends the enforcement of a number of civil rights laws that were restricted by a 1984 Supreme Court decision, *Grove City College v. Bell.* These laws prohibit discrimination on the basis of age, sex, race, color, national origin, and handicap in all programs receiving federal funding. The Civil Rights Restoration Act amends the civil rights laws by clarifying the definition of "program or activity" to ensure that discrimination is prohibited throughout the entire institution or agency if any part of the institution or agency receives federal assistance. The act covers state and local agencies, school systems, and corporations and other private groups.

14.  Do we have to provide services to undocumented immigrants?

   Yes. Legislation handed down from the U.S. Supreme Court in *Plyler v. Doe* stipulates that all children enrolled in U.S. public schools must be provided free public education, including equal access to appropriate instructional services. Status of parental documentation may not be taken into account in deciding access to services.

15.  ESL teachers are only available during lunch and after school. Is this arrangement legal?

   Probably not. Title VI of the Civil Rights Act of 1964 states that a recipient of federal funds may not "deny an individual an opportunity to participate in the program through the provision of services or otherwise afford him an opportunity to do so which is different from that afforded others under the program" (34 C.F.R. Part 100 § 100.3(vi)). To meet a curricular need for minority children that is inconsistent with practices used for nonminority children appears to violate this provision in the law. If the student or parents request that special language services (e.g., ESL, bilingual) take place during noncurricular classes or after school, it would be advisable for the school to obtain and keep on file a written, signed consent form specifying the request and times the services are provided.

16. Are private schools obligated to follow nondiscrimination laws and to provide special language services (e.g., ESL, bilingual) to language minority students?

A person investigating this issue would need to obtain information about the following:

- Does the private school receive school lunch funds directly from the U.S. Department of Agriculture?
- Does the private school avail itself of IASA Title I services?
- Does the private school avail itself of special education services provided by the public school district?
- Does the private school have a tax-exempt status from the Internal Revenue Service?
- Does the private school receive supplies or equipment from the public school district?
- Does the private school cowrite grants with the public school district?
- Is the cost of tuition for students from the public school paid to the private school that they are attending??

If any of these conditions apply to the private school, that school will need to contact the OCR and determine if the school is obligated to follow nondiscrimination laws and to provide special language services (e.g., ESL, bilingual education) to its LEP students.

17. What responsibilities do state correctional facilities have to educate language minority students of school age?

If the correctional facility receives federal funding, the educational responsibilities are very similar to those in regular education. The OCR recommends that language minority students be tested for their English language proficiency prior to trial and sentencing so that the correctional facility may determine what language will be needed to communicate (a) the rules of the correctional facility and (b) the legal proceedings and the type of appropriate educational programming for those students.

18. How can we find out about U.S. immigration laws that might affect some of our language minority students and their parents?

Nonimmigrant students (sometimes called "F-1" students) needing to petition the U.S. Immigration and Naturalization Service (INS) for approval for student attendance must file a Form I-17, which can be downloaded at http://www.ins.usdoj.gov/graphics/formsfee /forms/i-17.htm. Academic and language students (nonimmigrant students in the United States who are attending a U.S. school and/or studying English) who are F-1 may seek an eligibility certificate for full-time study in the United States by filing an I-20 form, which is available at http://www.ins.usdoj.gov/graphics/formsfee/forms/i-20ab.htm. For additional information about I-17s, I-20s, and other aspects of immigration law, ESL managers and other school representatives may call the INS district office. That office can supply interested persons with a booklet on general student and school regulations and answer specific questions. The toll-free number for the INS is 800-375-5283. For the hearing impaired, the number is 800-767-1833.

A well-respected publication, *Immigrant Students: Their Legal Right of Access to Public Schools (A Guide for Advocates and Educators)*, is available from the Immigrant Student Program, National Coalition of Advocates for Students, 100 Boylston Street, Suite 737, Boston, MA USA 02116-4610; Telephone: 617-357-8507; Web site: http://www.ncasl.org; E-mail: ncasmfe@mindspring.com.

19. Where are the regional offices for civil rights of the U.S. Department of Education located?

The national headquarters for the U.S. Department of Education's OCR is located at the following address: U.S. Department of Education, Office for Civil Rights, Customer Service Team, Mary E. Switzer Building, 330 C Street, SW, Washington, DC USA 20202; Telephone: 202-205-5413 or 800-421-3481; Fax: 202-205-9862; Web site: http://www.ed.gov/offices/OCR; E-mail: ocr@ed.gov.

# Suggested Resources on the Web

For the Office for Civil Rights (OCR) nearest you:
    Access to the OCR's 12 offices nationwide (http://www.ed.gov/offices
    /OCR/aboutus.html#five)

For the Immigration and Naturalization Service (INS) on-line:
    Immigration laws, regulations, and guides (http://www.ins.usdoj.gov)

For LEP students and Title I:
    *LEP Students and Title I: A Guidebook for Educators* (August, Hakuta,
    Olguin, & Pompa, 1995, http://www.ncbe.gwu.edu/ncbepubs
    /resource/lepguide)

For legislation passed or pending in the U.S. Congress:
    All legislation (http://thomas.loc.gov)
    *U.S. House of Representatives* (http://www.house.gov)
    *U.S. Senate* (http://www.senate.gov/legislative)

For politically oriented language policy issues:
    *James Crawford's Language Site & Policy Emporium*
    (http://ourworld.compuserve.com/homepages/jwcrawford/be.htm)

# Chapter 3
# Implementing the
# *Lau* Mandate

*Awareness of local things disappears in the crush of standardized
curricula, generic textbooks, and centralized test design. These practices
are invented by and for an urban industrial age.*

—Haas & Nachtigal, 1998, p. 5

## A *Lau* Plan: The Heart of ESL Policy and Practice

**M**atters of law described in the previous chapter provide a statutory
rationale for a school district to establish a structured comprehensive language and content support program for its LEP students.
Those laws have not specified what kind of service delivery models schools
must adopt. The school district, in essence, has the burden of proving the
effectiveness of any given model. So what does one do?

Indeed, there are many kinds of structured language support models that
are appropriate for LEP students. The ability of a district to provide some of
these programs depends on the availability of native-language-speaking personnel, the availability of instructional materials in students' native language
for regular content classrooms, and the student composition of the district's
second language classrooms. The keys to an effective and appropriate program
choice include careful consideration of the LEP child's needs, research into
the personnel or material resources available, full understanding of possible

program configurations, and adherence to equity issues demanded under Title VI of the Civil Rights Act and related federal and state legislation. State and local requirements are also necessary for all students to achieve predetermined academic standards (as described in chapter 4). LEP student achievement of such standards will be predicated in part on the institutional approach selected.

## Program Approaches

English language support programs (as illustrated in Table 3.1) include the following types.

### ESL Pullout

Sometimes called English for speakers of other languages (ESOL), this structured language support approach is designed to teach English to students whose native language is not English. In low-incidence situations, this instruction

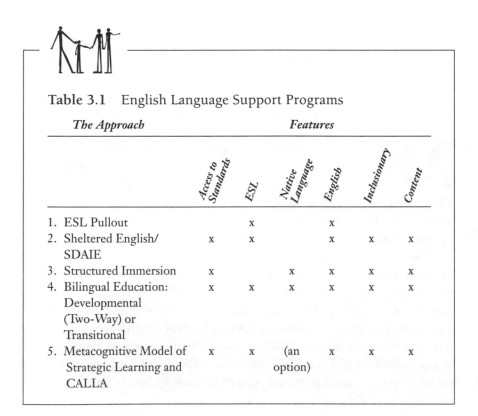

**Table 3.1** English Language Support Programs

| The Approach | Access to Standards | ESL | Native Language | English | Inclusionary | Content |
|---|---|---|---|---|---|---|
| 1. ESL Pullout | | x | | x | | |
| 2. Sheltered English/ SDAIE | x | x | | x | x | x |
| 3. Structured Immersion | x | | x | x | x | x |
| 4. Bilingual Education: Developmental (Two-Way) or Transitional | x | x | x | x | x | x |
| 5. Metacognitive Model of Strategic Learning and CALLA | x | x | (an option) | x | x | x |

may occur through an isolated tutorial program where students are pulled out from regular English literacy instruction for part of the day and are placed in mainstream subject areas for the rest of the school day. This tutorial program may include itinerant ESOL, where a teacher travels to more than one school to provide ESL instruction. Pullout services are usually provided or supervised by an ESL-credentialed teacher. It is not regarded as a viable approach (as illustrated in Figure 3.1, which identifies common approaches and their strengths and weaknesses). Because ESL pullout is so focused on only English, content in academic subjects grounded in state and local standards may not reach the LEP student until sufficient English fluency has been attained.

## Sheltered English

This approach utilizes the simplification of the English language to teach ESL and subject-area content simultaneously. Sheltered English permits LEP students to acquire state and local standards in comprehensible English. The actual content is the same as that taught to mainstream non-LEP students (not watered down), although key concepts and vocabulary are at a lower academic level, targeted to fit the ESL student's proficiency level in the English language. Sheltered English may be loosely referred to as content ESL.

## Specially Designed Academic Instruction in English (SDAIE)

This approach is comparable to sheltered English. However, the content is taught at its appropriate grade level by the regular content teacher.

## Structured Immersion

In this approach, instruction for LEP students is conducted in English in a setting where the teacher understands the student's native language. The student typically uses the native language as needed with the teacher, who usually responds in English.

## Bilingual Education

This program utilizes the students' culture and native language in instructing them in their academic subjects, except for English. Bilingual education does, in effect, enable LEP students to access the same local and academic standards required of all students. The difference for LEP students in bilingual education is that they can access the standards in two languages. Transitional bilingual

Figure 3.1  Common Approaches to Supplemental Language Support

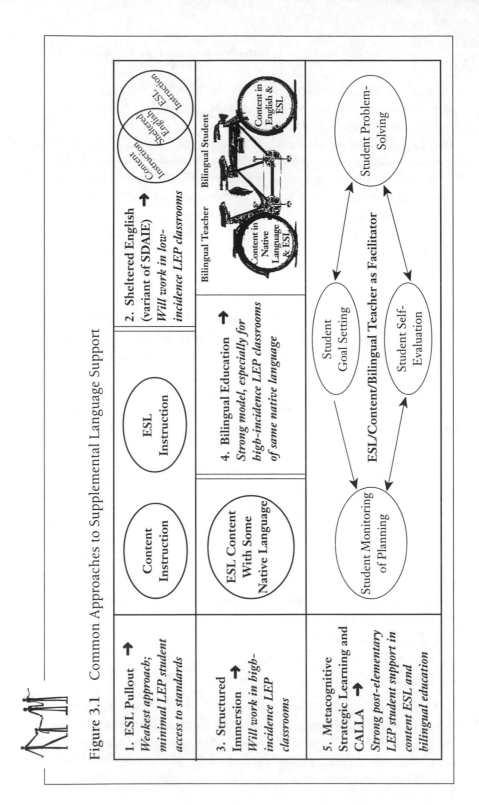

education programs phase out the native language once English is acquired; developmental bilingual education (also known as two-way bilingual education) programs sustain the native language and English for all students, regardless of their fluency level. Specially credentialed bilingual teachers provide instruction in both program models.

## Metacognitive Model of Strategic Learning

This is a social-cognitive learning inclusion model that emphasizes students' prior knowledge, collaborative and reflective learning, and awareness of self-regulated acquisition of English. CALLA (see below) is grounded on this model.

## Cognitive Academic Language Learning Approach (CALLA)

CALLA is a post-elementary-level approach that recursively combines language, content, and learning strategies through student preparation, presentation, guided practice, and strategic self-evaluation.

A structured language support program such as the program exemplars described previously must be provided based on what will most benefit LEP students. The goal is to provide the most appropriate services to the students so they may benefit fully from and succeed in an education conducted in English.

Figure 3.2 illustrates what the current research supports. Thomas and Collier (1997) examined the academic performance of students who began their exposure to English in kindergarten, attended either ESL pullout or sheltered English in elementary school, and received regular mainstream instruction in Grades 7–12. The results of their study are striking. The long-term scores from the schools' nationally normed standardized tests in English and reading were an average of 36 for the students in the sheltered English group and an average of 25 for the students in the ESL pullout group. Their analytic data research further notes that the final average scores for students in the ESL pullout setting are at the 11th national percentile by the end of their schooling. Among the students in sheltered English, the scores double to the 22nd national percentile—almost as well as the performance of students in a transitional bilingual education program with traditional teaching, which Thomas and Collier also examined. For rural schools, these findings are particularly welcome, as ESL managers weigh alternative ESL approaches, given the impracticality of implementing bona fide bilingual education programs with low-incidence LEP student enrollments.

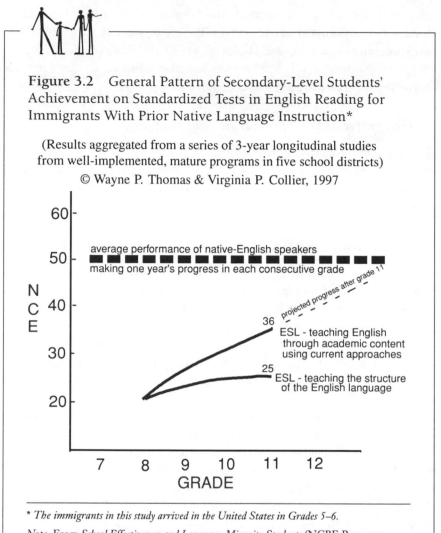

**Figure 3.2**　General Pattern of Secondary-Level Students' Achievement on Standardized Tests in English Reading for Immigrants With Prior Native Language Instruction*

(Results aggregated from a series of 3-year longitudinal studies from well-implemented, mature programs in five school districts)
© Wayne P. Thomas & Virginia P. Collier, 1997

* *The immigrants in this study arrived in the United States in Grades 5–6.*

Note. From *School Effectiveness and Language Minority Students* (NCBE Resource Collection Series, No. 9, p. 66), by W. P. Thomas and V. P. Collier, 1997, Washington, DC: National Clearinghouse for Bilingual Education. Copyright © 1997 by Wayne P. Thomas and Virginia P. Collier. Reprinted with permission.

In short, an inclusive English content model is the way to go. Ultimately, state and political realities may dictate that another approach prevail. Any approach must, of course, be consistent with law as discussed in the previous chapter. The ESL manager must, therefore, be well informed about both—the statutes and the research literature.

Another approach, not previously mentioned, is submersion, known popularly as *sink or swim*, and is not included in this discussion. As a do-nothing approach, the practice is illegal under Title VI of the Civil Rights Act. Relabeling submersion incorrectly as *immersion*, as some administrators may be tempted to do, does not alter that fact.

In short, the policy a school will follow in selecting an approach to program implementation is locally or sometimes state determined. Most state policies are derived from federal statute usually relating to bilingual education. Policies do, of course, affect hundreds or thousands of LEP students across each state. They should be developed and revisited frequently to ensure that the approach used best meets the needs of the LEP students served. Chamot and O'Malley (1987), well-established researchers on program design for the LEP student, recommend that the following three-question test be considered before deciding on a particular approach:

1. Is the approach grounded in well-controlled recent research?
2. Does the approach explain what and how the LEP student will learn?
3. Does the approach provide guidance for instruction?

Chamot, Barnhardt, El-Dinary, and Robbins's (1999) *Learning Strategies Handbook* with metacognitive strategic learning models offers an approach that offers a resounding "yes" to those questions. First, the research supporting instructional models for integrating content instruction with language learning is sound. The work of Chamot et al. (1999) draws in part from the work of Cantoni-Harvey's (1987) *Content-Area Instruction: Approaches and Strategies*; Mohan's (1986) *Language and Content*; and Snow, Met, and Genesee's (1989) "A Conceptual Framework for the Integration of Language and Content Instruction in Second/Foreign Language Instruction." Second, direct instruction using the approach in *Learning Strategies* focuses on ways students take responsibility for their own learning, including activating the student's prior knowledge of the topic for a learning task, summarizing the information, selecting details that will help the student perform the learning task, questioning (i.e., clarifying and verifying), and making inferences from knowledge gained. Third, teachers are guided through the applications of the *Learning Strategies* by applying Chamot and O'Malley's (1987) CALLA instructional model sequence as its framework. Recursive phases for following the framework with guidelines and sample activities are presented throughout the *Learning Strategies Handbook*.

# Crafting a *Lau* Plan

Under the law, a school district must have a procedure in place that outlines how it will serve LEP students under its jurisdiction. Named after the landmark Supreme Court case of *Lau v. Nichols* (see chapter 2), such a policy has come to be referred to as a *Lau* plan. The *Lau* plan is at the nucleus of almost all the ESL manager must know in overseeing a local ESL program. A *Lau* plan, usually formally adopted by a local school committee or school board, is the school district's vehicle for implementing Title VI of the Civil Rights Act and any other applicable statute previously described. Four principles should guide a manager's development of a *Lau* plan:

1. The plan cannot supersede federal or state law.
2. The plan is consistent districtwide, with no administrator having veto authority.
3. The plan delineates training and certification requirements it will follow in employing personnel who will implement the procedures and the language support program.
4. The plan will describe the following components of its equal access policy for the LEP students under its charge:
   - LEP student identification
   - a language assessment procedure (for first and/or second languages)
   - grade-level placement of LEP students
   - policy on the approach selected for English language support
   - criteria for student reclassification or exit from the language support program
   - language support program evaluation

The following is a sequence of steps that school districts may wish to follow as they develop a *Lau* plan to present to a school board or committee for adoption:

## *Step 1: Establish the Legal Basis for the Plan*

This step is primarily for the school committee's benefit as well as for the administration in understanding how important it is that a local policy be in place. The legal foundations that such a policy may cite are well detailed in chapter 2.

## Step 2: Create a Language Assessment Committee

The language assessment committee (LAC) is a group of school staff and parents of students that meets to develop an appropriate and effective structured language support program for LEP children. It is recommended that the LAC meet on a regular basis, such as quarterly, to review each LEP student's progress and the effectiveness of the program and to redirect certain instructional activities if necessary. The membership of the LAC should consist of a building-level administrator, the ESL professional, the child's standard-curriculum classroom teacher, a parent/guardian, and a school counselor (especially important if the child has experienced trauma from his or her native country). If there is no ESL professional on staff, a speech/language clinician may participate on the committee as a consultant to the committee and to the person providing the language support services. The membership of the committee may change periodically as the student is promoted to the next grade level or if new students who are LEP enroll at the school. An LAC convener needs to be determined at the outset. The list of responsibilities of the LAC would typically include

- reviewing the schoolwide home language surveys to identify potential LEP students in the school (those students who have not already been identified by other survey instruments, mandatory special education screening, or parent or teacher referral), circulating to the LAC the results of surveys that indicate minority language usage, and creating a language assessment file for each student identified (see the *Lau* plan model in Appendix A for an example of a comprehensive home language survey)
- notifying the parents in a language they comprehend of the date and nature of projected English-language proficiency testing
- administering multicriteria evaluation devices to potential LEP students each year
- making decisions from multicriteria evaluation devices about placement in a given program and appropriate ESL support
- meeting on a regular basis to monitor the LEP student's language and academic progress (grade reports, a portfolio, standardized tests when applicable, and parent and teacher observations)
- meeting with the entire school staff to provide information about LEP student enrollees and ESL support services
- recommending revisions and additions to the school district's *Lau* plan

- recommending modification of ESL support services or reclassification of a student from LEP to fully English proficient (FEP) or vice versa
- carrying out periodic monitoring for at least 3 years after a student's reclassification to FEP
- continually evaluating the ESL program as a whole

## Step 3: Determine Staff Responsibilities and Credentials for Instruction

The following roles or responsibilities of key staff should be described in the *Lau* plan:

- Determine roles of content teachers as partners to ESL.
- Determine roles of staff who serve on the LAC.
- Determine credentials of typical language support staff, which includes
  — credentials of districtwide ESL program director
  — ESL teachers (state certifications, endorsements)
  — education technicians (e.g., credentials for native languages)
  — independent ESL consultants and program evaluators
  — parent/community liaisons or coordinators

See the discussion in chapter 5 for more detailed information on ESL staffing.

## Step 4: Identify Test Instruments and Evaluative Devices to Be Used in Ongoing Assessments

Accountability guides much of the work of the ESL manager, and comprehensive assessment of the LEP student's performance is part of that responsibility. As part of a comprehensive assessment, an ESL manager should

- make language proficiency tests available for all grade levels
- establish the extent to which achievement tests will be used in LEP student assessment
- establish how student records will be maintained to gauge LEP student progress
- establish how teacher recommendations from student performance (e.g., writing samples, projects, portfolios) will be utilized

For additional information about assessments, see the discussion in chapter 7.

## Step 5: Set Limitations for Ongoing Testing

The following questions address limitations on testing:

- What time limitations will be placed on the identification process?
- What mechanism for record keeping, such as a language progress file (LPF) for identified language minority students, will be followed?
- Who will maintain and update student files?
- What components of multicriteria evaluation (entrance criteria) for identified language minority students will be established? Will it include native language evaluation? English evaluation tools?

## Step 6: Set Parameters for Language Support Services

ESL support is not the content teachers' panacea any more than submersion is to the uninitiated. The following questions need to be posed for the LAC's consideration:

- How much ESL will occur daily? Weekly?
- How much, if any, native language support will be provided?
- How will support services be carried out?

## Step 7: Establish Criteria for LEP Student Transition From Language Support Services

A significant function of the LAC involves consensus decisions on LEP students' exit from supplemental support. Multiple test measures will guide that decision-making process as previously noted in Step 4. The potential impact of the actions taken, as listed here, must be carefully weighed:

- Reclassify student for classroom placement.
- Transfer student to other support services or offerings.
- Schedule changes for student if applicable (e.g., band, clubs, and extracurricular activities).
- Partial exit for students who may be described as transitionally English proficient (i.e., ESL teacher monitoring of the academic performance of former LEP students in content areas in the absence of ESL pullout).
- Plan for the student's eventual full exit.
- Oversee the LAC's process for monitoring LEP student progress for at least 3 years after he or she exits the program.

## Step 8: Determine Program Effectiveness

To ensure that the most effective and appropriate structured language support programming for LEP children is occurring, a model for overall program evaluation should be developed and utilized. Chapter 8 provides greater detail on the matter of program evaluation. The *Lau* plan should propose that the following kinds of evaluation criteria be documented:

- attainment of program outcomes
- attainment of learner outcomes
- school climate and support for the program and children
- quality of instructional materials
- maintenance of information about students
- effectiveness of staff development activities
- amount and effectiveness of mainstream-ESL collaboration
- effectiveness of school and program communication with parents
- implementation of the district's *Lau* plan itself as approved by its school committee or board

The program accountability and demonstration of outcomes will enhance the program's legitimacy in the school and will consummate the work and methods of the program toward the ultimate goal of continually improving instruction to meet learner instructional needs. In all of the procedures involving the identification, assessment, provision of services, and exit from services for LEP children, thorough record keeping must be maintained. Such record keeping is necessary to keep track of the components of the individual learning plan and the child's progress within it. The child's LPF is also a valuable source of information for program evaluation. If the child's family moves to a different school, the information in the LPF can help the new teacher set up a language support program more expeditiously. The LPF is also a valuable tool for illustrating a school's commitment to quality services for LEP children. A member of the LAC needs to be designated as the person to maintain the LPF. Typically, such a file would consist of

- a copy of the home language survey that initially identified the child as a language minority student
- all test scores pertaining to program decisions
- recommendations for the individual child's program
- portfolio of literacy work done by the student
- individualized language support programs (with program goals and objectives) and outcomes

- parent interviews or questionnaire notes
- time line of LAC meetings
- recommendations for reclassification or exit from program
- notes for observations by school staff
- copies of report cards

Armed with a sound grasp of key statutes protective of LEP students, the program manager becomes well equipped to craft a *Lau* plan that a superintendent and school board can adopt. A model plan from a fictitious school district, Heartland Valley, is presented as one an ESL manager may wish to work from (see Appendix A).

## Potential Constraints in Managing ESL Local Policy

### Instructional Space

Of all the concerns that ESL managers express, instructional space has generated many horror stories. Perhaps this occurs because it is the most concrete proof that the program exists and that there is a need for it in the school. ESL teachers have worked in drafty halls, noisy boiler rooms, windowless janitors' closets with peculiar smells, libraries where students could not talk, and on auditorium stages while the band practiced below. They have begged supplies from "real" teachers (having been issued none), retrieved furniture from dumpsters, made secret deals with custodians, and wheedled and cajoled administrators to recognize the reality of their students' need for space and materials. It is a credit to the ingenuity and dedication of some teachers that their programs exist at all.

Establishing a high-quality ESL program demands that a school provide both a place for instruction to be carried out and adequate materials to support the instruction. Although this is a commonsense assertion, it is often in these two areas that schools fail to serve their LEP students. Adequate space for an effective ESL program is indeed an important component of local policy and should be included in the *Lau* plan.

The burden of proof of acceptable physical space for LEP students is on the school district. A helpful rule is to consider this space as it compares to that used by nonminority children. If all children, regardless of national origin, must utilize this space, then it is probable that such space is not a denial of equal education access.

Space intended for instructional purposes needs to be comparable to what is offered to mainstream students. That is, if the ESL program is relegated to a space at the back of the auditorium and no other program is relegated to that space, the classroom space is not comparable to other programs provided by the school. Instructional space must have the capability of being free of distraction. Its location should encourage integration of ESL instruction with that of the mainstream instruction because the interaction of both is crucial to student success (see chapter 4). In pullout arrangements of last resort, a language laboratory might be established for LEP students where they may work with an ESL tutor. The ESL classroom should be accessible to all of the building's resources such as the library, computer lab, gym, audiovisual equipment, auditorium, and stage. Table 3.2 identifies some of the places where LEP students find themselves throughout the school day and offers ESL teachers recommendations on how to best utilize those spaces.

The following scenarios depict environments that ESL teachers (either single-building teachers or itinerant ones) commonly encounter. The numbers and needs of students dictate what kind of setup is appropriate, and the key is flexibility—the flexibility to sense LEP students' needs and to advocate effectively for the kind of space that will best meet those needs. Any one of the situations that follow could provide a suitable environment for learning. The regular content-area classroom or self-contained elementary classroom must be at the core of an LEP student's daily experience at school. Many of those students' needs are best served in such a classroom. Ancillary support beyond that classroom involves decision making that the ESL teacher and the classroom teacher will jointly embrace after assessing each student's social, emotional, academic, and language needs, as outlined in the school district's *Lau* plan. The scenario that follows is a common one that has been reasonably managed in this instance. See chapter 5 for a more in-depth discussion of ESL collaboratives.

## Scenario

*In April, two Tagalog-speaking girls, ages 8 and 9, arrive from the Philippines. Neither child speaks nor understands any English. Their father was recently killed in a street attack. They are the youngest of eight children and have never been apart; therefore, the decision is made to place them together in one grade. The content-area teacher does not know how to help them or where to start but feels it is best for the girls to remain in the same classroom.*

*The ESL teacher goes into the classroom for an hour every morning to observe, help the girls participate in classroom activities, and assess what she should teach to help them meet with success. During the time she is in the classroom, the students participate with their classmates as activities permit. At other times,*

## Table 3.2 Spaces Where LEP Students May Find Themselves

| Spaces | Purpose of Spaces and Recommendations |
|---|---|
| Regular homeroom or advisory group | Called by a variety of names, this typically is an anchor base for all students. Integration of LEP students with non-LEP peers can occur here and can help to promote the social skills of LEP students. |
| Special subject areas (e.g., physical education, integrated arts, computer instruction, wellness and life skills, and sometimes mathematics) | Somewhat less language dependent, these subject areas can provide a comfort zone for LEP students (especially newcomers) to adjust to their new culture and to study with their non-LEP peers. |
| Resource room | A room with a stigma, this may be used for limited pullout activity to support short-term metacognitive activities of the regular content classroom. It may be used for individual testing or for short-term intensive ESL for newcomers. The resource room must not become the primary classroom for the LEP student in schools that boast of inclusive instruction. |
| Content-area classrooms | These are places where modified curriculum, including SDAIE, CALLA, bilingual education, and metacognitive learning strategies, occur and where LEP students are supported by ESL teachers and peer tutors. |
| Backstage, the boiler room, the storage closet, under the stairwell, the hallway | These are not appropriate learning venues for any children—let alone LEP children. |

*they are instructed in an area in that room set up for ESL. This might be a table with a bookshelf for materials. An area behind a folding partition minimizes visual and auditory distractions.*

Some situations will necessitate pulling out small groups of students for part of their school day. Sometimes a space with close proximity to regular classes helps to support LEP students as well as non-LEP students. A resource room may meet some students' needs, allowing for more flexibility. It is recommended that the ESL teacher who is given a book storage room, a custodian's closet, or a drafty hall space, whereas non-ESL teachers have their own spacious, well-equipped rooms, respond in kind. ESL teachers, managers, and administrators familiar with relevant statutes know that all students are entitled to equitable program spaces and facilities. Following are three scenarios the ESL manager may encounter, given a nondiscriminatory and equitable pullout arrangement that includes content ESL-content teacher collaboration. Indeed, creativity and good negotiation skills help.

## Scenario A

*In a low-incidence population, there are four first and second graders who are each in different classrooms. They have adequate conversational English skills, but their regular content classroom and ESL teachers note their difficulty following oral directions; they do not use correct tenses and pronouns when speaking or writing and have difficulty with vocabulary, particularly in worksheets with pictures that have to be identified. It does not seem appropriate to enter the classrooms to work with each student individually because (a) their instructional program will require an area free from auditory distractions and a place where their voices will not bother others and (b) they all have comparable needs. As a result, both teachers schedule all the LEP children for simultaneous ESL pullout instruction. After considering the options (a poorly lit but quiet open hall area that has no space for storage or electric outlets), the ESL teacher compromises by sharing the resource room when there is only one other group there. The resource room has a chalkboard, bookshelves, a table and chairs, a sink, two wall cabinets, and some counter space.*

## Scenario B

*The ESL teacher is at the middle school for three scheduled periods every day. There are eight ESL students with skills ranging from no prior education and no English to comparable academic programs in the native country and fluency in conversational English but inability to handle the regular classroom without assistance. This is a beautiful, brand-new school, but, as there was no ESL pro-*

*gram when the school was planned, there is no space dedicated to ESL instruc-*
*tion. The ESL teacher has been given a small windowless room originally planned*
*as a storage closet for special education materials. This room is just outside of the*
*special education resource room. The ESL teacher begs the custodian to find some*
*shelves and a chalkboard, and being the ally that she is, the custodian consents.*
*The room is so small that the door cannot be closed because the table is in the*
*way. However, if the door were closed, the students would shiver. Because the room*
*was designed for the door to remain closed, there are no heat vents. The staff of*
*the special education resource room keeps the door of the resource room open to*
*facilitate comings and goings of students. Raucous laughter, shouting, and occa-*
*sional temper tantrums punctuate the air. A resource room is available in the*
*afternoon, so the ESL teacher schedules a group of students with similar needs*
*for Period 7 and meets with small groups in their "closet" during Periods 5 and*
*6. This ESL teacher has been around though, and she has learned the ins and*
*outs of getting what she wants. She invites the principal, central office adminis-*
*trators, and the school board to participate in an ESL activity—to enlighten them*
*about the ESL instructional program. Within a month, the principal has met*
*with the ESL teacher to resolve space needs. There is a comparable closet room*
*used for enrichment tutorials for non-ESL students and another one for small-*
*group guidance counselor conferences.*

## Scenario C

*After 3 years of moving from one classroom to another, the ESL department has*
*been given half a mobile unit, its own ESL space for 12 students. There is a*
*teacher's desk, student desks, a file cabinet, and two old tables that are too high to*
*sit at but suitable for stacking materials. There are no bookcases. There is a beau-*
*tiful new whiteboard, and the room is carpeted, a plus for an ESL space. The*
*ESL teachers have requested hanging maps of the United States and world maps*
*as well as new texts for an ESL-sheltered history class. They are told that there*
*is enough money for texts and maps but not for bookshelves. They opt for the*
*maps and texts and stack the books and other material on tables. ESL occupies*
*this space for four periods a day. Two periods during the day, the ESL teachers*
*go into biology and social studies classes with the students. The mobile unit is*
*actually available two other periods, but the ESL teachers decide to hold other*
*classes in English and history classrooms that are not being used at the time.*

# Budget

Schools are obligated to provide not only instruction but also instructional
resources to benefit LEP students. A regular classroom is an enticing environment for promoting equitable participation for all students as described
in the anchor legislation, Title VI of the Civil Rights Act (see chapter 2).

As in large urban areas, LEP enrollee needs in rural and small urban schools can vary considerably. Hence, it may be difficult to anticipate what their needs will be when budgets are prepared months ahead of time. In fact, annual budgets do not tend to include contingencies for the possible arrival of newcomer LEP students or increases in present enrollments. Each ESL program must be given a reasonable budget so that the program can be carried out effectively and appropriately.

The ESL manager should be able to prepare an effective and appropriate program budget. Such a budget would include instructional materials comparable in quality to what non-LEP students enjoy, stipends for native language translators, opportunities to interact in real-life situations (i.e., field trips), and professional development opportunities. Note that staffing, translator, and instructional material needs for an ESL program can fluctuate greatly if the student population changes—usually with little or no notice. The budget should have the flexibility to accommodate expenditures that may arise when the LEP population fluctuates long after a budget is in place. If a budget does not have that flexibility, the ESL manager should at least alert the superintendent or the school committee or both that this possibility could occur. A rationale for typical budget items may look as follows:

| *Budget Item* | *Purpose* |
| --- | --- |
| Native language facilitators/translators | Provide (per Title VI) LEP parents/guardians access to school notices and meetings pertaining to their child's well-being and instructional program |
| | Provide support for the ESL teacher in the classroom |
| Professional development | Provide (per OCR Enforcement Policy of 1991; see chapter 2) ESL educators opportunities to participate in professional growth activities |
| Field trips | Give LEP students genuine opportunities to interact in the community |
| | Provide experience-based schemata for skills and activities |
| Instructional materials | Provide materials for ESL instruction that are especially developed for LEP students of different proficiency levels and with varying skill needs |

## Transportation

To state what appears obvious, LEP students are entitled to equal access to transportation to and from school. That access would include having equal access to before- and after-school programs that are made available to students who are not in an ESL program. The families of LEP students cannot be assessed a charge for transportation if non-LEP students are not similarly assessed.

Because many rural schools have a scattered population of LEP students, it is common and legal for the ESL program to be centralized in a magnet school for efficiency of services. If bus transportation arrangements to and from a magnet school ESL program result in the inability of LEP students to participate in before- and after-school activities, the arrangements may need to be altered to make those opportunities realistically available to those students.

Language minority parents need to be given the district's transportation policies in a language they comprehend; if the parents are themselves LEP, the policies will have to be provided either orally or in writing in a language they comprehend.

# Summative Guidance for the ESL Program Manager

This chapter serves as a segue from the previous chapter's emphasis on statutes, namely, crafting and implementing ESL program policy consistent with federal and state statutes. Although there appear to be some intelligent choices as to which program model to follow, the choice may be governed by the reality of a school district's low-density LEP student population rather than by the research that overwhelmingly favors variants of bilingual education, including metacognitive strategic learning. Forced to consider "second best," the ESL manager is advised to concentrate on ESL/content collaboratives as a viable model in the absence of bilingual education. The data presented earlier (Thomas & Collier, 1997) make this choice easy to defend.

A *Lau* plan, approved by the district's school board or committee, is at the core of a comprehensive equal access program for LEP students. It becomes the province of the ESL manager to work through the eight steps described in this chapter in developing the district's *Lau* plan. The Heartland Valley *Lau* plan serves as a sample for how those eight steps translate to actual policy development.

Issues that generally do not find their way to the *Lau* plan but receive highly contentious attention are matters relating to equitable instructional space as well as an ESL program budget. On the other hand, any ESL program feature ought to and can find its way to a *Lau* plan, which may include issues of ESL space and ESL budget among others.

Another feature that may be included in a *Lau* plan relates to schoolwide testing. A policy for granting waivers for schoolwide testing would, for example, have the effect of exempting LEP students from certain assessments. Test modification and alternative testing provisions for LEP students are other features that may be found in a *Lau* plan.

Another *Lau* plan policy may present a procedure for offering parental waivers (albeit reluctantly) for declining to enroll an LEP student in ESL. This circumstance presents itself, for example, when the ESL program does not serve the family's neighborhood school. It may also occur when a parent refuses ESL interventions altogether.

In any case, once the school committee approves the plan as local policy, no administrator can veto any of its provisions but the policy can—and should—be updated to reflect changing demographics, state policy, new scholarship from the literature on second language learning, and, of course, changing needs. If the manager knows how to craft a *Lau* plan that everyone can live with, that plan will make everyone's life at school a good deal easier.

The provision of adequate and equitable space, resources, and transportation is one of the building blocks with which effective programs are established. Although schools may face limitations in making these rudimentary provisions, it is always worthwhile for a school to do whatever is necessary to meet space and resources requirements. Support and understanding on the part of the school administration is crucial in providing adequate space and resources. Consider a school district's efforts satisfactory if the answer to each of the following questions yields a "yes" response:

- Is ESL instructional space comparable to that provided for other programs for a similar number of students?
  — Does the space have the capability of being quiet and free from distractions?
  — Is the space accessible to the school building's resources?
- Are ESL instructional materials comparable to those provided to other programs serving a similar number of students?
  — Are the materials appropriate for the instructional needs of the individual students?
  — Are the materials appropriate for the ESL teacher's needs?
- Is there an ESL program budget that
  — allocates money for instructional materials?

— takes into account the possibility of new students entering the ESL program at any time during the school year?

— contains a line item for translator services, school notices, and meetings pertaining to the LEP student's instructional program (e.g., LAC, pupil evaluation team [for special education referrals and placement])?

— contains a line item for professional development for the ESL teacher and ESL paraprofessional?

— contains a line item for field trips?

- Do LEP students have equal opportunities to school bus transportation?

- Do LEP students ride a school bus with peers?

- When LEP students do not attend a neighborhood school, do they have access to late buses so that they may participate in after-school programs?

- Are transportation policies distributed to other parents also distributed to language minority parents in a language they comprehend?

A "no" response to any of the previous questions would trigger a serious need for the ESL manager to convene the stakeholders for a reevaluation of the school district's *Lau* plan and submit a revised plan to the school committee for formal approval. Worse yet, a "no" response to any of the above could trigger a complaint to the district's regional OCR to resolve the inequities.


## Suggested Resources on the Web

For more samples of *Lau* plans:
> ESL/Bilingual Education Office at the Maine Department of Education (http://www.state.me.us/education/esl.htm)

For ESL help from ESL colleagues around the world:
> *Dave Sperling's ESL Café* (http://www.eslcafe/help/index.cgi)

For information on how the OCR ensures equal access to education and resolves complaints:
> (http://www.ed.gov/offices/OCR/ensure99.html)

For professional development programs and emerging ESL program models that support LEP students:
> Teachers of English to Speakers of Other Languages (TESOL) (http://www.tesol.org/edprg/index.html)

# Chapter 4
# Including LEP Students in Standards-Driven Curriculum

*Perhaps those "good" teachers succeeded because they gave optimal attention to linguistic goals and to the personhood of their students.*

—Brown, 1994, p. 138

There was a time when an LEP student's success was determined largely by self-motivation. A pullout program of ESL for the short term was the model. Anything beyond that remained the student's own crucible. This is no longer the case—standards for all students have arrived.

As ESL managers maintain a finger on the pulse of direction, policy, and accountability from the school district, they may query, "What shall the LEP student be accountable for? How high shall the bar of teacher expectations be placed?" In short, what are the local standards expected of all students? What standards, if any, does the school committee or the state (or both) expect of the LEP student? Are those standards different from the general standards expected of the non-LEP student?

# Standards Across the United States

The U.S. Department of Education (USDE) has vigorously promoted national standards since they were adopted in 1994. They are commonly referred to as the Eight National Education Goals prescribed by the USDE:

1.  By the year 2000, every adult American will be literate and will possess the knowledge and skills necessary to compete in a global economy and exercise the rights and responsibilities of citizenship.

2.  By the year 2000, every school in the U.S. will be free of drugs, violence, and the unauthorized presence of firearms and alcohol and will offer a disciplined environment conducive to learning.

3.  By the year 2000, the nation's teaching force will have access to programs for the continued improvement of their professional skills and the opportunity to acquire the knowledge and skills needed to instruct and prepare all American students for the next century.

4.  By the year 2000, every school will promote partnerships that will increase parental involvement and participation in promoting the social, emotional, and academic growth of children.

5.  By the year 2000, all children in America will start school ready to learn.

6.  By the year 2000, the high school graduation rate will increase to at least 90 percent.

7.  By the year 2000, all students will leave grades 4, 8, and 12 having demonstrated competency over challenging subject matter including English, mathematics, science, foreign languages, civics and government, economics, arts, history, and geography, and every school in America will ensure that all students learn to use their minds well, so they may be prepared for responsible citizenship, further learning, and productive employment in our nation's modern economy.

8.  By the year 2000, U.S. students will be the first in the world in mathematics and science achievement. (U.S. Department of Education, 1994, p. 3)

A National Education Goals Panel reports annually on the progress each state is making toward attainment of those national goals. For example, in its year-end findings for 1999, the Panel reported significant improvement nationally for these goal areas: ready to learn, student achievement and citizenship, mathematics and sciences, safe and drug-free schools (but with declines in some areas), school completion, adult literacy and lifelong learning, and parental participation. The highest performing states were Maine, Connecticut, and North Dakota, and Connecticut, North Carolina, and Washington, DC, were the most improved (National Education Goals Panel, 2000). The USDE has presented mounting evidence that far more rigorous levels of academic achievement will be required to equip all students for jobs of the 21st century. Individual state scorecards may be accessed on the Web at http://www.negp.gov/page7-1-5.htm.

Merely having standards is window dressing, or the warm-up before the show. Implementing the standards requires a command performance. Of course, whereas there is little research on the impact the national standards have had on learning in recent years, there is some data on states' performance on their standards, many of them derived from the national standards. According to Finn, Petrilli, and Vanourek's (1998) analysis of state standards for English, history, geography, math, and science, merely 18% of the states pass muster (a grade of "C" or better) in setting clear expectations and goals of their students. In Jerald's (2000) review for *Education Week* of states' performance on their standards 2 years later, states' previously abysmal numbers in achieving standards skyrocketed to 90%. Rankings from both sources are displayed state by state in Table 4.1.

## Standards and the LEP Student

What about LEP students and the brouhaha about standards? Under Goals 2000's "Accountability Challenge" national legislation, state education departments are required to submit plans on how their reform efforts will improve schooling for all groups, including LEP students. Excluding LEP children from state-mandated assessments, once a common practice, has traditionally relieved schools of their accountability for serving them. In surveys conducted by Rivera, Stansfield, Scialdone, and Sharkey (2000) for 1998–1999, 92% of the states permit some form of exempting LEP students from state assessments. Those days are numbered. Most states have no monitoring process to determine how well their schools are serving LEP students. Yet, most states address funding as well as instructional direction to be followed in educating LEP students. Variation of approach is considerable as evident in Table 4.2, which shows states' different requirements for educating LEP students.

Of course, the cynics may say of standards, "this too shall pass," and return to their cloisters and resist change. The seriousness with which states have

Table 4.1  Rankings for Achieving State Standards Across All Subjects in 1998 and 2000

(In order by cumulative grade point average [GPA] according to Fordham's analysis)

| | English (n = 28) (Fordham) | History (n = 38) (Fordham) | Geography (n = 39) (Fordham) | Math (n = 47) (Fordham) | Science (n = 36) (Fordham) | Cumulative GPA (Fordham) | Grade (Fordham) | State Grade (NAEP 2000)+ |
|---|---|---|---|---|---|---|---|---|
| Arizona | B | —** | — | B | A | 3.33 | B+ | B+ |
| California | — | B | D | A | A | 3.00 | B | B+ |
| Texas | B | B | A | B | C | 3.00 | B | B+ |
| Indiana | F | C | A | C | A | 2.40 | C+ | B |
| Utah | C | C | C | B | B | 2.40 | C+ | C |
| Virginia | B | A | D | B | D | 2.40 | C+ | A- |
| Massachusetts | A | B | D | F | C | 2.00 | C | A |
| No. Carolina | — | F | C | A | — | 2.00 | C | A |
| Rhode Island* | — | — | — | F | A | 2.00 | C | C- |
| West Virginia | — | C | B | B | F | 2.00 | C | B+ |
| Alabama | D | C | C | B | D | 1.80 | C- | B+ |
| Louisiana | — | C | C | F | B | 1.75 | C- | B+ |
| Dist. of Col. | — | C | C | D | — | 1.67 | C- | — |
| Georgia | B | D | F | B | D | 1.60 | C- | B+ |
| Illinois | B | F | D | D | B | 1.60 | C- | C+ |
| New Hamp. | D | C | B | C | F | 1.60 | C- | B+ |
| Connecticut | — | C | F | D | B | 1.50 | C- | B |
| Ohio | F | D | D | A | — | 1.50 | C- | B+ |
| Colorado | F | D | A | D | D | 1.40 | D+ | B |
| New York | C | F | F | B | C | 1.40 | D+ | A |
| Alaska | — | F | C | C | — | 1.33 | D+ | C- |
| Hawaii | F | — | — | F | A | 1.33 | D+ | D+ |
| Vermont | — | F | F | C | B | 1.25 | D+ | C- |
| Delaware | D | F | F | C | B | 1.20 | D+ | B |

| State | (1) | (2) | (3) | (4) | (5) | NAEP+ | (7) | (8) |
|---|---|---|---|---|---|---|---|---|
| Florida | D | C | C | D | F | 1.20 | D+ | A- |
| New Jersey | F | F | F | C | A | 1.20 | D+ | B- |
| Wisconsin | C | F | F | C | C | 1.20 | D+ | C |
| Mississippi | D | F | F | B | F | 1.00 | D | C+ |
| Oregon | F | — | — | D | C | 1.00 | D | A |
| So. Carolina | — | — | — | D | D | 1.00 | D | B |
| Kansas | F | D | D | D | C | 0.80 | D- | A- |
| Missouri | F | C | C | F | C | 0.80 | D- | C+ |
| Washington | D | F | F | F | B | 0.80 | D- | C+ |
| Michigan | F | B | B | F | — | 0.75 | D- | B |
| Oklahoma | C | F | F | F | — | 0.75 | D- | A- |
| Idaho | F | F | C | F | — | 0.67 | D- | C |
| Tennessee | F | D | F | C | F | 0.60 | D- | D |
| Maine | — | D | F | F | D | 0.50 | D- | C+ |
| Pennsylvania | — | F | — | D | — | 0.50 | D- | B |
| Nebraska | — | F | F | F | D | 0.33 | F | C- |
| North Dakota | — | — | F | D | F | 0.33 | F | D+ |
| Kentucky | — | F | F | D | F | 0.25 | F | B+ |
| Arkansas | — | F | — | F | F | 0.00 | F | B+ |
| Maryland | F | — | F | F | — | 0.00 | F | C- |
| Minnesota | — | F | F | — | — | 0.00 | F | C- |
| Montana | — | — | — | F | F | 0.00 | F | D- |
| New Mexico | — | F | — | F | — | 0.00 | F | A |
| South Dakota | — | — | F | F | — | 0.00 | F | C+ |
| Iowa | — | — | — | — | — | — | — | F |
| Nevada | — | — | — | — | — | — | — | A- |
| Wyoming | — | — | — | — | — | — | — | C- |

+ *National Assessment of Educational Progress (NAEP)*

* *Italicized states have grades for two subjects or fewer.*

** *The dashes denote academic fields in which states lack standards.*

Note. The data in columns 1–7 are from *The State of State Standards*, by C. E. Finn, Jr., M. J. Petrilli, and G. Vanourek, 1998, retrieved August 13, 2000, from the World Wide Web: http://www.edexcellence.net/standards/summary.html. Copyright © 1998 by the Thomas B. Ford Foundation. Reprinted with permission. The data in column 8 are from *Quality Counts 2000: Who Shall Teach* (p. 1), by C. D. Jerald, 2000, retrieved June 8, 2000, from the World Wide Web: http://www.edweek.com/sreports/qc00/tables/gradesum-t1b.htm. Copyright © 2000 by Education Week. Reprinted with permission.

accepted the accountability challenge is clearly implicit in the 1998/2000 shift in grades illustrated in Table 4.1. With standards mandated by legislation in virtually every state, teachers are advised that they must incorporate the standards in local curriculum. Human nature would suggest that there are those who are skillful at creating the illusion of adopting new procedures by closing their classroom doors and ignoring the requirements sans their performance evaluation. Engaging them at the outset, then, becomes critical. If the ESL teacher is not supported and engaged in the standards adoption process, the disaffected teacher may ultimately have the unfortunate upper hand in a more cavalier implementation of the standards.

ESL instruction is commonly absent in state standards policy discussion. Yet, it is becoming increasingly relevant in the broader discussion. Indeed, research has only just begun on the impact standards have on learning for the typical non-LEP student. Action research on standards and the LEP student remains an emerging groundbreaking challenge, especially for rural schools. The Northeast and Islands Regional Educational Laboratory at Brown University is pioneering initiatives in this area. These pioneering initiatives include investigating standards and learning practices, conducting case-study assessments of LEP students (including LEP students in statewide assessments), and studying the influence of culture in mathematics and science reasoning.

The lack of research on standards and the LEP student is a dilemma that projects across the United States are seeking to address. Some of the larger states are developing their own assessment tools in minority languages; others are working on accommodations in English language testing. Long-term solutions, however, will demand substantial resources that so far do not appear significantly forthcoming for rural schools.

The Center for Research on Education, Diversity & Excellence (CREDE), based at the University of California-Santa Cruz, is pursuing research on standards for the LEP student. Its research mission is, in fact, to assist the United States' culturally diverse students in achieving high academic standards. Eight premises govern its mission:

1.  All children can learn.

2.  All children learn best when challenged by high standards.

3.  English proficiency is a goal for all students.

4.  Bilingual proficiency is desirable for all students.

5. Languages and cultural diversity can be assets for teaching and learning.

6. Teaching and learning must be accommodated to individuals.

7. Risk factors can be mitigated by schools that teach the skills that schools require.

8. Solutions to risk factors must be grounded in a valid general theory of developmental, teaching, and schooling processes. (Center for Research on Education, Diversity & Excellence, 1997, p. 1)

In 1996, the Center for Equity and Excellence in Education, based at The George Washington University, addressed six imperatives in its standards discussion. The Center's six guiding principles are comparable to those described for CREDE:

1. English language learners must be held to the same high expectations of learning established for all students (see Premise 2 for CREDE).

2. English language learners must develop full receptive and productive proficiencies in English in the domains of listening, speaking, reading, and writing, consistent with expectations for all students.

3. English language learners are taught challenging content to enable them to meet performance standards in all content areas, including reading and language arts, mathematics, social studies, science, the fine arts, health, and physical education, consistent with those for all students.

4. English language learners receive instruction that builds on their previous education and cognitive abilities and that reflects their language proficiency levels.

5. English language learners are evaluated with appropriate and valid assessments that are aligned with state and local standards and that take into account the language acquisition stages and cultural backgrounds of the students (see Premises 5 and 6 for CREDE).

6. The academic success of English language learners is a responsibility shared by all educators, the family, and the community.[1]

---

[1] From *Promoting Excellence: Ensuring Academic Success for Limited English Proficient Students* (p. 11), by the Center for Equity and Excellence in Education, 1996, 2000, Washington, DC: The George Washington University. Copyright © 1996 and 2000 by The George Washington University. Adapted with permission.

Table 4.2   State Requirements for Educating Limited English Proficient (LEP) Students

| State | Mandates Bilingual Education | Prohibits Bilingual Education | Statute Imposed for LEP Students | Funding Limited to Bilingual Education | Funding Limited to Non-Bilingual Education | No Funding for LEP Student Instruction | Content Standards Specific to LEP Students | No Statutes Relating to LEP Student Instruction |
|---|---|---|---|---|---|---|---|---|
| Alabama | | | | | | | | X |
| Alaska | X | | X | | | | | |
| Arizona | | | X | | | | | |
| Arkansas | | X | | | | | | |
| California | | | X | | | | X | |
| Colorado | | | X | | | | | |
| Connecticut | X | | X | | | | | |
| Delaware | | X | | | | X | | |
| Florida | | | X | | | | | |
| Georgia | | | X | | | X | | |
| Hawaii | | | X | | | | | |
| Idaho | | | X | | | | | |
| Illinois | X | | | | | | | |
| Indiana | X | | X | | | | | |
| Iowa | | | X | | | | | |
| Kansas | | | X | | | | | |
| Kentucky | | | | | | X | | X |
| Louisiana | | | | | | X | | X |
| Maine | | | X | | | | | |
| Maryland | | | X | | | | X | |
| Massachusetts | X | | X | | | | X | |
| Michigan | | | X | X | | | | |

| State | | | | | | | | |
|---|---|---|---|---|---|---|---|---|
| Minnesota | | | | | | | | |
| Mississippi | | | X | | | X | | X |
| Missouri | | | X | | | X | | X |
| Montana | | | | | | | | |
| Nebraska | | X | | | | | | |
| Nevada | | | X | | | X | | |
| New Hamp. | | | X | | | X | | |
| New Jersey | X | | | | | | X | |
| New Mexico | | | | X | | | | |
| New York | X | | X | | | | X | |
| No. Carolina | | | X | | | X | X | |
| No. Dakota | | | | | | | | X |
| Ohio | | | X | | | X | | |
| Oklahoma | | | X | | | | | |
| Oregon | | | X | | | X | | |
| Pennsylvania | | | X | | | X | | |
| Rhode Island | | | X | | | | | |
| So. Carolina | | | | | | X | | |
| So. Dakota | | | | | | X | | X |
| Tennessee | | | X | | | X | | |
| Texas | X | | X | | | | | |
| Utah | | | X | | | X | | |
| Vermont | | | | | | | | X |
| Virginia | X | | X | | X | | | |
| Washington | X | | X | | | | | |
| West Virginia | | | X | | | | | X |
| Wisconsin | X | | | | | X | | |
| Wyoming | | | | | | | | X |

*Note.* From *A 50 State Survey of Requirements for the Education of Language Minority Children* [Abstract], by A. Garcia and C. Morgan, 1997, Washington, DC: READ Institute, retrieved July 26, 2000, from the World Wide Web: http://www.read-institute.org/50state.html. Copyright © 1997 by the READ Institute. Adapted with permission.

# Implementing the TESOL Standards

Among the first professional organizations to respond to the national call for state standards was Teachers of English to Speakers of Other Languages (TESOL). In *Promising Futures* (TESOL, 1996), the introduction to *ESL Standards for Pre–K–12 Students* (TESOL, 1997), the ESL Standards Project Committee clearly articulated its 4-point purpose, arguing that ESL standards can indeed complement state standards across the United States. The project committee stated the following:

1. Schools and communities throughout the United States are facing increased linguistic and cultural diversity.

2. ESOL students vary greatly in proficiency levels and academic needs.

3. The *ESL Standards* describe the language skills necessary for social and academic purposes.

4. The *ESL Standards* provide the bridge to general education standards expected of all students in the United States. (TESOL, 1997, pp. 1–2)

Beyond the rationale described here for the ESL standards, the organization has noted three other compelling arguments:

1. LEP students have different needs in learning English from those of native English speakers.

2. The needs of LEP students are not addressed in most other content-area standards documents.

3. The ESL standards provide a much-needed service to and for the ESL profession.

The rationale for ESL managers' proactive role in the standards discussion is persuasive: They must become more visible in brokering local standards. The days when isolationism of ESL teachers has been the standard are numbered; the pressures are acute. For example, the accreditation process for K–12 schools will now include the ESL standards as recommended by the National Study of School Evaluations. Schools will also become increasingly dependent on ESL teachers, in collaboration with content-area teachers, in accommodating the needs of LEP students in statewide assessments. The stakes have never been higher.

The ESL standards presented in Table 4.3 apply to all grade levels pre-K–12 for LEP children. Accompanying each grade cluster level (pre-K–3, 4–8, and 9–12) are the listed overarching goals. Several subcategories are not listed in Table 4.3, because that is readily available at TESOL's Web site: http://www.tesol.org/. Those subcategories for the goals and standards are

- descriptors: categories of behaviors students can demonstrate when a standard is met
- sample progress indicators: assessments of how well students are doing
- vignettes: classroom-based, real-life scenarios with descriptive background information for these vignettes
- sequence: a description of how the lesson in the vignette is carried out
- discussion: connecting the vignette to the standard and progress indicators

There is a surfeit of data, analyses, and scorecards on the continuing national standards debate. One must note that the ESL standards are, of course, not the only standards. There are scores of Web sites on the Internet that the reader may want to explore for other standards (see the end of the chapter for additional Web site addresses). Where, therefore, should the ESL teacher/manager be positioned in implementing standards-based education in his or her school district? The following guidelines warrant consideration:

1. Become familiar with TESOL's ESL standards as well as state, regional, and local standards that best apply to your school community.
2. Participate in a steering committee with subject-area colleagues in discussions about standards.
3. Find out how the national ESL standards align with the state content-area standards as the core or nucleus for local standards. For a searchable database that includes information on states, districts, and schools that are involved in using the ESL standards, see http://www2.cal.org/eslstds/.
4. Find out how the ESL standards align with English language proficiency levels set for each standard, corresponding, of course, to pre-K–12 grade-level state standards. Three goals are noted in Table 4.3 with their accompanying standards for LEP students.
5. Identify assessment tools to be used for setting interim benchmarks for which LEP students would be held accountable at their English language proficiency levels.
6. Join TESOL's ESL standards electronic discussion list to share your insights and learn from others nationwide who are working through this process. (See the end of this chapter for the Web site address to access this list.)

August and Pease-Alvarez (1996) point to four examples of classroom practices reflective of standards-driven systemic change:

1.     The learning environment is collaborative, challenging, and responsive but not threatening, and it fosters student independence.

**Table 4.3**    ESL Standards for Pre-K–12 Students

|  | *Goal 1: To Use English to Communicate in Social Settings* | *Goal 2: To Use English to Achieve Academically in All Content Areas* | *Goal 3: To Use English in Socially and Culturally Appropriate Ways* |
|---|---|---|---|
| **Standard 1** | Students will use English to participate in social interaction. | Students will use English to interact in the classroom. | Students will use the appropriate language variety, register, and genre according to audience, purpose, and setting. |
| **Standard 2** | Students will interact in, through, and with spoken and written English for personal expression and enjoyment. | Students will use English to obtain, process, construct, and provide subject matter information in spoken and written form. | Students will use nonverbal communication appropriate to audience, purpose, and setting. |
| **Standard 3** | Students will use learning strategies to extend their communicative competence. | Students will use appropriate learning strategies to construct and apply academic knowledge. | Students will use appropriate learning strategies to extend their sociolinguistic and sociocultural competence. |

*Note.* From *ESL Standards for Pre-K–12 Students* (pp. 9–10), by Teachers of English to Speakers of Other Languages (TESOL), 1997, Alexandria, VA: Author. Copyright © 1997 by TESOL. Reprinted with permission.

2. A variety of instruction methods permits generous interaction among LEP/non-LEP students and facilitates the acquisition of a new language concurrent with new knowledge.
3. The context for instruction is comprehensible and conceptually appropriate.
4. Opportunities are provided that value contributions from students using both English and their heritage language (August & Pease-Alvarez, 1996).

In sum, LEP students must achieve all standards. All students, including LEP students, ultimately need to know and meet challenging state and local standards that are set for them. Differences in focus on everyday topics will vary, of course, among LEP and non-LEP students. More readily obvious, perhaps, is the range of topics tailored to the unique environment and experience of the LEP newcomer student. Besides the standards expected of all students, there are additional key skills and knowledge that the LEP student must learn that the non-LEP student already possesses. These skills and knowledge, which are given in greater detail in the first column in Table 4.4, can be condensed into the following four topic areas:

1. school topics (the library, cafeteria, emergencies, playground, rules, safety, bus procedures)
2. community topics (the neighborhood, money, clothes, grocery store, streetwise language, local/state agencies, jobs)
3. culture (attire, hygiene, mores, religious practices, the arts, shelter, cultural survival)
4. basic literacy skills, study skills, interpersonal communication skills, and higher order thinking skills

From Table 4.4, one may reasonably note that standards inevitably become extended for LEP students at varying English proficiency levels. The reader is reminded that the first column (non-English proficient student) refers to newcomers with very little (if any) comfort with the English language. The newcomer's temporary challenge is twofold: (a) the acquisition of survival skills and orientation to a new culture and (b) communicative competence in English. The second column in Table 4.4 emphasizes the integration of content skills for the transitionally English-fluent student. As the newcomer's proficiency in English improves, greater attention is placed on language and content acquisition needs. An excellent source for understanding these complex language proficiency distinctions and their implications for academic instruction is Hakuta, Butler, and Witt's (2000) paper, "How Long Does It

Take English Learners to Attain Proficiency?" Access to curriculum crosses all language proficiency levels (as shown in both columns in Table 4.4). The needs listed under each column are a sampling, not an exhaustive list, and neither column is rigidly defined but is rather an outline of the natural continuum of the LEP student's journey toward reaching English proficiency and competence in the content areas on a par with his or her non-LEP peers.

**Table 4.4** Achieving State Standards (and Much More) for Limited English Proficient (LEP) Students

| Beginner (Non-English Proficient) New Arrivals Need to Know About . . . | Intermediate and Advanced Second- or Third-Year Students Need to Know About . . . |
|---|---|
| 1. Food, clothing, and shelter and how to ask for it | 1. Formal grammar and metalanguage |
| 2. Survival vocabulary, for example, how to ask to go to the bathroom | 2. Learning strategies and metacognition (e.g., note taking, outlining, questioning) |
| 3. Communicating health and safety needs | 3. Test-taking skills |
| 4. Following directions | 4. Following directions from school personnel |
| 5. Requesting information | 5. Reading comprehension and reading strategies |
| 6. Communicating emotions | 6. Study skills |
| 7. Appropriate indoor/outdoor behavior | 7. Writing process and product |
| 8. Social rules | 8. Public/formal speaking |
| 9. Cafeteria foods and how to eat them | 9. Information-gathering skills |
| 10. Nutrition | 10. Research strategies and project processes/learning strategies |
| 11. Personal hygiene/health | 11. Cooperative learning and group dynamic skills |
| 12. Specific vocabulary and directions related to the classroom | 12. Idiomatic English |
| 13. Student expectations, teacher expectations, and classroom agenda | 13. Affective-sharing skills |
| 14. Being streetwise at school and in the community | 14. Cultural exchanges |
| | 15. Language of power/ empowerment |
| | 16. Vocabulary related to health and legal issues and the media |

*Continued on p. 77*

Table 4.4 *continued*  Achieving State Standards (and Much More) for Limited English Proficient (LEP) Students

| *Beginner (Non-English Proficient)*<br>*New Arrivals*<br>*Need to Know About . . .* | *Intermediate and Advanced*<br>*Second- or Third-Year Students*<br>*Need to Know About . . .* |
|---|---|
| 15. Being streetwise about advertising | 17. Learning about culture |
| 16. Money | 18. Connecting the known to the unknown |
| 17. The geography of the school and the town | 19. Integration into the school community |
| 18. School and community resources | 20. Street savvy |
| 19. Appropriate attire | 21. Advanced content vocabulary concepts and processes |
| 20. Basic content vocabulary and concepts | 22. Nonverbal communication |
| 21. Basic literacy skills | 23. Cognitive/academic language proficiency |
| 22. Basic interpersonal communication skills, such as listening and speaking | 24. Paralinguistic features, such as intonation and stress |
| | 25. Complex discourse features |

*Note.* From an unpublished worksheet by R. Parker, Providence, RI: Education Alliance at Brown University. Adapted with permission.

## Holistic Approaches

Holistic, integrative instruction that is tied to standards is a very suitable approach for instructing LEP students. Such an approach emphasizes meaningful and enjoyable communication that focuses on the LEP student's natural language acquisition while the student acquires the necessary knowledge and skills prescribed in curriculum. Once again, the ESL manager may turn to the statutes. The requirement of Title VI of the Civil Rights Act of 1964 for equal provision of services has been interpreted to include that LEP students must have equal access to the regular content-area curriculum. Also, the *Lau v. Nichols* concern with "meaningful education" has been interpreted as education that is comparable to the mainstream in terms of the subject-area skills taught. An excellent defense for the need to engage content teachers in the ESL profession points toward equity as well as second language development.

Inequities of approach to classroom instruction where LEP and non-LEP students learn together are well documented. Research conducted by Verplaetse (1998), for example, revealed that non-ESL teachers tended to limit their verbal exchanges to LEP students to points of procedural directives (e.g., "Do you know what this assignment requires?") rather than cognitive interactions (e.g., "How were the founding fathers of the United States different from today's legislators?"). The result was quite understandably a reduction of LEP student engagement, limited chances for LEP students to co-construct knowledge with peers, and a perhaps unintended devaluing of the diversity that results from social interactions among LEP students and their non-LEP peers. Enright and McCloskey (1988) and Y. S. Freeman and D. E. Freeman (1992) have identified certain principles necessary to implement a whole language program for ESL students. These include

- acquiring language as a total process; the language skills of listening, speaking, reading, and writing should be taught as a whole process rather than as a series of isolated skills
- exploiting language as a tool that can help students think, problem solve, and successfully attack other learning tasks
- developing English proficiency and academic competence simultaneously
- managing a classroom atmosphere that is conducive to language acquisition

Language is, of course, a total process. Its acquisition is facilitated when all of the skills are used together: listening, speaking, reading, and writing. LEP students acquire their new language more quickly when they use it to accomplish specific tasks. LEP students need a welcoming as well as a purposeful atmosphere that encourages them to experiment with language and literature. A popular holistic approach to creating an atmosphere conducive to language acquisition is by bringing real-life, interesting objects into the classroom. Children enjoy being involved with situations representative of life outside of the school. This helps second language learners acquire "natural" language. In sum, "when whole language is defined correctly, it is a consistent winner" (Krashen, 1999, p. viii).

# Specially Designed Academic Instruction in English (SDAIE) Approach

Quality instruction is, of course, key to the success of LEP students. One must always keep in mind that LEP students have a double task in school. First, they must master content skills that are age- and grade-level appropriate, just as their native-English-speaking peers must master. In addition, they must learn English, both for purposes of everyday conversational interaction and for academic purposes in the classroom. Thus, in a sense, the ideal situation is to make standards-driven curriculum accessible to LEP students, either through bilingual instruction or through ESL methods that take into account the learners' current level of English proficiency and further develop their English language skills. Such ESL instructional methodologies are based on content and emphasize active learning, using the student's cultural background as a resource. The ESL teacher should be encouraged to employ visuals, manipulatives, and graphic organizers to reduce the language load of content-area lessons. This kind of instructional strategy is referred to as specially designed academic instruction in English (SDAIE) (sometimes more loosely called *sheltered English*).

Y. S. Freeman and D. E. Freeman (1998) make a distinction between sheltered English and SDAIE. With sheltered English, content teachers are limited because students at varying grade levels and varying levels of English proficiency are in the same lower academic-level classes. Some succeed; some do not. The focus is largely on English language development. Enter SDAIE for those students who are midway in their level of English proficiency and academic content knowledge, generally at the secondary level, where the focus is largely on academic development.

SDAIE grew from the scholarship introduced by the work of at least four celebrated scholars in the field of second language learning. These scholars include Stephen Krashen, Jim Cummins, Spencer Kagan, and Kenji Hakuta. Krashen (1982) explained that the second language learner must receive comprehensible input through strategies that make content in the new language comprehensible; he further advances an input hypothesis, suggesting that when language is acquired, it is comprehensible. Cummins (1994) posited that there are two broad and complex levels under which second language learners demonstrate fluency in the new language: (a) basic interpersonal communication skills (BICS) through which students become familiar with the oral/aural conventions of the new language at the conversational level and which take about 2 years to achieve; and (b) cognitive academic language proficiency skills

(CALPS), which involve the development of more complex language proficiency and require an average of an additional 4–6 years to acquire. Kagan (1985), another scholar in the arena of second language learning, has helped teachers progress their students beyond the passive acquisition of knowledge to the now-common strategies for applying learnings in highly interactive, low-anxiety collaborative environments. Of course, cognitive and communicative skills development are interrelated, suggesting that BICS and CALPS are not definitive or separate processes on the road to English proficiency. Hakuta, Butler, and Witt (2000) and others sorted out some of the exogenous variables such as context, environment, sociocultural considerations, and the like about the learner that make the lines separating the two levels difficult.

Both sheltered English and SDAIE require some degree of collaboration between the ESL teacher and the regular education teacher or teachers, making the quality of ESL-mainstream collaboration a key consideration in establishing an effective program. If LEP students are to have a successful school experience, the transition from ESL classes to the mainstream classroom requires that collaboration between ESL and mainstream teachers involve training, mentoring, and monitoring to reach the most desirable classroom environment. The following discussion and the accompanying Tables 4.5, 4.6, and 4.7 suggest workable strategies for such collaboration.

When mainstream teachers take fundamental course work that is required for ESL teachers, the genesis for collaborative work in assessment (alternative and traditional), teacher expectations, coteaching, and sheltered English instruction is likely to emerge. At least two course work topics would be advisable for mainstream teachers: second language acquisition theory and ESL teaching methods. When mainstream teachers have a thorough understanding of those two topics, the mainstream teachers and ESL teachers can form a collaborative team that is positioned to develop individual learning plans for LEP students, whether they are in the mainstream classroom or in ESL/content pullout support situations. Some teacher training institutions already require some introductory ESL course work for all prospective teachers.

In the early grades, including middle school, sheltered English is recommended to help LEP students have a greater understanding of academic vocabulary and language structures. Content-area support comes as a result of that interaction. SDAIE approaches involve exploiting (a) the LEP student's academic knowledge; (b) operational skills such as study, affective, or thinking skills; and (c) English communicative skills already acquired, such as listening, speaking, reading, and writing, to carry out learning assignments. In SDAIE, teachers identify what content emphases non-LEP mainstream stu-

## Table 4.5   Typical Elementary/Middle School Schedule for Sheltered English*

| *English Proficiency Level* | *Curricular Area* |
| --- | --- |
| NON-ENGLISH PROFICIENT/ LEVEL 1 | ESL LANGUAGE ARTS (emphasis on all domains) Sheltered MATH, SCIENCE, HEALTH, SOCIAL STUDIES/HISTORY INTEGRATED rest of school day w/peer guide |
| LIMITED ENGLISH PROFICIENT/ LEVEL 2 | ESL LANGUAGE ARTS (emphasis on all domains) Sheltered SCIENCE/HEALTH (w/aide if possible) Sheltered SOCIAL STUDIES/HISTORY (w/aide if possible) MATH – MAINSTREAMED INTEGRATED rest of school day |
| LIMITED ENGLISH PROFICIENT/ LEVEL 3 | ESL LANGUAGE ARTS (emphasis on all domains) Sheltered SOCIAL STUDIES/HISTORY MATH – MAINSTREAMED SCIENCE/HEALTH – MAINSTREAMED CONTENT-AREA TUTORING INTEGRATED rest of school day |
| TRANSITIONAL ENGLISH PROFICIENT/ LEVEL 4 | ESL LANGUAGE ARTS (emphasis on higher level oral, reading, and writing skills) INTEGRATED/MAINSTREAMED rest of school day |
| TRANSITIONAL ENGLISH PROFICIENT/ LEVEL 5 | ESL LANGUAGE ARTS (emphasis on higher level reading, writing, and literary skills, especially for students with native language schooling before emigrating to the United States) INTEGRATED/MAINSTREAMED rest of school day CONTENT-AREA TUTORING (especially for students with native language schooling before emigrating to the United States) |

* *The limited English proficient (LEP) student is enrolled in an English language classroom with same-age peers. This may be a self-contained ESL/content classroom for one grade or a cluster of two or three grades.*

*Note.* From an unpublished worksheet by R. Parker, Providence, RI: Education Alliance at Brown University. Adapted with permission.

dents are expected to learn against those set for LEP students. In this approach, teachers use strategies that incorporate modified instruction and utilize a variety of instructional approaches. They also consider what preteaching needs the LEP student may have as well how support services can be provided.

Use of graphic organizers such as charts, diagrams, and pictures assist students in both sheltered English and SDAIE. The ESL manager and the collaborating content teacher are advised to consider the two schedules described in Tables 4.5 and 4.6 in implementing sheltered English and SDAIE.

When a school district enrolls LEP students, the Office for Civil Rights (OCR) would, in its appraisal of statutory compliance, typically look for a formal program that is appropriate to that student's content skills and language acquisition needs. As mentioned in chapters 2 and 3, a school district must document and justify the special language services (e.g., ESL) programming decisions made regarding LEP students. Presenting schedules as those in Tables 4.5 and 4.6 may help the ESL manager in addressing such a concern.

How much time does it take each day to teach SDAIE or sheltered English? Based on the language assessment committee's (LAC's) multicriteria evaluation of an individual LEP student (see chapter 3), an English language proficiency level is described for the LEP student. Those levels might apply differently to the various skill areas needed for full fluency (i.e., low intermediate speaking skills, high beginning reading skills). Those levels may be used as guidelines for the LAC to determine special language services (e.g., ESL, bilingual) programming and program time allotments, types, and instructional focus on a case-by-case basis. A general spectrum and suggested time allotments may appear as shown in Figure 4.1.

SDAIE enables the ESL teacher to collaborate with the LEP student's academic subject-area teachers. Together, they can develop pedagogies that support student access to comprehensible input and greater English fluency as well as collaborative learning. The SDAIE plan, as detailed in Table 4.7, works across all subjects by meeting these six integrative authentic learning practices:

1. exploiting the student's previous knowledge and expanding them to meet high standards
2. maximizing the use of curriculum and related resources commonly aligned to standards
3. facilitating greater understanding of subject matter and in achieving high standards
4. enhancing organizational aptitude

**Table 4.6** Typical Secondary School Schedule for Specially Designed Academic Instruction in English (SDAIE)*

| English Proficiency Level | Curricular Area |
|---|---|
| NON-ENGLISH PROFICIENT/ LEVEL 1 | ACADEMIC ENGLISH (all domains)<br>SHELTERED MATH<br>SHELTERED SCIENCE/HEALTH<br>SHELTERED SOCIAL STUDIES/HISTORY<br>INTEGRATED rest of school day w/peer guide |
| LIMITED ENGLISH PROFICIENT/ LEVEL 2 | ACADEMIC ENGLISH<br>SHELTERED SCIENCE/HEALTH<br>SHELTERED SOCIAL STUDIES/HISTORY<br>MATH in English<br>INTEGRATED rest of school day |
| LIMITED ENGLISH PROFICIENT/ LEVEL 3 | ACADEMIC READING AND COMPOSITION<br>SHELTERED SOCIAL STUDIES/HISTORY<br>MATH or ELECTIVE in English<br>INTEGRATED rest of school day |
| TRANSITIONAL ENGLISH PROFICIENT/ LEVEL 4 | ACADEMIC READING AND COMPOSITION<br>SOCIAL STUDIES/HISTORY or<br>ELECTIVE in English<br>MATH or ELECTIVE in English<br>SCIENCE/HEALTH or ELECTIVE in English<br>INTEGRATED rest of school day w/peer guide |
| TRANSITIONAL ENGLISH PROFICIENT/ LEVEL 5 | Higher level reading, writing, and literary skills (especially for students with native language schooling before emigrating to the United States)<br>SUPERVISED STUDY HALL<br>INTEGRATED rest of school day |

* *The limited English proficient (LEP) student is enrolled in an English language classroom with same-age peers.*

*Note.* From an unpublished worksheet by R. Parker, Providence, RI: Education Alliance at Brown University. Adapted with permission.

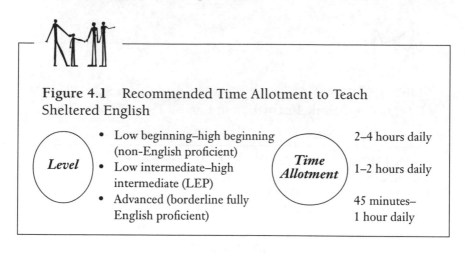

Figure 4.1   Recommended Time Allotment to Teach Sheltered English

**Level**
- Low beginning–high beginning (non-English proficient)
- Low intermediate–high intermediate (LEP)
- Advanced (borderline fully English proficient)

**Time Allotment**
2–4 hours daily

1–2 hours daily

45 minutes–1 hour daily

5.   varying approaches to assessments
6.   transforming classrooms into lively and positive learning environments

## Cognitive Academic Language Learning (CALLA) Approach

Chamot and O'Malley (1987) developed the cognitive academic language learning approach (CALLA), which approximates SDAIE methods for teaching content and language tailored to the higher elementary- and secondary-level LEP student (who typically has intermediate or advanced levels of English fluency).

CALLA is a task-based model for assisting LEP children in transitioning from an English as a second language program into the mainstream curriculum by teaching them the learning strategies needed to successfully handle content-area materials. Students use these strategies to perform learning tasks from CALLA-content lessons. These strategies consist of three parts:

1.   The content of each lesson is determined by the appropriate grade level for the basic science, math, social studies, or health curriculum.
2.   The language consists of whichever language students need to handle the content of the lesson successfully.
3.   The learning strategy is the technique for managing content that will be heavily emphasized during the lesson.

**Table 4.7**　Specially Designed Academic Instruction in English (SDAIE) Strategies That Work

| *Plan* | *Method* |
| --- | --- |
| 1. **Exploiting Student Knowledge** | • brainstorming student knowledge and wants for learning (KWL)<br>• group discussions<br>• home-based projects about the student (esp. in native language)<br>• assessment of previous knowledge and skills<br>• identification and affirmation of culture norms<br>• folk tales<br>• personalization of the lesson<br>• field trips<br>• providing choices for students<br>• schoolwide culture fair<br>• journals<br>• interviews<br>• use of the Internet<br>• realia |
| 2. **Maximizing Curriculum Usage and Classroom Resources** | • listing or isolation of key vocabulary<br>• visuals (charts, maps, realia)<br>• demonstrations<br>• role play—student interaction<br>• modification of tests (bold, label, draw, highlight)<br>• high-interest material appropriate to fluency level<br>• summarization of the chapter; framing of questions<br>• reading aloud (paraphrase; read captions)<br>• group reading; pairing<br>• support with glossary and index<br>• outlining chapters<br>• scanning for visuals and headings<br>• chapter headings cast as questions<br>• highlighting with removable tape |

*Continued on p. 86*

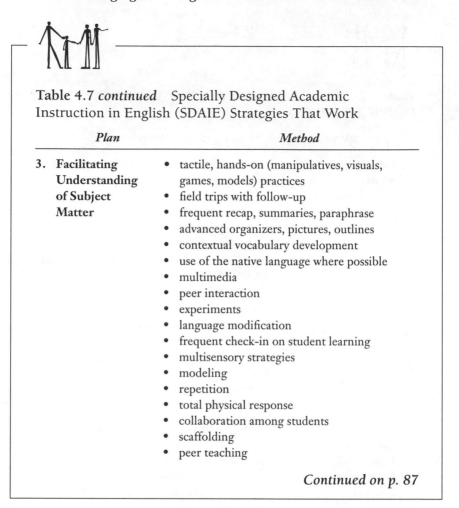

**Table 4.7** *continued*    Specially Designed Academic
Instruction in English (SDAIE) Strategies That Work

| Plan | Method |
|------|--------|
| 3. **Facilitating Understanding of Subject Matter** | • tactile, hands-on (manipulatives, visuals, games, models) practices<br>• field trips with follow-up<br>• frequent recap, summaries, paraphrase<br>• advanced organizers, pictures, outlines<br>• contextual vocabulary development<br>• use of the native language where possible<br>• multimedia<br>• peer interaction<br>• experiments<br>• language modification<br>• frequent check-in on student learning<br>• multisensory strategies<br>• modeling<br>• repetition<br>• total physical response<br>• collaboration among students<br>• scaffolding<br>• peer teaching |

*Continued on p. 87*

CALLA lessons may cover almost any topic or area from state or local standards. For example, students may complete an itinerary for a hypothetical 10-day trip across the United States. The content objective of this lesson may be found in a social studies standard for U.S. geography. The language structures necessary for students to handle the content would be prepositions; two of the necessary language skills could be following directions and asking questions for clarification. The strategies that students would use might be elaborating and identifying resources: elaborating by expanding on existing knowledge of cross-country travel and identifying resources such as bus, plane, and train tables or travel agents. See Appendix B for a detailed variation on this CALLA lesson.

Table 4.7 *continued*   Specially Designed Academic
Instruction in English (SDAIE) Strategies That Work

| Plan | Method |
|------|--------|
| 4. Enhancing Organizational Aptitude | • scaffolding<br>• graphic organizers (visuals, outlines)<br>• peer support with an English-fluent buddy<br>• portfolio development<br>• scheduling structures, time management<br>• countdowns (as in counting the days to the New Year)<br>• assignment booklets<br>• teacher modeling: cause and effect<br>• oral/written directions<br>• note taking<br>• checklists<br>• student feedback (oral)<br>• study-skill templates, prioritizing, calendars<br>• color-coded content folders<br>• periodic debriefing<br>• requests from students about useful strategies that work well<br>• home/school folder<br>• taking turns for classroom jobs |

*Continued on p. 88*

In a different CALLA lesson called "Our Solar System," students might follow given directions for completing a chart of the solar system. The content/objective of the lesson is found in the science standards for the solar system. The language structures necessary for students to manage the content are prepositions and question formation; two of the needed language skills are following directions and asking questions for clarification. The strategies that students use are elaborating and making inferences: elaborating by expanding on existing knowledge of the sky and the solar system and making inferences by reading the directions and determining planet placement.

As suggested by the format of the lesson presented in Appendix B, one

**Table 4.7** *continued*   Specially Designed Academic Instruction in English (SDAIE) Strategies That Work

| Plan | Method |
|------|--------|
| 5. **Varying Approaches to Assessments** | • student-generated assessments<br>• limited short-answer assessments<br>• manipulatives<br>• portfolios<br>• pictures: multimedia technologies<br>• story writing, drawing, acting<br>• oral assessments, interviews<br>• audio and video<br>• collaborative student projects<br>• music, games, plays<br>• role playing<br>• dialogue journals<br>• checklists<br>• rubrics<br>• conferencing<br>• peer teaching<br>• student publications |
| 6. **Transforming Classrooms Into Lively, Positive Learning Environments** | • engaging students with music, games, plays, songs, dances, and laughter<br>• scaffold, reinforce student successes and goals<br>• validation of student culture with student centered presentations; culture days<br>• prizes, stickers, other rewards<br>• replaying student work<br>• using the community as the classroom<br>• emphasizing content, not form<br>• waiting time<br>• native language usage whenever possible<br>• informal conferencing<br>• peer tutors and buddies<br>• bright, colorful classroom<br>• variations for teacher/learner styles<br>• varied work stations<br>• safe environments<br>• soft, ambient music |

may structure a CALLA framework to develop methods by which the LEP student, not the teacher, is empowered to assume control of integrative teaching and learning. This classroom-based research model presents a workable path to the learning strategies of metacognition (as suggested by TESOL's ESL standards) by permitting learners to reflect on their own learning and ultimately to control that metacognitive process. Students at all grade and English proficiency levels can be supported by this model of effective strategies instruction. The following are five recursive phases that permit students to organize and plan instruction:

1. Planning: What does the student want to gain from the instructional task? The student reflects on matters such as prior knowledge, sets goals, and maps out strategies for reaching those goals.
2. Presentation: How can the new material be made comprehensible? Multiple techniques such as scaffolding and those listed previously under SDAIE are appropriate.
3. Self-Evaluation: Is the input comprehensible? This is an inquiry and tracking of understanding and progress.
4. Monitoring/Problem Solving: How might the task have been differently managed? The learning strategy for managing language and content are reviewed in this reflective phase.
5. Application/Expansion: How does the given task translate to real life? It must make sense linguistically, culturally, and in the context of community life.

A rationale from theory to practice is presented in *The Learning Strategies Handbook* (Chamot, Barnhardt, El-Dinary, & Robbins, 1999) with a CALLA step-by-step sequence to preparing LEP students for independent learning at all grade and English language proficiency levels.

## Summative Guidance for the ESL Program Manager

From guiding principles for student learning to the ESL standards as "promising futures," this chapter has sought to assist the ESL manager in practicing the universal imperative of "all means all" for LEP students. Once the ESL manager has reviewed what his or her state expectations are by way of standards and ESL-program permissibility, he or she may then examine which models may best help in ensuring that LEP students may reach those standards.

A good place to start may be to align local standards with the ESL standards developed for LEP students. Note that the ESL standards provide detailed descriptors for each standard as well as sample progress indicators by grade-level clusters—a format that is compatible with several state standards documents.

Holistic, integrative curriculum design and classroom methodologies are advanced in this chapter as an approach for aligning ESL to content instruction. Embraced are three approaches that offer greatest promise, absent a developmental (two-way) bilingual education program: (a) SDAIE, including a scheduling plan by grade level that, through simplified English, supports comprehension of unaltered academic content; (b) CALLA, where mastery of learning techniques at the secondary level permits the LEP student to acquire English fluency and academic content; and (c) a CALLA-companion metacognitive model presented in Chamot, Barnhardt, El-Dinary, and Robbins's *The Learning Strategies Handbook* (1999)—a must for the ESL manager committed to implementing well-researched and effective strategic learning systems.

It will be up to the ESL manager to present those models to colleagues to advance the premise that all does indeed mean all. To expect a lowering of standards for LEP students borders on racism at worse; at best, it is a lazy approach to gauging student progress. As noted by Merino and Rumberger (1999), members of California's English Language Proficiency Assessment Project Advisory Committee, "the major task in not establishing standards for English learners lies in the failure to perceive progress when it is occurring and in the failure to measure a real lack of progress" (p. 1). The SDAIE and CALLA approaches and the approach presented in Chamot, Barnhardt, El-Dinary, and Robbins (1999) support ESL/content collaboratives and help ensure that LEP students will achieve high, challenging state and local standards, helping rural schools pull out of arguably the least effective ESL practice—ESL pullout.

## Suggested Resources on the Web

For accessing policy and resources for LEP students from state departments of education:

The National Clearinghouse for Bilingual Education's state resources (http://www.ncbe.gwu.edu/states/index.htm)

For ongoing projects with standards, assessment, and instruction for
LEP students:

> *The Lab at Brown University* (http://www.lab.brown.edu [click on
> Standards])

For the ESL standards on-line:

> Teachers of English to Speakers of Other Languages (TESOL)
> (http://www.tesol.org/assoc/K12standards/index.html)

To subscribe to the *ESL Standards Implementation Electronic Discussion List*:

> Send an e-mail to: request – eslstds@cal.talk.cal.org. In the subject line,
> type: subscribe. Leave the rest of the e-mail message blank.

For the identification of needs of LEP students for achieving challenging
standards:

> "Changing Instruction for Language Minority Students to Achieve
> National Goals" (Chamot, 1992, http://www.ncbe.gwu.edu/ncbepubs
> /symposia/third/chamot.htm)

For articles and documents on school reform and LEP students—
exemplary practices and ideas:

> "Education Reform and Language Minority Students" (Rennie, 1998,
> http://www.cal.org/ericcll/minibibs/edreform.html)

For CREDE's standards and the LEP student as well as other
CREDE resources:

> *Center for Research on Education, Diversity & Excellence (CREDE)*
> (http://www.cal.org/crede)

# Chapter 5
# Staffing the ESL Program

*Do you like me? Sometimes I'm scared of you though. The way you look, the way you smile—when I'm scared.*

—Cullum, 1971, p. 42

**E**ducating everyone takes everyone: administrators, counselors, tutors, teachers, parents, and volunteers. As with other specialists, personnel with ESL credentials are needed to support ESL instruction because they are trained to provide a specific service. However, it is common, especially in rural schools, to see teachers with no training in ESL working with LEP students. Hiring qualified ESL personnel is at least as important as hiring a credentialed principal. Why so? It is the law. Recall this Office for Civil Rights (OCR) policy statement (as quoted in chapter 2):

> A recipient may not in effect relegate LEP students to second-class status by indefinitely allowing teachers without formal qualifications to teach them while requiring teachers of non-LEP students to need formal qualifications. (Office for Civil Rights, 1991, p. 4)

This policy, commissioned by the U.S. Supreme Court in 1991, has the force of law. Recruitment of ESL teachers must adhere to a state's requirements for the ESL profession. Gone are the days when well-intended interest in cultural diversity by itself once opened the doors for many prospective and now practicing ESL teachers. So much more is at stake.

A National Research Council Commission (August & Hakuta, 1998) released a descriptive study that revealed some seemingly dramatic statistics:

- Fifteen percent of all public school teachers in the United States had at least one LEP student in the classroom.
- Sixty-six percent of the teachers of LEP students were non-ESL teachers; 18% of these non-ESL teachers had primary responsibility for those LEP students.
- Eight percent of teachers of LEP students were certified in ESL (10% in literacy education).
- Forty-two percent of the teachers of LEP students could speak their students' native language.
- Fifty-five percent of the teachers had received professional development or college courses relevant to ESL.

Such data begs the question, "Just how skilled in ESL does one have to be to teach LEP students?" The answer, of course, is that it depends on the requirements of the individual state. Regardless of the requirements of a particular English support program, teachers will find the following skills and competencies important to carry in successfully providing appropriate services:

- insight into the cultural and linguistic backgrounds as well as the academic experiences of the students
- a special knowledge of the sounds, syntax, semantics, and prosody in the target language to help the students learn these features as well as knowledge of the linguistic features in the target language and native language
- experience in the methodology of successful second language instruction
- accessibility to individual or agency resources available to teachers of non-English-speaking students
- knowledge of the current issues and research in second language pedagogy, psycholinguistics, bilingual education, and applied linguistics
- awareness of the dynamics of individualized instruction and how to use them in ESL instruction
- skills for adapting and developing relevant instructional materials for ESL instruction
- familiarity with ways to provide a learning atmosphere that promotes not only second language skills but also enhances the sense of self in second language students

All of these noted skills and competencies are necessary for ESL teachers. In the first place, ESL teachers often must provide instruction to LEP students with a wide range of abilities, experiences, and levels in both their native and second language. Secondly, immigrant students may enroll in school at varying points, forcing the school to make almost spontaneous decisions throughout the school year (see the discussion on *Lau* planning in chapter 3). Hence, the ESL teacher or manager, knowledgeable about the linguistic and cultural variables the newcomer brings to the school environment, becomes a pivotal influence in making those decisions. The ESL manager is the liaison between the non-English-speaking students, their ESL teacher, and their English language teachers. The research literature is conclusive: There is a positive relationship between English language proficiency and academic achievement measured in English. A level of quality and quantity of English competency plus academic skill for achievement in English-only instruction is essential for those students.

In 1975, TESOL adopted guidelines for the certification and preparation of ESL teachers in the United States. These five categories were recommended as minimal:

1. academic preparation in English grammar and language learning
2. ESL methodology
3. LEP student assessment
4. practical experience
5. knowledge of another language

In the decades that followed the publication of the guidelines (TESOL, 1975), all but 14 states established credentials (licensures and endorsements) for aspiring ESL professionals as noted in Table 5.1. Most states require many of the categories TESOL had initiated in its guidelines. For example, California and Nevada both require language acquisition and development as well as ESL methodology and a course in culture to teach ESL. Maine requires these as well as ESL curriculum development and LEP student assessment among other courses. For most states that have requisite ESL credentials, it is a common requirement that an ESL teacher will carry 15–18 credit hours beyond his or her initial teacher certificate in ESL-specific areas such as those noted previously.

In many rural areas, the provision of ESL support services to students who have limited English proficiency is a new issue. As a result, there may be a lack of teachers who are trained and certified in ESL. If this is the case, it is essential that teachers who are hired to work with LEP students complete state requirements for certification (also called *licensure*) and endorsement (if they exist) in a timely manner as required by the OCR enforcement policy previously noted.

Census projections indicate that as of 2000, nearly one third of the U.S. population will be speakers of English as a second language. From that, we learn that teachers will likely continue to encounter students of limited English background. As a minimum, aspiring teachers as well as teachers currently in service ought to consider taking a course in multicultural education and a course in basic linguistics and language development/acquisition and should consider attending workshops and conferences offered in ESL as well as in culture-specific topics.

**Table 5.1**    States That Require ESL Teacher Certification or Endorsement

| | | |
|---|---|---|
| Alabama | Arizona | Arkansas |
| California* | Colorado* | Connecticut* |
| Delaware | District of Columbia | Florida |
| Georgia | Hawaii | Illinois* |
| Indiana* | Iowa | Kansas* |
| Kentucky* | Maine | Maryland* |
| Massachusetts* | Minnesota | Missouri* |
| Montana* | Nebraska* | Nevada* |
| New Hampshire | New Jersey* | New Mexico |
| New York* | North Carolina | Ohio* |
| Oregon | Tennessee | Texas* |
| Utah* | Virginia* | Washington |
| Wisconsin* | | |

*These states not only offer ESL certification but also require ESL certification by statute.

Note. From *State Survey of Legislative Requirements for Educating Limited English Proficient Students*, by A. McKnight and B. Antunez, 1999, Washington, DC: National Clearinghouse for Bilingual Education, retrieved July 31, 2000, from the World Wide Web: http://www.ncbe.gwu.edu/projects/state-legislation/index.htm. Copyright © 1999 by the National Clearinghouse for Bilingual Education (NCBE), The George Washington University. Reprinted with permission.

Who, then, are the adult models for LEP children at school? Do those models even look like some of the cultures represented in a given ESL classroom? The fact is that teachers and administrators rarely look like the racial or ethnic minorities they serve, and they often do not speak the native languages of the LEP children in their classrooms. Furthermore, many of the teachers do not come well prepared to teach these children to their unique linguistic and academic needs, given their students' limited English proficiency. Data as shown in Table 1.3 in chapter 1 reveal demographic distribution differences by race among teachers, principals, and students.

What is known of the racial/ethnic distribution of the adult models for LEP children is remarkably disproportionate as one moves up the leadership ladder. While it is very difficult to locate credible data on the race/national origin demographics for superintendents of schools, Keller's (1999) report places superintendents' minority representation at 5%.

National Education Association (1997) data also reveal that 46% of U.S. teachers work in rural and small towns and that 46.1% of them have an average teaching experience of 16 years. This is significant, given that when these teachers received their initial training, the minority demographics in the United States were dramatically different from what they are now. Their training probably did not prepare them well for their work with LEP students. In fact, in a speech before the U.S. Department of Education, the commissioner of the National Center for Education Statistics revealed that only 20% of U.S. teachers feel well prepared to teach students of limited English proficiency (Forgione, 1999). In addition, only 30% of U.S. teachers have spent more than 8 hours of professional development addressing the needs of LEP or culturally diverse students. That noted, the ESL managers and teachers are LEP children's closest advocates, and training in linguistic and cultural diversity is essential for ESL professionals.

Collier and Thomas (1999) offer an instructive 4-point test for defining membership in a profession:

1. advanced education and training
2. standards of practice and certification
3. an agreed theoretical and empirical base
4. advocacy for the profession

Do educators throughout the disciplines meet this 4-point test? Of course they do. Do ESL teachers meet the same test? Indeed, yes. The profession of teaching must, then, be one—one dedicated to meeting the diverse needs of all children. ESL would appear indistinguishable in that gestalt.

# The Rationale for Having ESL-Credentialed Teachers

A strong, well-trained staff is the cornerstone of a school's ESL program that is consistent with the law. In light of this, it is crucial that properly credentialed teachers are those seasoned in the study of ESL methods, culture, authentic assessment (see chapter 7), ESL curriculum development, and linguistics. ESL teachers must be knowledgeable about second language acquisition and linguistics so that they may most effectively work with LEP students to raise their ESL instructional levels. ESL teachers should be well versed in implementing the dynamics of alternative classroom management styles. They should be able to develop curriculum and adapt varying ESL materials and resources to LEP students' needs. ESL teachers must, of course, be proficient in all of the communicative English skill areas (writing, speaking, listening, and reading). ESL teachers should also have, to the extent possible, insights and knowledge on the culture and linguistic backgrounds and the academic experiences of their LEP students. Important, too, is having experience in providing a sound environment for acquiring English concomitant with enhancing self-esteem. Not lost on most ESL teachers is their role as advocates for the LEP student and his or her family; the ESL teacher is often the most visibly influential figure in that student's daily life away from home.

ESL teachers perform a range of functions on behalf of LEP students. These functions include teaching ESL and developing appropriate assessments, collaborating with mainstream teachers and administrators on policy and curriculum development, and serving as liaison with parents. To be prepared to carry out those functions, ESL teachers do need training in second language acquisition, ESL methods, and culture knowledge that will facilitate their interaction with the community. In addition to these roles, ESL teachers frequently supervise paraprofessionals who work with LEP students.

# Recruitment of ESL Teachers

Rural communities often find that recruiting a qualified ESL teacher can be a daunting challenge. Urban schools frequently offer better wages and working conditions that discourage stronger candidates from applying for ESL positions in the rural schools. It is common for rural schools to nurture ESL teachers through "growing their own" staff from within. Sometimes this can mean providing incentives that would encourage staff to pursue ESL professional development. This generally occurs through the university system in the state or through institutes offered by state education agencies or similar ESL support centers. Schools seeking ESL teachers may well need to be more creative in recruiting staff than relying solely on traditional advertising.

That said, traditional advertising, such as in the Sunday newspapers, is still needed. That medium reaches a wide audience of readers and satisfies legal requirements connected to equal employment opportunity access. The problem with newspapers serving these rural communities is that the readers in the circulation area often do not happen to be qualified candidates for ESL employment. As a result, rural communities need to pursue less common sources for finding potential ESL teachers in addition to newspaper advertising. The bottom line is that the professional standing for degreed ESL teachers must be comparable to that of regular teachers. Among the possibilities for circulating position vacancy announcements are the following sources:

- senior citizen groups, including American Association for Retired Persons (AARP)
- state organizations for teacher retirees
- part-time or substitute teachers already employed by the district
- community leaders, volunteer organizations (e.g., Literacy Volunteers), and school/parent volunteers
- work-study students from area colleges
- state department of education offices who hold data on potential part-time ESL teachers or tutors
- a local ecumenical council or similar religious organization
- the organization of Returned Peace Corps Volunteers (RPCV)
- host families for international students
- refugee resettlement and immigrant service agencies

The Internet also offers a wealth of options for the manager or administrator looking to find qualified ESL staff. The ESL manager should begin by looking at some of the larger markets, such as the state professional associations that are affiliated with the National Education Association (NEA) and the Association for Supervision and Curriculum Development (ASCD). Web sites for state education agencies (particularly their sections on teacher certification) and teacher-training colleges in each state are another valuable source. The Web site address for the National Clearinghouse for Bilingual Education (http://www.ncbe.gwu.edu) features a biweekly "Newsline," which lists ESL and bilingual education vacancies as a free service, and TESOL's Career Services department advertises ESL vacancies around the world as well (http://

careers.tesol.org). Finally, the ESL manager is advised to consider the multitude of ESL Web sites, many of which will also post ESL job openings. Many of these Web site addresses are listed in chapter 9.

Not to be overlooked is a readily available ESL job description, which is a valuable recruitment tool for the administrator or ESL manager. This document serves the job-searching ESL teacher as a reference in discussing day-to-day duties with his or her future employer. It also clarifies expectations and can be referred to when questions arise. If there is no job description, the ESL teacher may want to network with peers to find out the process by which their districts formulated their job descriptions. If a job description is in place, the ESL teacher is advised to examine and discuss it with the employer, measuring the expectations as compared with the realities of the job situation. An administrator or ESL manager may want to consider the following questions when drafting an ESL position description:

- What will be the role of the ESL teacher?
- How many students will the teacher be expected to provide services for? (Is there a maximum?)
- How many hours will be expected as part of the daily schedule?
- Will there be compensation for travel time and expenses (if applicable)?
- Will preparation time be compensated?
- If the position is for itinerant ESL, how many buildings are to be serviced?
- What is the total budget for ESL support that the position can expect?
- Will there be ESL space for storage and instruction in all facilities that the teacher serves?
- How will the ESL program be evaluated?
- Are there non-ESL duties (e.g., lunchroom, bus, study hall, teaching other subject areas)?
- What level of support for professional development can the position expect?
- To whom will the ESL teacher be answerable?
- What will the ESL teacher's role be in implementing the district's *Lau* plan? (See chapter 3.)
- What will the ESL teacher's role be in implementing the district's or the state's curriculum standards with the LEP students?
- How great an advocate will the ESL teacher be for the LEP student under his or her charge?

The ESL manager will face some contentious issues along the way in re-cruiting suitable ESL staff. For example, should the manager hire a part-time ESL tutor or a full-time ESL teacher? How might a certified teacher who is employed as an ESL tutor create a full-time teacher position for her- or him-self? The decision about who shall be hired would depend on several factors, including the different English language proficiency levels of the LEP stu-dents being provided ESL services, the number of students receiving ESL services, the grade levels of the students, and the geographical layout of the school district. For a beginning ESL student, the teacher would need to spend 2–4 hours with that student. If the teacher also has students at other profi-ciency and grade levels, which is likely, and if the teacher is itinerant (where traveling time between schools is needed), he or she might not be able to pro-vide adequate services to the other students on a daily basis.

An LEP student population of 10–12 students in a school district (in light of the previously mentioned factors) would merit the hiring of a full-time ESL teacher. The teacher could be employed in an itinerant capacity or have a core program (based on a *Lau* plan) where students are transported to the teacher for certain time allotments during the school day. Another option would be for two school districts to form a consortium to share a special language ser-vices (e.g., ESL) teacher and provide the teacher with classroom spaces in both districts.

The OCR prefers that LEP students be provided special language ser-vices (e.g., ESL, bilingual) by a certified and appropriately trained (e.g., ESL, bilingual) teacher. A school district, regardless of having a low-incidence LEP student population, should pool its resources to provide quality, appropriate special language services to those children to ensure that they acquire the course work and skills necessary to benefit from an education conducted in English. The children's education should not suffer because they are in a low-incidence population.

# ESL Paraprofessionals

Like teachers, paraprofessionals (e.g., tutors/teacher aides, native language facilitators, peer tutors/language informants) who work with LEP students should be acquainted with current practices in educating students whose first language is not English. Because paraprofessionals are sometimes themselves members of the language minority community, they represent an important resource that should be utilized to the fullest extent possible. This means offering opportunities for advanced training through college courses, career ladders, and workshops in both ESL and mainstream education. Paraprofessionals should be encouraged to undertake a comprehensive educational program so that they may eventually become certified teachers.

Whenever possible, schools should hire teachers and paraprofessionals who are members of the language minority groups represented in the school population. These individuals commonly offer native proficiency in the languages of some of the students and can give assistance in promoting intercultural understanding. For both ESL teachers and ESL paraprofessionals, a school should make an effort to ensure parity with mainstream educators in the building, which requires that teachers and paraprofessionals meet the same standards for hiring as non-ESL teachers and paraprofessionals. It also implies equity of working conditions, such as equivalent teacher/student ratios for ESL teachers as well as for mainstream staff.

## Native Language Facilitators

Native language facilitators act in concert with the ESL teacher in a variety of ways. They may provide interpretive assistance to students in following directions and may help students in checking for comprehension or completing assignments. Some school districts assume that because a native language facilitator can speak English, he or she can teach it. Rarely is this true. Such ESL paraprofessionals must be knowledgeable in the pedagogical and linguistic development methods and techniques appropriate for the student population.

Whether the school district hires a paraprofessional as a tutor or teacher's aide (sometimes called an education technician) or native language facilitator, it is advised that expectations be made at the outset. As discussed earlier regarding ESL teaching positions, paraprofessional positions warrant the same kind of treatment. A job summary and duties should be readily available as illustrated in the model in Figure 5.1. It may also be helpful to have job descriptions for all ESL positions appended in the district's *Lau* plan.

## Peer Tutors/English Language Informants

Using English language peer tutors has been recognized as an effective means to assist second language learners. Whether in cooperative learning groups or assigned to buddies, second language learners benefit from exposure to activities that are rich in language usage. Peer tutors can assist LEP students in student-friendly language with their assignments, particularly in areas of complex concepts and new vocabulary. Peer tutors can also assist LEP students in social situations that may arise. Comparable to the peer tutor is the English language informant. In this peer tutoring approach, English-fluent students are trained as ESL tutors. They may be given high school elective credits as an incentive and be provided transportation to the school where the LEP student is enrolled.

The peer tutor/English language informant reinforces what has been taught in the ESL class, assists the LEP student with subject-area assignments, and guides the student through the educational processes and requirements of the local school system. The peer tutor/English language informant works closely with the ESL teacher/manager. Providing extra ESL services to the LEP student such as those noted in the previous paragraphs should result in the acquisition of communicative competencies and the development of English cognitive academic skills.

## Cross-Age Tutors

The use of tutors who are not peers of LEP students is also an appropriate service support. These tutors can provide supplemental instruction, whether in the classroom or in after-school settings. The older tutor can act as a mentor, review homework, and provide guided instruction, while also having the opportunity to talk with the student about his or her culture, homeland, or similar supportive assistance. Some cross-age tutors may have the advantage of bilingualism. A word of caution is in order: It is neither effective nor appropriate for ESL tutors to use materials designed for a native-English-speaking student when teaching LEP students reading or grammar.

## Volunteers

Community volunteers are valuable in filling a gap in instruction or in adding context to the learning students are engaged in, whether in the classroom or in the student's orientation to his or her new environment. Their services must be consistent and they need to be reliable. Otherwise, the LEP students' skills they serve to improve will not accelerate. All volunteers should receive training in what they are likely to encounter in their assignments. They should have some comfort in following the ESL and the standard curriculum if they are to support instruction. Volunteers are typically used as classroom aides, tutors,

**Figure 5.1**   Position Description for Professional Tutors:
A Model From the Public Schools in Aurora, Colorado

**Position Title:** Professional Tutor for Multilingual Students

**Reports To:** ESL/bilingual education consultant and home school
principal (The professional tutor is under the direct supervision of a
certified teacher who is endorsed in bilingual education and ESL.)

**Job Summary:** Assists teachers in identifying needs of language minority
students, defining measurable objectives for such students, providing
instruction to equip them with adequate English language skills, and
evaluating the progress of such students toward the defined objectives.
Also assists the principal and staff in communicating with the home
ethnic community.

**Supervisory Duties:** None

**Major Duties:** 1. Identifies, assesses, monitors, and places language
minority students in the appropriate levels of the ESL/bilingual
education program, and maintains appropriate records and files on
each student according to federal, state, and district guidelines.

2. Supplements and reinforces classroom teacher's
objectives and district curriculum by scheduling and working with
individuals or small groups according to their needs in English or the
content-area subjects.

3. Provides students with input that reinforces language
skills such as listening comprehension, oral production, language
structure and patterns, communication, and reading and writing by
following the district curriculum and utilizing district-approved
materials and methodology.

4. Acts as a resource person for the building staff;
communicates regularly with classroom teachers, the principal, and the
ESL/bilingual education consultant; keeps parents informed of the
students' needs and progress through phone calls, home visits, or
conferences; interprets and translates the students' native language or
arranges interpreters as requested by staff or parents; attends parent/
teacher conferences; and assists with parent advisory council meetings.

5. Gathers and generates the necessary data for evaluation
of the program.

*Note.* From *Professional Tutor's Handbook for Multilingual Students* (p. 39), by
J. Golden, 1994, Aurora, CO: Project TALK. Copyright © 1994 by Project TALK.
Reprinted with permission.

special guests, or as translators for families. Volunteers may need training in second language acquisition or cultural influences that affect LEP students. See also chapter 6 on strategies for strengthening parent and community inclusion in ESL programs.

## Mainstream Staff

As suggested in the previous chapter, mainstream (i.e., regular content-area) teachers play a crucial role in the academic success of all language minority students. Administrators must make an effort to include mainstream teachers in understanding issues surrounding language minority education and in sharing responsibility for the education of LEP students. LEP students can spend significant amounts of time in mainstream classrooms, and mainstream teachers must be able to work effectively with these students. They must not, for example, exclude LEP students in academic instruction or postpone that instruction pending greater fluency in English. Not only would that practice result in long-term academic failure (Collier & Thomas, 1999), but it would also be a denial of access occasioned by national origin—hence, illegal under Title VI of the Civil Rights Act. Besides, the National Education Goals and the Improving America's Schools Act (IASA) stress the importance of shared educational objectives and collaboration among mainstream educators and adjunct programs such as Title I, ESL, special education, and education of the homeless.

Enabling mainstream teachers to work with LEP students may be approached in different ways. First is their need for university training. University teacher training programs in general education have not generally required course work that addresses linguistically and culturally diverse populations. In effect, this has left mainstream teachers with little opportunity to engage in the study needed to acquire methods of effectively working with LEP students. What is needed is the inclusion of course work in teacher training programs that will prepare preservice teachers to work with LEP students in their future classrooms. For mainstream teachers who are currently teaching, workshops, institutes, and college courses that address the issues of second language acquisition, instructional modifications, and diversity issues should be made available.

The second way of building the capacity of mainstream teachers to work with LEP students is through ongoing sharing of information and teaching strategies with ESL staff. This practice has two benefits: Mainstream staff may begin to practice instructional techniques in which ESL teachers should have expertise, and ESL teachers stay abreast of how to support the content-area instruction that the LEP student is receiving from the mainstream staff. Mingucci (1999) raises the bar for all policy makers in suggesting that teachers be given the time and resources to collaborate with their ESL colleagues in areas such as action research. This practice would enable them to better understand and improve their own teaching. Such collaboration between the ESL and mainstream staff must be constantly maintained to meet the often rapidly changing needs of LEP students as discussed in chapter 4. Table 5.2 offers a sampling of the tools mainstream teachers use in educating LEP students.

# Administration

Principals and district-level administrators play a pivotal role in overseeing and supporting high-quality ESL, language development, and content-area instructional programs for all students. Indeed, effective school leaders must be adequately informed of issues involving second language learning, too. Collier and Thomas (1999) have stressed that the acquisition of English is not the only goal, the only need LEP students' have. According to Collier and Thomas, a knowledgeable and caring administrator must address more than just the students' language acquisition; he or she must address the cognitive, emotional, social, and physical development needs of these learners in order to serve the instructional needs of the whole child.

Administrators must be aware of the state and federal requirements and policies for the education of language minority children and must take appropriate action so that these requirements are met. An administrator who is an advocate for the LEP student collaborates with the ESL manager and teacher in making decisions about staffing, allocation of space, and budgeting for supplies. Such an administrator assures parents that they will be informed and advised of their children's progress. Administrators work with the ESL manager and teacher to ensure program coordination among all disciplines.

Holding fast to high expectations of all students has been shown to produce positive student performance outcomes and overall school success (Meier, 1995). What administrators can do to enable teachers to challenge students goes beyond the rhetoric of the politically popular sound bite about high standards. The challenge imposed by the standards must be carried out for successes to become manifest (Adger & Peyton, 1999).

**Table 5.2**   Some Tools for the Mainstream Teacher in Educating the Limited English Proficient (LEP) Student

| *Inclusiveness* | *Advocacy* |
| --- | --- |
| Engage ESL teacher with students in the whole classroom (not "back of the room ESL") | Culture-connected high-interest books for all children |
| Cooperative learning and decision making | Affirmations of diversity |
| ESL/content curriculum development teaming | Civil rights activity |
| Specially designed academic instruction in English (SDAIE); sheltered content | Intimate knowledge of the LEP student and family (culture, previous schooling) |
| Cognitive academic language learning approach (CALLA) | |

| *Materials* | *Resourcefulness* |
| --- | --- |
| Technology | Collaboration |
| Realia | Engage buddies, interpreters, and cross-age tutors |
| Support systems with colleagues for LEP students | Use LEP students as an instructional resource |
| Interesting print material for LEP and non-LEP students to share | Use LEP students' parents as guest speakers and volunteers |
| Authentic materials | |
| Games | |
| Books for pleasure reading (intended for either LEP or non-LEP students) | |

*Continued on p. 108*

**Table 5.2 *continued***   Some Tools for the Mainstream Teacher in Educating the Limited English Proficient (LEP) Student

| *Professional Development* | *Pedagogy* |
| --- | --- |
| Ongoing staff development | Comprehensible content (no watering down subject matter) |
| Time and resources to visit model programs elsewhere | Thematic interactive units |
| Support for ESL/content action research initiatives | Active learning |
| | Model appropriate and natural English usage without embarrassing the LEP student |
| | Employ a variety of teaching styles to accommodate varying learning styles |
| | Conduct holistic and alternative assessments (portfolios, test modification, test to improve instruction) |
| | Employ metacognitive learning strategies |

As schools move increasingly toward systemic reform, administrators will need to break with past practices of deferring all ESL professional development opportunities to ESL staff. In-service staff development programs are needed for all faculty and instructional leaders, including administrators.

## Continuous Professional Improvement for All

Most notable in many rural schools that enroll LEP children is the ESL teacher's or tutor's unfortunate isolation. Such balkanization manifests itself physically in the teacher and students' separation from the center of school activity and from the academic program and faculty. Regrettably, the LEP student is too often viewed as the sole responsibility of the ESL staff. This presents itself most commonly in ESL pullout scenarios where the ESL teacher's contact with the LEP student is limited. The result? The LEP student is significantly disadvantaged in both understanding content instruction due to dysfluency and falling victim to an otherwise competent and caring teacher who knows almost nothing about the LEP student's special learning needs. To establish a high-quality program, LEP students should have access to the full grade- and age-level appropriate curriculum and should be engaged in meaningful activities to master that curriculum all day, every day. A well-trained staff is central to the fulfillment of this goal. In short, collaborative schools are effective schools.

In order for activities to be meaningful, teachers, both ESL and mainstream, must know how to make content accessible to their LEP students. This vision of ESL and mainstream teachers working together to provide high-quality instruction to LEP students aligns well with the goals of systemic education reform, such as the National Education Goals, state-based standards, and high-stake assessments for all students.

Staff development is attainable through the engagement of ESL specialists at the school. Such specialists may be consultants skilled not only in ESL instruction but also in culture-connected testing and other ESL-related instructional support. Certainly, college-level study in ESL should be encouraged for all staff, including administration. Reimbursement for such courses is common for most school districts, dependent on local contracts and union-negotiated benefits as applicable. As Table 5.3 illustrates, the colleges and universities in nearly every state in the United States offer ESL-related courses, also called *teaching English as a second language (TESL)*, whether it be undergraduate, graduate, or certification/endorsement support—or a combination of these. Rural schools frequently depend on distance learning because commuting to colleges in the state may be prohibitive. Teachers can contact university or state education personnel to learn of ESL-related course offerings on interactive television or can access *Dave's ESL Cafe* on the Web under the main menu's "Teacher Training Options" at http://www.eslcafe.com.

When university courses are treated as one-shot events, they will have limited long-range classroom benefits. Hence, it behooves the teacher to follow through on implementing techniques acquired in training. Teachers may incorporate new skills into their teaching repertoire to follow up on previous training by two mechanisms, which are either geared toward transmission of information or based in sharing among teachers. These mechanisms include (a) mentoring, whereby an ESL teacher or paraprofessional can be paired with an experienced staff member who can impart teaching information in a work setting; and (b) peer teaching, whereby the ESL teacher can access other professionals in the content classroom via observation and coteaching activities.

**Table 5.3**    ESL Teacher Education Programs in State Institutions of Higher Education*

| State | Undergraduate Degree? | Graduate Degree? | Certification/ Endorsement? |
|---|---|---|---|
| Alabama | Y | Y | Y |
| Montana | N | N | Y |
| Alaska | N | N | Y |
| Arizona | Y | Y | Y |
| Arkansas | N | N | Y |
| California | Y | Y | Y |
| Colorado | Y | Y | Y |
| Connecticut | N | Y | Y |
| Delaware | Y | Y | Y |
| District of Columbia | N | Y | N |
| Florida | Y | Y | Y |
| Georgia | Y | Y | Y |
| Hawaii | Y | Y | N |
| Idaho | Y | Y | Y |
| Illinois | Y | Y | Y |
| Indiana | Y | Y | Y |
| Iowa | Y | Y | Y |
| Kansas | N | Y | Y |
| Kentucky | Y | Y | Y |
| Louisiana | Y | Y | Y |
| Maine | Y | Y | Y |
| Maryland | N | Y | Y |
| Massachusetts | Y | Y | Y |
| Michigan | Y | Y | Y |
| Minnesota | Y | Y | Y |
| Mississippi | N | Y | N |
| Missouri | Y | Y | Y |

Continued on p. 111

**Table 5.3** *continued*  ESL Teacher Education Programs in State Institutions of Higher Education*

| State | Undergraduate Degree? | Graduate Degree? | Certification/ Endorsement? |
|---|---|---|---|
| Nebraska | Y | Y | Y |
| Nevada | N | Y | Y |
| New Hampshire | N | Y | Y |
| New Jersey | Y | Y | Y |
| New Mexico | Y | Y | Y |
| New York | Y | Y | Y |
| North Carolina | Y | Y | Y |
| North Dakota | N | Y | N |
| Ohio | Y | N | Y |
| Oklahoma | Y | Y | Y |
| Oregon | Y | Y | Y |
| Pennsylvania | N | Y | N |
| Rhode Island | N | Y | N |
| South Carolina | N | N | N |
| South Dakota | N | N | Y |
| Tennessee | N | N | Y |
| Texas | Y | Y | Y |
| Utah | Y | N | Y |
| Vermont | N | Y | Y |
| Virginia | Y | Y | Y |
| Washington | N | Y | Y |
| West Virginia | N | N | N |
| Wisconsin | N | Y | Y |
| Wyoming | N | N | N |

*Data may reflect one or more institute of higher education per state.

Note: From *Teacher Education Programs in the U.S.: Bilingual & ESL*, by the National Clearinghouse for Bilingual Education, 2000, Washington, DC: National Clearinghouse for Bilingual Education, retrieved July 31, 2000, from the World Wide Web: http://www.ncbe.gwu.edu/links/teachered/index.htm. Adapted with permission.

Information in this table is based on information available at the referenced Web sites and may be incomplete or out of date. Please contact the institution directly to obtain the most current information.

# The Family of Stakeholders: A Commitment to Professional Growth

Taking the opening premise from this chapter, "Educating everyone takes everyone," collaboratives throughout the school bode well for LEP students. The ESL manager and administrator are first among the collaborators. They will need to exact a strategy that engages their colleagues. Doing so is, of course,

**Table 5.4**   A Collaborative ESL Manager's Appraisal of Stakeholders

| Pivotal stakeholders (as appropriate) | List issues (wants, needs, or goals) | List barriers (fears, resistant behaviors) to collaboration | List strategies to make collaboration work | List resources needed by the school |
|---|---|---|---|---|
| LEP student(s) | | | | |
| ESL manager | | | | |
| ESL teacher/tutor | | | | |
| Content teacher(s) | | | | |
| IASA Title I-A (Disadvantaged) | | | | |
| IASA Title I-C (Migratory) | | | | |
| Special education | | | | |
| Guidance | | | | |
| Principal | | | | |
| School committee | | | | |
| Central administration | | | | |
| Parent | | | | |
| Community at large | | | | |

not easy—there are resistors and devotees of the status quo. On the other hand, there are also colleagues who genuinely care about all the students in the school and want to be approached for their expertise and sagacity. Table 5.4 offers a working grid for a collection of issues that may serve as an icebreaker for a collaborative at its embryonic stage. Using that grid for examining issues and their stakeholders, take, for example, the following as a hypothetical scenario:

Pivotal Stakeholder: Principal

Issues (wants, needs, or goals): To discontinue ESL support for newcomers after one year

Barriers (fears, resistant behaviors): The ESL teacher wants to save her job; she will likely call in parents to her side

Strategies to Make Collaboration Work: Agree to meet and hear out ESL teacher, content teachers, and parents to consider the principal's proposal, its rationale, pros/cons, and review students' portfolios and assessments; discuss principal's alternatives; discuss the research literature that would raise doubt over the principal's position; review *Lau* plan for language regarding program exit consistent with statute

Resources Needed: *Lau* plan as approved by the board; results of language proficiency tests; students' portfolios; research articles (e.g., from such authors as Collier, Cummins, Hakuta, and Krashen; see References)

An ongoing step is training—especially for the scenario posed here. Indeed, for collaboratives to work, high-quality training for persons involved in the education of LEP students will include the administrators, ESL staff, mainstream teachers, guidance personnel, and support staff, among others. Top-quality training programs will showcase the following two characteristics:

Comprehensive: Training for all staff will include learning about a variety of topics pertaining to ESL and mainstream education. It will include, as a minimum, second language theory, ESL methods, diversity awareness, ESL curriculum design, and authentic assessments.

Ongoing: Training will be offered frequently during the school year to continually acquaint all staff with current issues relating to second language acquisition. Training must be ongoing to maintain a high level of effective practices and to troubleshoot when needed. Teachers who are implementing a new instructional strategy need adequate time to practice and refine their skills. Consider the effect that diverse teacher training practices have on teacher learning. Doctoral research conducted by Bennett (1995) at the University of Toronto reveals much about what is already known of the dramatic effect collaborative learning has on students—that coaching is good for everyone. What is subsequently needed is mainstream/ESL professional development to enhance the teachers' collaborative coaching potential.

## Summative Guidance for the ESL Program Manager

Good teaching truly does matter, especially when all teachers and their leaders work toward making a difference in educating LEP students. This chapter has presented the role of the ESL manager in the context of a comprehensive, collaborative school team. The ESL program cannot be a fissure of the school. If it were, high standards for LEP students would be indeed difficult to pursue. Those disjunctive kinds of programs of the past across the United States appear to be gradually disappearing.

To establish and manage an ESL program as prescribed in this volume will require broad-based recruitment of new staff as needed and the engagement of current staff whose demonstrable commitment to the school district of learning for all students will illuminate the ESL program. Paraprofessionals and volunteers, to be included in staffing, will become essential participants among those teams.

A quality ESL teacher, like any other good teacher, thirsts for good ideas that improve instruction. Where do so many of these teachers get those ideas? The temptation is to respond almost instantly with "course work" or "research," which is not true. In a study by Crookes and Arakaki (1999), those good teachers cited the following idea sources, in order of popularity:

- accumulation of teacher experience
- informal consultation with colleagues
- printed resources that support instruction
- spontaneous self-generation
- preservice training
- in-house workshops

Neither research nor conference attendance appears in this listing. A relatively small sampling of teachers from that study reveals that these teachers trusted their own expertise or that of their peers before turning to the outside experts. This revelation should not be startling to the ESL manager or teacher. After all, the reasons why some teachers remain complacent would appear self-evident: burnout (especially among itinerant teachers), boredom with training, not enough time, not enough money, and not much practical application from the experts.

Schools need to reach those teachers less inclined to read the resources that support instruction or to solicit advice from the so-called experts. Recycling of decades-old ideas or enhancing these ideas through faculty lounge conversations may be healthy. On the other hand, there is more to good teaching than that. There is a growing base of knowledge about how children learn, how second languages are acquired, and what makes our diverse cultures different from each other. Accessing that knowledge responsibly is key, and well-trained ESL teachers possess that knowledge.

Good teachers, like good physicians, remain current, and they improve their practice by keeping it grounded in sound ideas. For schools, incentives need to be in place for that to occur. The major incentives to pursue include financial supports, professional leave time for ESL teachers and their collaborators, defrayment of expenses in teachers' attending training events, encouraging teachers to visit other schools, and valuing ESL as far more than a temporary dead-end job.

Teacher enthusiasm for using an effective instructional technique learned in training is commonly followed by a demonstrable competence in using that technique in the classroom. Therefore, it would seem that in order for teachers to improve their skills in making content-area instruction accessible and strengthening their students' English language acquisition, they must have training that offers them adequate time, practice, knowledge, skills, and opportunities for transfer of learning. Sometimes teachers assume that if they attend a conference or two on ESL-related topics, they bring a credible presence to the school's ESL program. Such efforts, though useful, are superficial. Training must be a part of continuous improvement. State departments of education frequently provide conferences as do universities and professional organizations, to name a few. The value of those events is limited without follow through.

Continuous professional improvement through staff development is by definition, ongoing. One-shot training events are futile. Schools of excellence are distinguished for their philosophical and fiscal support for continuous quality improvement for their staff through ongoing training. For the ESL professional, the additional training germane to this part of the profession is no less important. Individual states' requirements for ESL credentials and the availability of university courses will need to be examined in that process.

One of the keys to establishing a successful ESL program is having a school staff—including administrators, mainstream teachers, ESL and other resource teachers, guidance counselors, and support staff—who understand issues in the education of LEP students. The entire staff must be committed to improving the learning outcomes of these students, and sufficient training must be provided toward that end.

## Suggested Resources on the Web

For the OCR's guidelines regarding staffing resources needed to support ESL:

> *Programs for English Language Learners: Resource Materials for Planning and Self-Assessments* (Office for Civil Rights, 1999, http://www.ed.gov /offices/OCR/ELL/index.html)

For interaction with ESL teachers on-line:

> *EFL Teachers Lounge for Teachers of English as a Foreign or Secondary Language* (http://www.capaho.com/efl/cgi/rst_config.cgi)

For guidance on content instruction challenges with teaching LEP students:

> "Meeting the Challenge of Content Instruction in K–8 Classroom: Part 1 and Part 2" (Haynes & O'Loughlin, 1999, http://www.tesol.org /isaffil/intsec/columns/199904-ee.html [Part 1] and http:// www.tesol.org/isaffil/intsec/columns/199906-ee.html [Part 2])

For a unique project on ESL collaboratives with bilingual teachers:

> "Teamworks: Mainstream and Bilingual ESL Teacher Collaboration" (Sakash & Rodriguez-Brown, 1995, http://www.ncbe.gwu.edu /ncbepubs/pigs/pig24.htm)

For a paper on reducing failures of LEP students in mainstream classrooms:

> "Reducing Failure of Limited English Proficient Students in the Mainstream Classroom and Why It Is Important" (Cornell, 1995, http://www.ncbe.gwu.edu/miscpubs/jeilms/vol15/reducing.htm)

For guidance on preparing mainstream teachers to teach LEP students:

> "Preparing Mainstream Classroom Teachers to Teach Potentially English Proficient Students" (Hamayan, 1990, http:// www.ncbe.gwu.edu/ncbepubs/symposia/first/preparing.htm)

# Chapter 6
# Parents and the Community

*Many immigrant children throughout the world . . . bring with them
the attitude that they must render respect and obedience to the teacher
in the same way they respect their parents. When children leave home,
they are entrusted to the teacher. Teachers then become their
"educational parents." The teacher becomes not only an ally but a
person whose voice is respected and obeyed.*

—Igoa, 1995, p. 100

Parental and community involvement in the school is a very timely topic.
As one of its National Education Goals, the U.S. Department of Education (1994) proclaimed that "every school will promote partnerships
that will increase parental involvement and participation in promoting the
social, emotional, and academic growth of children" (p. 3). A volume by itself
is warranted in addressing the role of parents and communities in the education of LEP children. Resources are legion, and cyberspace is a virtually limitless resource for understanding and supporting families regardless of culture,
language, and size of the community. In an increasingly heterogeneous society, the importance of joint efforts among parents and schools working together to ensure quality education for LEP youth cannot be overstated. One
method for achieving this is the creation of an ESL advisory board for the
school system. The purposes and function of such as board are discussed later

in this chapter. Having noted that, this chapter provides a few matters of importance about parents in rural and small urban communities that the ESL manager is advised to consider.

## A Compelling Rationale

August and Hakuta (1998) report that the research is conclusive: Ongoing parental/community involvement is an important contributor to effective schools. Cited as most effective in parent and community involvement is the encouragement of home-based learning opportunities and home/school comprehensive connections: the more types of positive connections, the more powerful the effects. For all this, language minority families must be considered as pivotal players too. The Center for Equity and Excellence in Education (1996) at The George Washington University has captured one of six conditions that exist in schools where LEP students are succeeding academically. It states that "the academic success of LEP students is a responsibility shared by all educators, the family, and the community" (p. 11). Such a condition must be created to achieve excellence in the education of students acquiring English as their new language. At least seven core beliefs surface at the outset in enabling empowerment of the language minority family:

- The family is the child's first teacher.
- Learning is life-long.
- Families can and want to learn.
- In our global world bilingualism is an asset, not a liability.
- Families, regardless of ethnicity or socioeconomic status, want to make a positive impact on their children's education.
- Education is the shared responsibility of the home and school.
- A child's education at home or at school is powerfully defined by culture. (Center for Equity and Excellence in Education, 1996, p. 11)

How do parents participate in their children's education, given the influences previously noted? Among middle-class Americans, parent participation means helping with homework, having conferences with the teacher, and being active in parent-teacher associations (PTAs). Because most parents, including those from newly arrived families, are taxpayers, they believe that the school should be responsive to their ideas and that their voice in defining how the school educates their children is valued. The differences in beliefs are probably marginal, but the differences in how those beliefs are expressed are likely formidable.

Immigrant parents may have a range of beliefs and attitudes about what parent participation should entail. For example, some Hispanic and some Asian groups tend to see their role as parents as focusing on how the child behaves and see the teachers as professionals, much like doctors or lawyers, who have expert knowledge and whose practices and suggestions should be accepted almost without question. Thus, what is expected from one culture's point of view may be seen as intrusive from another culture's viewpoint. School personnel must be sensitive to cultural beliefs and practices when they plan for genuine involvement of language minority parents. This becomes increasingly relevant for rural communities, especially where nonminority residents are unaccustomed to a populace that is culturally different from the mainstream. The ESL manager must be aware that leaving language minority parents to their own devices will lead to their isolation. It has been well established that immigrant groups have historically demonstrated a strong desire for their children to acquire English and take full advantage of the opportunities that are opened to them by the U.S. educational system—a good foundation on which the ESL manager can help build parent involvement for the entire school community.

Because class and cultural differences among groups of language minority parents can lead to complex school issues, such differences should be acknowledged. In order to present current U.S. school expectations to parents new to the United States, language minority parents should indeed be encouraged to become involved at all points of their child's entry into school. Such engagement of parents is essential for an effective program for LEP students and should not be considered as something extra. As noted in chapter 2, Title VI of the Civil Rights Act of 1964 states that:

> No person in the United States shall, on the ground of race, color, or *national origin* [italics added], be excluded from participation in, be denied the benefits of, or be subjected to discrimination under any program or activity receiving federal financial assistance. (§ 2000d)

This requirement has been broadly interpreted to require equal access to educational services for language minority students and parents.

Parental noninvolvement is popularly attributable to language barriers, lack of transportation, economics, or feelings of alienation. Issues surrounding majority and minority parent involvement in schools are complicated and varied; some school personnel are reluctant to share their power in decision making. Mandating parental involvement in ESL programs does not, of course, guarantee success. What seems to make a difference are such factors as community and school support for appropriate educational services for LEP children, teachers' active involvement with parents, and parents' attendance at school and board meetings. Although it is true that civil rights legislation has enabled parents of LEP children and other advocates to file formal complaints against schools whose programs for their children are perceived as inadequate, parents' involvement in schools limited to confrontational relationships is understandably not a desired goal. Indeed, when their concerns go unheeded, there remains every right for the parent to seek due process. Highly vocal and active parents have typically appeared at the core of many U.S. court cases from 1970–1979—and most notably in the *Lau* Supreme Court decision of 1974. Though regrettably adversarial, these methods have been remarkably effective. Remaining proactive and supportive is in everyone's better interest.

## Parents' Rights and Responsibilities

It is by now an axiomatic reminder that parents and school personnel must be partners in the education of children. The responsibility of administrators and teachers who are involved in this partnership is a function of their specific roles. Roles parents can actively play in the education of their children include, but are not limited to, learners, teachers, decision makers, counselors, resources, and agents of social change. The single greatest barrier to LEP parent participation at school is the parents' lack of English skills. It is essential that interpreters be available at all meetings. Providing regular program updates on the child's progress and activities in a language parents can comprehend will help bridge the communication gap and facilitate better communication between the teachers and the home. When LEP students participate in this ongoing assessment process, it becomes more authentic and meaningful.

The ESL manager, in liaison with individuals who speak the parents' language and who have some knowledge of the parents' culture, can help start a rich partnership within the community. To ensure that parents are aware of what their rights and responsibilities are, there must be communication between the school and the home in a mode that parents can understand. That is an inviting and proactive first step. Because some parents have limited English skills, school notifications concerning school programs, school policies, parent/teacher conferences, homework, language surveys, and other documents need to be provided to language minority families in a language they comprehend. In legal parlance, if the parents/guardians of language minority children are themselves limited English proficient, "school districts have the responsibility to adequately notify national origin-minority group parents of school activities which are called to the attention of other parents. Such notice in order to be adequate may have to be provided in a language other than English" (Pottinger, 1970, p. 1). In most cases, written notification in the home language will suffice, but schools should be sensitive to the possibility that some parents may have limited literacy skills in their native language. Whether or not a school district ensures that parents who are not proficient in English are provided with understandable information about school activities, the regional Office for Civil Rights (OCR) would take note of that school district's shortcomings when it is monitored for compliance with Title VI of the Civil Rights Act or when a complaint is filed.

LEP parents should have access to information to school activities such as discipline codes, field trips, alerts about health hazards, and school cancellations. The school may need to provide LEP parents/guardians the services of an interpreter-translator for school meetings that address their child's instructional program, such as language assessment committee (LAC) meetings and parent-teacher conferences. Schools may not be required to provide interpreters, on the one hand, for parents of students 18 years of age or older. That student, on the other hand, may wish to request involving his or her parents in a school meeting such as a pupil evaluation team (PET), which is responsible for negotiating referrals to students who may be candidates for special education placement. Should that occur, the meeting should include an interpreter for the parents. The use of interpreters must be strictly professional. Using relatives of the parents is inadvisable, especially where school matters may be not only confidential but sensitive as well. It takes a trained interpreter to provide accurate information both orally and in writing, as appropriate. The school should have a plan in place for accessing qualified interpreters.

The OCR encourages parents to attempt to solve communication problems with the schools locally first. Should that fail, the parents have the right to file a complaint with the OCR at any time. The ESL manager is advised to let parents know that if they feel that their child is not receiving proper supplemental language services (e.g., ESL) in the school, they should begin at the school level by notifying the LAC contact person (see chapter 3) and ask that a meeting of the committee be convened. The parents should be invited to participate in that meeting to the extent they are comfortable. If they are LEP, an interpreter must be brought in. If the parents remain unsatisfied, they may opt to pursue the hierarchical chain of command in the school district (e.g., principal, special language services director, superintendent, school board). They may lean heavily on the ESL manager to help shoulder that burden. If, after key personnel have been contacted with assistance from the ESL manager, the parents still do not feel appropriate action has been taken with regard to their child or children, they may contact the state's education department for assistance or advisement. More dramatic than that, they may file a formal OCR complaint. In order to file such a complaint with the OCR's enforcement offices, parents can call the OCR's customer service team at 800-421-3481 or contact the OCR at its national Web site (http://www.ed.gov /offices/OCR/). No credential is needed to file a complaint with the OCR; anyone may file a complaint.

Language minority parents have a right to attend any meetings concerning placement and progress of their children. These meetings might include a PET meeting, an LAC meeting, or parent-teacher conferences. It is the responsibility of the school to hold meetings at times convenient to ensure parent attendance and to provide translators or interpreters if necessary. Attending meetings may be a struggle for some parents because they have younger children who cannot be left at home alone or because they lack transportation. Some immigrant parents may not understand the school's expectations. The ESL teacher can act as a liaison between the home and the school, encouraging the language minority parents to participate at these meetings.

There is a plethora of reasons frequently attributed to parents who remain invisible in their children's school. Work, busy schedules, lack of child care and transportation, discomfort with the school environment, attitude, boredom, and their estrangement from other parents are only a few of these reasons. The newly arrived parents' absence may include any of the examples listed here or it may include additional factors such as discomfort with English, discomfort with the new culture (depending on their length of residence in the United States), absence of school personnel who can speak with them in their own language, and the appearance of an unwelcoming school environment. It becomes, then, particularly crucial that those parents' circumstances be taken into account as ESL program managers seek their involvement at school. It is not sufficient that one simply affirms the diversity such families bring to school. The values and their cultures must factor into school policy and practice. Note Figure 6.1, for example, which illustrates how one Virginia public school district transitions newly arrived parents toward culture in the United States.

**Figure 6.1**    ESL Manager Strategies for Involving Newly Arrived Families

---

**ACCULTURATION PHASE 1:**
**Families New to the System**

The Challenge: Families require orientation and information about the school community, enrollment procedures, and educational programs.

The Response: Whenever possible, provide information in the native language.

⇩

**ACCULTURATION PHASE 2:**
**Culture Shock**

The Challenge: Families' energies may be exhausted during this emotionally stressful time.

The Response: Encourage personal contacts from school personnel and minimal demands on families' time.

⇩

**ACCULTURATION PHASE 3:**
**Accommodation and Adjustment**

The Challenge: Families begin to become familiar with the new cultural system.

The Response: Encourage their participation in school activities and provide specific tasks and responsibilities for them.

⇩

**ACCULTURATION PHASE 4:**
**Integration and Acculturation**

As families feel comfortable in their new setting, encourage participation in all activities. Provide opportunities for leadership and mentoring of other family members. Acquaint them with options for participation in community opportunities.

---

*Note.* From "Process of Acculturation" [chart] in *ESOL High-Intensity Language Training,* by Arlington Public Schools, 1992, Arlington, VA: Author. Copyright © 1992 by the Arlington Public Schools. Adapted with permission.

Many language minority parents do not attend school functions or meetings because of the problems with scheduling, child care, and transportation. To overcome these problems, the school must be flexible, to the extent possible, to accommodate parents' work schedules. If child care is a problem, the school should consider encouraging the parents to bring their younger children to the school for meetings and utilizing some of the school's older students as babysitters. For parents new to the United States who likely will not have driver's licenses or cars, their lack of transportation will prohibit the parent involvement in the schools that is essential for their children's success. Thus, it may be necessary to seek public transportation sources for them. By connecting new families with local bus and van schedules or by putting them in touch with more established language minority families, getting to school might not be as difficult.

# Critical Parent Engagement

## Preschool Planning

Preschool programs, such as Head Start, are language-rich environments for children from 3–5 years old. These venues are ideal for supporting parents in encouraging use of their native language along with the acquisition of English. This is true of both adoptive parents or guardians and the biologically natural parents. LEP children's biological parents represent a rich resource for integrating multicultural concepts and their home language into the preschool curriculum. In addition, many local programs, such as Head Start and Even Start, form liaison committees with public schools to help kindergarten teachers become aware of the needs of their new minority students and to facilitate the children's transition to school. Preschool is also an ideal time for encouraging these parents to join parent committees or to volunteer their time at the local community center.

## Kindergarten Screening

The ESL manager or teacher carries an important role on the kindergarten screening team. Among parents who are LEP, often only those most comfortable speaking English will attend their child's kindergarten screening. This can cause pertinent information about the child's background, native language proficiency, and health information to be omitted from the interview with the screening team. The ESL teacher or manager must remind the school district of its legal responsibilities for providing an interpreter to ensure that parents can answer questions fully and accurately. Adoptive parents generally have these materials in hand more readily than do immigrant parents. The ESL manager should also take responsibility for ensuring that every parent completes a home language survey as part of the screening process. As noted in previous chapters, this is the first step in identifying potential students of limited English proficiency.

## Classroom Visibility

Language minority parents represent perhaps the best resource of firsthand knowledge about their native culture. Parents of adoptive LEP children need to be nurtured as well in this area, permitting them to share in their children's heritage. This resource can be shared within the ESL classroom as well as in the mainstreamed classes. Whether the parent is facilitating an activity in the native language or serving as a guest speaker/artist for a day, encouraging such participation promotes parental ownership in his or her child's education. Classrooms that are envisioned as a community of learners nurture the cultural knowledge that children bring from home. Consequently, these classrooms establish an environment in which cultural diversity is a valued asset, rather than a barrier to be overcome.

## Ongoing Advisement From Parents

One way for the ESL manager to ensure continuing parental involvement and support for their families is to establish an ESL advisory board. This board would consist of a representative from many potential community service groups, as well as the ESL manager, teachers, principals, the curriculum coordinator, the Title I director, the special education director, the Head Start director (or other special preschool project), a representative from the school board, the superintendent, and a parent representative. The ESL advisory board might choose to meet monthly or bimonthly in a school or at the superintendent's office and work through a well-planned agenda. Even if there is not an area of compelling concern to discuss, such meetings do serve to validate the local ESL program and the ongoing needs of the language minority students. This advisory board can provide the visibility necessary to promote the celebration of multiculturalism and diversity throughout the community. A chair for the advisory board should be named. Often that role will rotate, as a matter of fairness.

Rural schools where language minority parents are visibly treated as a valued resource are well on their way to addressing the needs of all students. For example, soliciting parents of language minority students to participate on various elementary, middle, high school, and districtwide committees ensures that social, psychological, and educational proximity will exist and that cultural barriers will be lowered. As representation from the various sectors within a school or school district promotes diversity and leads to empowerment, parents can contribute greatly at PTA meetings and on parent advisory boards, school curriculum committees, and school board committees as well. Often they need only to be asked.

The literature on parental engagement is replete with ideas on ways that parents can be valued in their child's education. Schools engage parents for a wide range of reasons initiated by the school or initiated by the parents themselves. Table 6.1 illustrates several kinds of roles parents can be encouraged to pursue in making a difference in their child's schooling. Building relations with parents in these ways helps families help themselves as well as the school in ensuring the best possible educational experience for their child. Those relations must focus squarely on the needs of the family, driven by the parent and family rather than by the school. Such engagement extends to school-sponsored parent training grounded in the language minority community's needs and interests, including those of adoptive parents or guardians.

## Creating a Welcoming Environment

Many parents are apprehensive about schools. Some may have had unfortunate experiences during their own childhoods. Some may have dropped out. The credentials of their children's teachers may intimidate them. Therefore, it behooves the school to recognize a kind of balanced expectation. In Violand-Sánchez's (1991) monograph for developing a framework for home-school partnerships, she notes four factors that help determine the extent to which language minority parents emerge in their children's schools. These four factors include

1. Length of residency here: Parents in Acculturation Phase 1 will first need a great deal of orientation to the new culture of that school and community.

2. English language fluency: The barrier of intimidation due to language is indeed real. LEP parents must be gently nurtured in a visibly welcoming environment.

## Table 6.1   Common Time-Tested Parental Practices

- advisement to teachers and administration
- advocacy
- art/science activities
- bulletin boards
- calling other parents
- celebrations and awards
- classroom speaker
- clerical activities
- coffees
- cultural events
- expert parent/speaker
- extracurricular activities
- "family of the week"
- field trips
- fund-raising
- homework management and support
- learning a new language
- math and science fun
- mentoring
- model learning and technology
- newsletters
- open house
- parent resource center
- photography
- pot lucks
- reading
- school garden
- selected television viewing (with parental guidance)
- special events
- story telling
- supervising learning centers
- training opportunities
- translator/interpreter
- tutoring
- writing projects
- young author's day

3. Access to support of other parents: Bilingual representatives will strengthen this bond and so may adoptive parents and guardians.

4. Prior experiences: The energy to which schools around the world seek to involve parents varies widely among cultures. Sensitivity and understanding of those differences is essential in nurturing their acculturation.

The physical environment should be visibly welcoming. Positive evidence of the schools' diversity should be apparent at the point of physical entry. For rural schools, this is telling, because the demographics of most rural areas do not mirror the current diversity in the United States. Encouragement of parental contributions to the school should be sincere. When it is, parents respond favorably to invitations from their child's school. They will indeed sign up to volunteer and support school activities.

Rural community schools welcoming their newfound diversity will want to access Jolly, Hampton, and Guzman's (1999) collection of useful parent tools designed as welcoming information notes. These are available in Spanish, French, Portuguese, Russian, Chinese, Vietnamese, and Korean. Below is a sampling of those notes:

> I enjoy teaching your child. Although I don't speak your language well, you are welcome to visit my classroom at any time. Feel free to bring a friend or interpreter. (p. 36)

> We know that it is sometimes difficult to communicate because of different languages. If you have information about your child that is important to share with us, please write us a letter. We will locate a translator and translate your letter. (p. 38)

> At [our] school, we provide a safe place for your child. If your child is worried or concerned about something, he/she can visit with _____ (Name of principal, counselor, or teacher) (p. 39)

> Welcome to our community. I'm glad your child is in our classroom. We are interested in learning more about your culture. You are welcome to share a tradition from your family or culture with our class. Can you come next week?
> Date:_____Time:_____ (p. 41)

> Our class is having a special event on _____ (date) at _____ (time). Could you please provide cookies or a dessert? You are also welcome to join us. (p. 45)

## Should LEP Parents Use Their Native Language at Home?

A misguided view held by many otherwise intelligent and culturally sensitive educators is that parents should raise their children solely in a community's dominant language. This view can come as well from both biological and adoptive parents and guardians. Many monolingual and bilingual Americans believe that bilingualism confuses, even harms children—a throwback to the flawed literature of the 1950s and the early 1960s. Yet, well-controlled research literature (Cummins & Swain, 1986) compellingly argues the need to encourage early childhood bilingualism. The consensus appears to be that when a child is of school age, the second language acquisition process is strong enough so that second language acquisition does not occur at the expense of losing the native language along the way.

Some current literature does suggest that the advantages of bilinguals are marginal, but there is more that attests to the benefits of bilingualism. For example, Collier (1995a) has found that bilingual children attain higher academic achievement in later years than students who lose their first language to learn English. Bialystok (1997) found that bilingualism, in fact, expedites the reading process. Credible literature of the 1980s and 1990s suggests that bilingualism is associated with a plethora of wonderful advantages such as positive scholastic outcomes, higher cerebral function, advanced processing of verbal material, higher IQ scores, higher scores on tests of mental flexibility, and strengthened reading and writing development in the nonnative language.

One must also remain mindful of the other bilingual benefits, which include eventual employment advantages, greater ease in meeting university language requirements, opportunities overseas as well as in North America, linkages to family heritage, and positive self-identity. The list goes on. How rare (and silly) it is to imagine that an American might exclaim, "I am so happy that I don't have a second language," or "A goal for my child is to remain monolingual."

The more bilingual families maintain their native languages, the more intellectually successful their children are likely to become. Many parents who were themselves reared bilingually recall the gradual loss of their native language over time and feel that the same loss will inevitably occur with their children, citing peer pressure at school. They would reasonably discourage any practice that may cause their bilingual toddler embarrassment with peers. Many parents regret that kindergarten was the point at which they lost their native language. Many among them have struggled to renew their native language as an adult after rigorous study.

To press parents to speak English only at home is to disempower them, albeit with the best of intentions (Bérubé, 1992). The best literacy development training programs for parents are those that support children's native language as they acquire a new language. In short, policy should not discourage parents to continue to use their native language at home. To subtract this aspect of the LEP child's home environment is to subtract the value of the child's native language and culture. It will also likely reduce the pace at which the child will acquire English. Teachers of LEP children should affirm the family's native language and culture as a readily available skill the child brings to his or her new experiences with English and suggest ways parents may keep the language not only alive but also enjoyable in normal everyday routines. Some possibilities are suggested in Table 6.2.

# Parent and Community Resources

The resources available in today's cyberspace are limitless in helping to support parents of LEP children by utilizing resources in their native languages. It should become increasingly easier for culturally diverse communities to access the Web—whether through local libraries, home, school, or the workplace.

Parents of non-English backgrounds often find themselves alone, especially in rural communities where only English is routinely heard. However, parents who become skilled surfers on the Internet can access almost anything in their own language. When parents can utilize media in their native language and English, they can potentially transfer that resourcefulness in helping their school-age children in using English and their native language. The very concept of accessing resources in hundreds of languages and dialects around the globe seems mind-boggling. One can access a limitless number of Web sites through a variety of search engines. For example, a search for "language resources" will result in a gargantuan alphabetical listing of Web sites from around the world. One of these sites, called *World Language Resources*, matches its products to scores and scores of languages. This site can be downloaded at http://www.worldlanguage.com/search/language/130.html.

A similar site, called *GlobalSurf*, allows Web and e-mail users to access Internet information in at least 23 different languages. A tool available at this site integrates into Netscape and Microsoft browsers to correctly display Web pages in other languages. Web pages are not translated into English. Rather, the original language is displayed. Languages supported by *GlobalSurf* include Arabic, Czech, Greek, Hebrew, Russian, Swedish, Turkish, and Thai as well as the major European languages, two types of Chinese, and other languages. A customizable interface lets users explore the Internet in any of the languages, through an intuitive floating toolbar. In addition, the user can view, process, and print international e-mail messages at this site, which supports cc:Mail, Eudora, and other Netscape Messages e-mail packages. An onscreen keyboard enables the user to input text in any of the languages. On-line Chinese/English and Japanese/English dictionaries are also available at this site. This site can be downloaded at http://www.dynalab.com (write 625 on the inquiry card).

To reach second language communities for Spanish, Portuguese, French, Italian, or German, at no cost, parents can draft information to their chosen community in their language by clicking on either http://www.freetranslations .com or http://www.babelfish.altavista.digital.com. Then, they can write text in the box provided in English and click when ready for a translation within seconds. The reverse may also be done in the same way (non-English to En-

## Table 6.2   Practical Practices From a Bilingual Home

- *Consistency:* One language is the "family language," even if there are two or more languages in the home. Absolute consistency in the simultaneous use of the native language will ensure a child's natural motivation to acquire that language without the appearance of coercion.
- *Harmony:* The warmth and security of the family unit makes for easy bilingual language management. Parents should sustain a positive, natural communicative experience.
- *Read and write:* Tell stories and acquire books in the native language. Create a dictionary with the children, using magazine cutouts, their drawings, and labels in the native language. When presenting gifts, include print-dependent items. Help the children to create greeting cards using the native language. Many conventional games are accessible in multiple languages.
- *Reinforcements:* Seek out activities conducted by native speakers of the heritage language. For example, our children are taught piano lessons by a native Québecois who lives in our community; the language of instruction is French.
- *Television:* Seek out programs and videos produced in the native language. Even commercials and chantable jingles help children develop complex language structures. Engage the child in amusing situations using the camcorder. Playbacks can be hilarious and will reveal a good deal about the progression of language acquisition over time.
- *Music:* Sing or make up songs and acquire music tapes in the native language. Enjoy popular children's sing-alongs.
- *Technology:* Exploit the tremendous potential available in current technologies. Computer software in non-English languages is widely accessible. The potential available on the Internet is limitless.
- *Travel:* Take family excursions to communities that use the native language exclusively. For example, we travel to Québec each summer where our children camp with francophone playmates.
- *Attitude is everything:* Reassure school personnel of your support of the school language (even though it is not the language of the home) with school work. There is nothing to gain from adverse posturing against the language of the community. Work to prevent xenophobia; affirm diversity.

*Note.* From "Two Polyglots, Three Languages," by B. Bérubé, 1998, *The Bilingual Family Newsletter 15*, pp. 3–5. Copyright © 1998 by B. Bérubé. Reprinted with permission.

glish, except that Italian and Portuguese [with Free Translations] do not have this feature).

Talk Systems, Inc., based in Georgia, appears to be a cost-effective use of technology to increase parental involvement. Interpretation in up to six languages can occur simultaneously without disrupting the primary presentation. Parents who once were segregated into separate language groups can be integrated into a single audience under Talk Systems. With this program, invited speakers need only present once and need not be bilingual; all parents receive the same message at the same time and can ask questions in their native language. Conferences and meetings with bilingual and multilingual parent populations that once took several days to complete can now be accomplished in one meeting, presumably saving money, staff time, space, and resources. Talk Systems can be accessed toll-free at 888-468-4552.

There are, of course, several other cost effective translation services accessible on the Web. JKW International boasts coverage of all major languages in a variety of media. It is accessible at http://www.jkwintl.com. There is also the popular AT&T Language Line. A toll-free phone call (800-752-6096) can access non-English speakers to over-the-phone interpretation services 24 hours a day. No reservations are required. The service is, however, not free. Users simply call the AT&T Language Line Services communication center, specify the language needed, and provide billing information. Within moments, an interpreter is added to the call. Language Line draws from a pool of full- and part-time AT&T trained interpreters who work from their homes in communities across the United States. AT&T offers Language Line in both subscribed and nonsubscribed services. The former is designed for organizations with multiple users; the latter is designed for an unanticipated need for the service. The Language Line Web site address is http://www.att.com/business/global /language .html.

The George Washington University, in Washington, DC, has a long history of supporting schools in the area of parent and community involvement. It offers full text documents and other resources on this topic at no cost. The following on-line resources are available at http://www.ncbe.gwu.edu/library /parent.htm.

- *Bilingual Brochures for Parents* (University of Illinois at Chicago (UIC) Center for Literacy, 1995) (nine practical brochures in English and Spanish)
- *Helping Parents and Children Understand Each Other in Their New Life in the United States: Tacoma Story* (2000) (story of Khmer parent support group in Tacoma, Washington)

- "Promoting Partnerships With Minority Parents: A Revolution in Today's School Restructuring Efforts" (Rosado, 1994)
- Links to organizations that work with parents such as
  — the national PTA (330 N. Wabash Avenue, Suite 2100, Chicago, IL USA 60611; Telephone: 312-670-6782 or 800-307-4782; Fax: 312-670-6783; E-mail: info@pta.org; Web site: http://www.pta.org)
  — the Parent Advocacy Coalition for Educational Rights (PACER) Center (4826 Chicago Avenue South, Minneapolis, MN USA 55417-1098; Telephone: 612-827-2966 or 888-248-0822; Fax: 612-827-3035; E-mail: pacer@pacer.org; Web site: http://www.pacer.org)
  — the U.S. Department of Education (400 Maryland Avenue, SW, Washington, DC USA 20202-0489; Telephone: 800-USA-LEARN; Fax: 202-401-0689; E-mail: usa_learn.ed.gov; Web site: http://www.ed.gov/index.html)

National research centers, such as the North Central Regional Education Laboratory (http://www.ncrel.org), offer links to several resources for youth and family information, including information on rural education, promising practices in parent involvement programs, school partnerships with families and community groups, a parent information network, parent books and audiotapes, and family-friendly school resources. Other laboratories that specialize in language and cultural diversity include the Northeast and Islands Regional Educational Laboratory at Brown University (http://www.lab.brown.edu) and Southwest Educational Development (http://www.sedl.org).

# Summative Guidance for the ESL Program Manager

Whereas schools are almost universally described as a place where all children must feel welcome, that sentiment does not always appear to apply to their parents or caregivers at home. There have been many reasons for this gross omission of so important a player and stakeholder in a student's education. This chapter has highlighted some of the barriers that face caregivers, from lack of English to personal discomforts with school grounded in their own childhood experience to the more common challenges from home life (e.g., lack of transportation and child care). The ESL manager has been presented with a range of resources to help in the process of making parental and community engagement at school a very high management priority.

Table 6.3 offers additional Web sites that provide resources for parents. Still more Web sites about engaging parents useful to both the ESL manager and parents appear at the end of this chapter.

The ESL manager must play a pivotal role in meeting the challenges, welcoming parents, and engaging the community on behalf of the school's LEP students. Most practical among the measures are program planning, advisement, and a community visibility in classrooms where parents' roles can enrich instruction. The ESL program manager, well tooled in the academic understanding of language acquisition as part of prior training, must defend and encourage parents in nurturing the resource of their family's native language and culture. Their language and culture follow the student to school each day, and the family's native language must never take second place to English in the home.

Leadership in the education of language minority children comes from a shared vision among ESL program managers, teachers, parents, and, more broadly, the community. The leadership and the shared vision are defined by a wide array of variables unique to the diversity of the communities and the families served by their schools. One has only to listen to the nation's most exemplary public and private school teachers, who, in a National Teachers' Forum (U.S. Department of Education, 1998), identified more than a dozen markers and exemplars of their efforts in building teacher leadership. Among them were five that directly connect to shared visions with the community: (a) school/home parent linkages, (b) teacher/community partnerships, (c) teacher/businesses and organizational partnerships, (d) teachers as community leaders, and (e) political engagement.

Those five markers are easily understood in a U.S. school culture, though rarely in the context of cultures less known to Americans. Connecting those visions beyond an ethnocentric lens is a greater challenge, as posited by Fadiman (1999), a culture broker for a Hmong family in a medical crisis:

> If you can't see that your own culture has its own interests, emotions, and biases, how can you expect to deal successfully with someone else's culture? (p. 261)

## Table 6.3 Recommended Web Sites for Parents and Communities

Adult Literacy and Technology
  Network
http://www.otan.dni.us

Alliance for Parental Involvement
  in Education
http://www.croton.com/allpie

America Goes Back to School
http://www.ed.gov/Family
  /agbts_old/agbts98/index.html

Children, Youth and Family
http://www.cyfc.umn.edu

Families and Education
http://www.rmcres.com/famed

Family and Community
  Involvement
http://www.mcrel.org/resources
  /links/family.asp

Family Education Network
http://www.familyeducation.com

Family Literacy
http://www.ed.gov/pubs.FamLit

Family Planet
http://www.family.com

National Coalition of Advocates for
  Students
http://www.ncas1.org

National Parent Information
  Network
http://www.npin.org

Parents and Children Together
  On-line
http://www.indiana.edu/~eric_rec/fl
  /pcto/ish1.html

U.S. Department of Education Office
  for Civil Rights
http://www.ed.gov/offices/OCR

U.S. Department of Education
  Publications for Parents
http://www.ed.gov/pubs/parents

*Note.* From *Resource Links: Parent, Family, and Community Involvement*, by Intercultural Development Research Association, 1998, retrieved June 13, 2000, from the World Wide Web: http://www.idra.org/Links/Links.htm. Copyright © 1998 by Intercultural Development Research Association. Adapted with permission.

# Suggested Resources on the Web

For a paper on model strategies in working with bilingual families:
"Introduction to Model Strategies in Bilingual Education" (McCollum & Russo, 1993a, http://www.ncbe.gwu.edu/miscpubs/used/familylit /approach.htm)

For helping LEP parents in becoming active participants in their children's learning:
*Critical Issues in Parent and Family Involvement* (North Central Regional Educational Laboratory, 2000, http://www.ncrel.org/sdrs/areas /pa0cont.htm)

For developing ESL curriculum that addresses parenting issues:
"Profile 8: Florida International University Family Literacy Project" (McCollum & Russo, 1993b, http://www.ncbe.gwu.edu/miscpubs /used/familylit/profile8.htm)

For school-based management for ESL teachers:
"School-Based Management: What Bilingual and ESL Program Directors Should Know" (McKeon & Malarz, 1991, http://www.ncbe.gwu.edu/ncbepubs/pigs/pig5.htm)

For family and workplace adult literacy:
*The National Clearinghouse for ESL Literacy in Education* (http://www.cal.org/ncle)

For an article on raising children bilingually:
"Raising Bilingual Children" (Rosenberg, 1996, http://www.aitech.ac.jp/~iteslj/Articles/Rosenberg-Bilingual.html)

For problems of bilingual families and myths about bilingualism:
Kandolf's *Bilingual Families Web Page* (http://www.nethelp.no /cindy/special.html)

On raising children bilingually:
*Bilingual Upbringing of Children in the Home* (http://www.bklein .de/buc_home.html)

For NCBE's list of links to a wide range of topics of interest to bilingual parents:
(http://www.ncbe.gwu.edu/links/holding.htm)

# Chapter 7
# Authentic,
# Comprehensive
# Student Assessment

*Standardized testing is especially harmful to language minority students.*

—Y. S. Freeman & D. Freeman, 1992, p. 217

## What Is Authentic Assessment?

To gain a comprehensive appraisal of an LEP student's academic and language performance requires the obvious: a comprehensive approach to assessment. Authentic assessment differs from the traditional psychometric model of assessment. In the psychometric models of the past, there was a tendency to perform one-time measurements of student characteristics that were largely internal to the student. Authentic assessment, on the other hand, emphasizes ongoing assessment of factors that are both internal and external to the student, with the goal of using information obtained from assessment to optimize the learning environment. The conventional testing culture in the United States was grounded on the theory that intelligence was fixed. Students were compared to each other with little or no variant, as evident on popular curve equivalents normed on preset scales. Enter criterion-referenced achievement that emphasizes learning and informs teaching. The differences between the two measurement cultures are described in Figure 7.1. Such a culture for authentic assessment should guide policy.

Authentic assessment of LEP students must have at least four characteristics. First, it must take into account the student's cultural and linguistic background. The student's English language proficiency and cultural experiences with assessment inevitably affect how that learner will perform on a given assessment and should always be considered when assessments are designed and implemented. Second, authentic, comprehensive assessment must examine both internal and external factors that affect the learner's achievement. Persons carrying out assessment should always consider the learner's opportunity to master what is being tested in addition to his or her achievement. Third, authentic learner assessment makes use of multiple measures of student achievement. The call for multiple measures entails the use of instruments that are both formal and informal as well as traditional and alternative. Seeking a holistic barometer of how the LEP student performs on different kinds of assessments allows the teacher to use professional judgment in deciding which combination of instruments gives the most accurate portrayal of that student's abilities and achievement. Finally, authentic learner assessment is holistic and integrative.

## Conducting Authentic Assessments for English Language Proficiency

Combining reliable information sources together with testing helps the ESL manager and teacher determine the LEP student's instructional needs. To make decisions regarding the identification, classification, and appropriately tailored instruction to the needs of any student, it is necessary to obtain as much information as possible. Depending on the situation, the following information should be secured at the outset:

- background information about the student, including both educational history and descriptive information, for guidance in interpreting test and other performance data
- the student's dominant language, to identify the appropriate language(s) in which to conduct diagnostic and placement activities
- the student's oral language proficiency in English as a baseline for additional assessment and placement activities

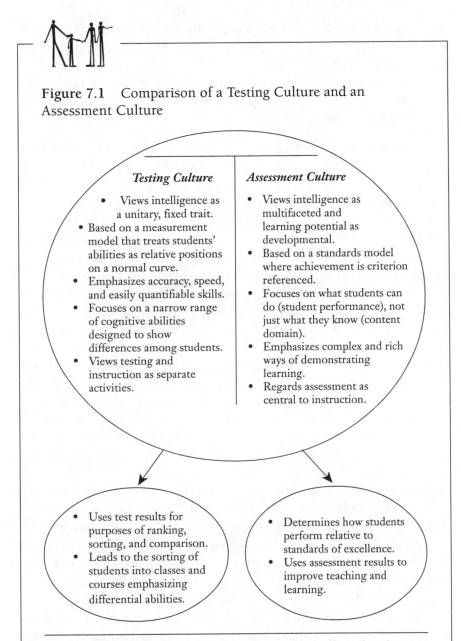

**Figure 7.1** Comparison of a Testing Culture and an Assessment Culture

*Testing Culture*

- Views intelligence as a unitary, fixed trait.
- Based on a measurement model that treats students' abilities as relative positions on a normal curve.
- Emphasizes accuracy, speed, and easily quantifiable skills.
- Focuses on a narrow range of cognitive abilities designed to show differences among students.
- Views testing and instruction as separate activities.

*Assessment Culture*

- Views intelligence as multifaceted and learning potential as developmental.
- Based on a standards model where achievement is criterion referenced.
- Focuses on what students can do (student performance), not just what they know (content domain).
- Emphasizes complex and rich ways of demonstrating learning.
- Regards assessment as central to instruction.

- Uses test results for purposes of ranking, sorting, and comparison.
- Leads to the sorting of students into classes and courses emphasizing differential abilities.

- Determines how students perform relative to standards of excellence.
- Uses assessment results to improve teaching and learning.

*Note.* From *What Policymakers and School Administrators Need to Know About Assessment Reform and English Language Learners* (pp. 14–21), by M. Lachat, 1997, Providence, RI: Northeast and Islands Regional Educational Laboratory at Brown University. Copyright © 1997 by the Northeast and Islands Regional Educational Laboratory at Brown University. Adapted with permission.

- the student's level of functioning in the native language as well as in English in all four communicative skills areas (reading, writing, speaking, and listening)
- the student's level of functioning in relevant subject matter areas (e.g., mathematics, social studies, science) in the native language and in English, if appropriate

Authentic testing is indeed one of a school's greatest multipurpose functions. There are a variety of questions and issues that only authentically secured assessment data can help resolve. Such assessments help determine if interventions for LEP students are working. They also help identify the general kinds of programs that will meet the identified linguistic and academic needs of LEP children. These assessments identify instructional components that are effective as well as areas where program improvements might be required. Collectively, authentic assessments document for administrators and school boards the effects that an ESL program is having. At the student level, results from any authentic assessments can also be used to identify and place students in the most appropriate types of programs. Authentic assessment practices should appear in *Lau* plans because they help plan instructional programs that are responsive to individual and group needs, both on a short- and long-term basis. As part of the exit criteria, such assessments help determine whether students have the academic skills necessary to benefit from an education conducted in English. Those uses, however, can only be accomplished if a given assessment is reliable, valid, and can provide the types of information suitable for its intended use. From the time a student first enters school, a cycle of assessment should be implemented to guide instruction and track student progress. Such an assessment practice would ensure that statutes (recall *Rios v. Read* in chapter 2) protective of LEP students are met. Indeed, assessments for English language proficiency come in many forms. The annual reports from state departments of education (also known as state education agencies) to the U.S. Department of Education (1995–1998 data) noted that U.S. schools used a wide range of tools for identifying or classifying potential students of limited English proficiency, which is illustrated in Table 7.1.

At least nine criteria have been identified nationally to determine that a student is of a non-English heritage language. As noted in chapter 3, every state in the United States uses the home language survey. All but one state report using some kind of language proficiency test. In general, states use multiple procedures for identifying LEP students. State departments of education report up to eight methods for classifying students as LEP. The methods departments of education use, in order of frequency by state, include home language surveys, language proficiency tests, parent information, teacher observations, achievement tests, student records, teacher interviews, referrals, and grade reports. These methods are detailed in Table 7.2. In using authentic assessments that identify and teach LEP students, the ESL manager is advised to follow the three steps detailed over the next several pages.

## Step 1: Gather Preliminary Information

Identify students from language minority backgrounds through the home language survey, as illustrated in the Heartland Valley *Lau* plan in Appendix A. As part of local policy, vis-à-vis a *Lau* plan, the survey should be part of the registration process for all students. If a home language survey is being implemented for the first time, as is often the case in rural districts that find themselves unexpectedly enrolling LEP students, there is a need to administer it to all the students in the school district as a proactive measure. The home language survey should be available in the non-English languages that are represented in the community. State departments of education are a good resource for securing surveys in non-English languages.

Students identified from the survey as having another language at home may or may not be English proficient. Hence, all students reporting a non-English language at home must be tested to determine which of those students may have limited English proficiency and, thus, in need of ESL services. Further information will need to be gathered for newly arrived students of non-English backgrounds. For example, previous school testing results for English and academic achievement will be valuable. Literacy skills testing in the first language, if included in the student's dossier, will also provide rich information.

There are several commercially published tools for testing English language proficiency. The most popularly used measures across the United States for identifying LEP students are listed in Table 7. 2. Table 7.3 provides a summation of popular language proficiency tests now in use.

Among those listed in Table 7.3, three are limited to measuring only oral English language proficiency: the Basic Inventory of Natural Language, the Bilingual Syntax Measure, and Phone PASS. Of course, those tests are limited in that they measure how well a student is functioning in regard to a specific spoken language. These three tests cover a wide range of language acquisition skills, ranging from those necessary for conducting basic interpersonal communications to those required for conducting more difficult activities, such

Table 7.1  Criteria Used by State Education Agencies to Identify Limited English Proficient Students, by State, 1995–1998

| State | Non-English Language Background | | | | | | | English Difficulty | | Academic Achievement | | |
|---|---|---|---|---|---|---|---|---|---|---|---|---|
| | Foreign Born | Non-English Home Lang. | Non-English Environment | Non-English Mother Tongue | Speaks Non-English | Native American in Non-English Environment | Ancestry/Ethnicity | Oral English | Reading/Writing English | English Reading Language Arts Test | Math Achievement Test | Grades in Core |
| Alabama | | X | | | | | | X | X | | | |
| Alaska | | X | | | X | | | X | X | | | X |
| Arizona | | X | | | X | | | | | | | |
| Arkansas* | | | | | | | | | | | | |
| California | | X | | | | | | X | X | | | |
| Colorado* | | | | | | | | | | | | |
| Connecticut | | | | | | | | | | | | |
| Delaware | X | X | X | X | | X | | X | X | | | |
| DC | | X | | X | X | | | X | X | | | |
| Florida | X | X | | X | | X | | X | X | | | |
| Georgia | | | | | | | | | | | | |
| Hawaii | | X | | X | | | | | | X | X | X |
| Idaho | | | | | | | | | | | | |
| Illinois | | | | | | | | | | | | |
| Indiana | | X | | X | | | | X | X | | | |
| Iowa | X | X | | | X | | | X | X | | | |
| Kansas | | | | | X | | | X | X | | | |
| Kentucky | | X | | X | X | | | X | X | | | |
| Louisiana* | | | | | | | | | | X | | |
| Maine* | | | | | | | | | | | | |
| Maryland | X | | X | X | | X | | X | X | | | |
| Mass. | | | | | | | | | | | | |
| Michigan | | X | | | | | | | | X | | |
| Minnesota | | X | | X | X | | | | | X | | |

| | 7 | 19 | 4 | 11 | 10 | 5 | 2 | 22 | 20 | 8 | 2 | 2 |
|---|---|---|---|---|---|---|---|---|---|---|---|---|
| Mississippi* | | | | | | | | X | X | | | |
| Missouri | | X | | | | | | X | X | | | |
| Montana* | | | | | | | | | | | | |
| Nebraska* | | | | | | | | | | | | |
| Nevada | | | | | | | | | | | | |
| New Hamp. | | | | | | | | | | | | |
| New Jersey | X | | | | X | | | X | | | | |
| New Mexico | | X | | X | X | | X | X | X | X | X | |
| New York | | | | | | | | | | | | X |
| N. Carolina* | | | | | | | | | | | | |
| N. Dakota | | | | | | | | | | | | |
| Ohio | X | | X | X | | X | | X | X | | | |
| Oklahoma* | | | | | | | | | | | | |
| Oregon | | | | | | | | | | | | |
| Pennsylvania | | | | | | | | | | | | |
| Rhode Island | | | | | | | | | | | | |
| S. Carolina | | | X | X | | X | | X | X | | | |
| S. Dakota | X | | X | X | | | | X | X | | | |
| Tennessee | | | | | | | | X | X | | | |
| Texas | X | | | | | | | X | X | | | |
| Utah | X | | | | | | | X | X | | | |
| Vermont | | | | | | | | X | X | | | |
| Virginia | | | | | X | | | X | X | | | |
| Washington | | | | | | | | | | | | |
| W. Virginia | X | | | | | | | X | X | X | | |
| Wisconsin | | | | | | | | | | X | | |
| Wyoming* | X | X | | | | | | | | X | | |
| Guam | X | X | | | | | | | | | | |
| Micronesia | | | | | | | | | | | | |
| N. Marianas | | | | | | | | | | | | |
| Palau | | | | | | | | | | | | |
| Puerto Rico | X | | | | | | X | X | | | | |
| Virgin Islands | | | | | | | | | | | | |
| **Totals** | **7** | **19** | **4** | **11** | **10** | **5** | **2** | **22** | **20** | **8** | **2** | **2** |

*States that adopt the federal definition for limited English proficiency

Note. From Summary Report of the Survey of the States' Limited English Proficient Students and Available Educational Programs and Services, 1995–96 (Appendix 1, Table A1.3), by R. Macías, 1998, Washington, DC: National Clearinghouse for Bilingual Education. Adapted with permission.

**Table 7.2**  Methods Used by States to Identify Limited English Proficient Students

| Criteria | States Responding | Percent Total Responses |
|---|---|---|
| Total responses | 52 | 100.0% |
| Home language survey | 50 | 96.2% |
| Language proficiency test | 49 | 94.2% |
| Parent information | 42 | 80.8% |
| Teacher observation | 41 | 78.8% |
| Achievement test | 40 | 76.9% |
| Student records | 39 | 75.0% |
| Teacher interview | 37 | 71.2% |
| Referral | 36 | 69.2% |
| Student grades | 35 | 67.3% |
| Informal assessment | 32 | 61.5% |
| Criterion-referenced tests | 25 | 48.1% |

| Language Proficiency Tests | States Responding | Percent Total Responses |
|---|---|---|
| Total responses that identified language proficiency test | 49 | 100.0% |
| Language Assessment Scales (LAS) | 36 | 73.5% |
| IDEA Language Proficiency Test (IPT) | 16 | 32.7% |
| Language Assessment Battery (LAB) | 15 | 30.6% |
| IDEA Oral Language Program | 15 | 30.6% |
| Woodcock-Muñoz | 11 | 22.4% |
| Bilingual Syntax Measure (BSM) | 8 | 16.3% |
| Basic Inventory of Natural Language (BINL) | 8 | 16.3% |
| LAS-Oral | 5 | 10.2% |
| Pre-LAS | 4 | 8.2% |
| LAS-Reading and Writing | 3 | 6.1% |
| Student Oral Language Observation Matrix (SOLOM) | 1 | 2.0% |
| Spanish Assessment of Basic Education (SABE) | 1 | 2.0% |

*Continued on p. 145*

**Table 7.2** *continued*  Methods Used by States to Identify Limited English Proficient Students

| Achievement Tests | States Responding | Percent Total Responses |
|---|---|---|
| Total responses that identified achievement test | 26 | 100.0% |
| Iowa Test of Basic Skills | 15 | 57.7% |
| California Achievement Test (CAT) | 11 | 42.3% |
| Stanford Achievement Test | 10 | 38.5% |
| Comprehensive Test of Basic Skills | 10 | 38.5% |
| SRA-McGraw-Hill | 5 | 19.2% |
| Metropolitan Achievement Test | 5 | 19.2% |
| Spanish Assessment of Basic Education (SABE) | 4 | 15.4% |
| Woodcock-Muñoz | 3 | 11.5% |
| Brigance Inventory of Basic Skills | 2 | 7.7% |

*Note.* From *Summary Report of the Survey of the States' Limited English Proficient Students and Available Educational Programs and Services, 1995–96* (Section 2.0, Tables 2.7–2.9), by R. Macías, 1998, Washington, DC: National Clearinghouse for Bilingual Education. Adapted with permission.

as learning in academic subjects. Detailed information on the validity, reliability, and theoretical foundations for many of the tests listed in Table 7.3 are available through Del Vecchio and Guerro's (1995) *Handbook of English Language Proficiency Tests* and other sources listed at the end of this chapter.

In general, the results of an oral language proficiency test can be used to help determine whether a student is LEP. However, one must keep in mind that the results only make a general classification about selected listening and speaking skills. The results should not be overinterpreted. Additionally, because of the range of skills assessed in different oral language proficiency tests, it is important to carefully review the skills tested before using the results for instructional decision making.

One other very important caution: The results of an oral language proficiency test do not provide any information regarding the student's ability to

Table 7.3   Commonly Used Language Proficiency Instruments*

| Test | Contact Information | Grade Level | What It Measures | Comments |
|---|---|---|---|---|
| Basic Inventory of Natural Language (BINL) | CHECpoint Systems Inc. 1520 North Waterman Ave. San Bernardino, CA 92404 800-635-1235 | K–12 (Ages 5–18) | Oral English proficiency | • Developed in 1979<br>• Analyzes oral storytelling from large color pictures<br>• Scoring depends heavily on traditional grammatical structures and is difficult to do<br>• Useful for at least 32 language backgrounds<br>• Takes 10 minutes per child to administer<br>• Approximately $60 for full kit |
| Bilingual Syntax Measure (BSM) I & II | Psychological Corporation P.O. Box 839954 San Antonio, TX 78282 800-228-0752 | BSM I: Grades K–2 BSM II: Grades 3–12 | Oral English proficiency | • Has not been revised since 1975, when it was developed<br>• Language range is limited to short answers<br>• Takes 10–20 minutes per child to administer<br>• Hand scoring required<br>• Full kit (BSM I or II) is approximately $305 |
| Bilingual Verbal Ability Tests (BVAT) | Riverside Publishing Houghton & Mifflin 425 Spring Lake Drive Itasca, IL 60143-2079 800-323-9540 http://www.riverpub.com | Ages 5 to adult | Combines proficiency in English and first language to measure overall verbal ability | • Developed in 1997<br>• Jim Cummins, bilingual education expert, is one of its authors<br>• Takes 20–30 minutes per child to administer<br>• Intended to measure cognitive/academic language abilities in English and another language (up to 16 languages are available)<br>• Free training video accompanies the test<br>• Useful for entry and exit criteria for bilingual programs<br>• Complete BVAT kit (Windows or MacIntosh) costs $575 |

| Test | Publisher/Address | Grades/Levels | Purpose | Features |
|---|---|---|---|---|
| IDEA Language Proficiency Test (IPT) | Ballard & Tighe Publishers<br>480 Atlas Street<br>Brea, CA 92621<br>800-321-4332 | IPT I:<br>Grades K–6<br>IPT II:<br>Grades 7–12 | Oral English proficiency, reading English proficiency, and writing English proficiency | • Developed in 1978; revised in 1994<br>• Oral testing is done individually but reading and writing can be done in small groups<br>• All forms available in Spanish and English<br>• Pre-IPT available for preschool student<br>• Average testing time is 14 minutes per child<br>• Full set costs $105 |
| Language Assessment Battery (LAB) | New York City Board of Education;<br>Document Scan Center<br>44-36 Vernon Blvd.<br>Room 207<br>Long Island City, NY 11101<br>718-349-5600<br>Fax: 718-349-5642 | Level I:<br>Grades K–2<br>Level II:<br>Grades 3–5<br>Level III:<br>Grades 6–8<br>Level IV:<br>Grades 9–12 | English proficiency in reading, writing, speaking, and listening | • Normed on Spanish and English populations in 1982 and 1990<br>• Available in short LAB and full LAB<br>• Measures of writing and reading appear to measure grammatical usage instead.<br>• Full sample set costs $36<br>• Average testing time is 30 minutes per child |
| Language Assessment Scales (LAS) | Edward DeAvila<br>ETB MacMillan<br>McGraw Hill<br>2500 Garden Road<br>Monterey, CA 93940<br>800-538-9547 | Pre-LAS<br>Pre K–1<br>LAS Reading/<br>Writing 2–6<br>LAS Oral/<br>Reading/<br>Writing 7–12<br>Adult LAS | English proficiency in reading, writing, speaking, and listening | • Developed in 1990<br>• Reading and writing testing time is approximately 50 minutes per child and small group<br>• Kit with answer sheets costs approximately $130 |

*Continued on p. 148*

Table 7.3 continued  Commonly Used Language Proficiency Instruments*

| Test | Contact Information | Grade Level | What It Measures | Comments |
|------|---------------------|-------------|------------------|----------|
| Maculaitis Assessment Program (MAC) | Jean D'Arcy Maculaitis<br>Alemany Press<br>Prentice Hall Regents<br>1 Lake Street<br>Upper Saddle River, NJ 07458<br>800-643-5506<br>201-236-7000 | K–12 | Selection, placement, diagnosis, proficiency, and achievement (oral-listening-vocabulary-reading-writing) | • Developed in 1982<br>• Tests multiple subskills in all communicative skills areas for Grades K–12<br>• Based on motional, functional language syllabus<br>• Reusable test booklets<br>• Reliability range: .94–.99<br>• Predictive validity is high<br>• Average testing time is 25 minutes per child/small group in the lower grade levels; in the upper grade levels, testing time is up to 109 minutes<br>• Full kit costs approximately $600 |
| Phone PASS | Brent Townshend, Ph.D.<br>Ordinate Corporation<br>140 Noel Drive, Suite 102<br>Menlo Park, CA 94025<br>650-327-4449<br>http://www.ordinate.com | Older students, LEP students | Oral English proficiency (automated English language testing) | • Test does not measure advanced English skills<br>• Takes 10 minutes to administer per person<br>• Validity unknown<br>• Based on Likert Scale<br>• Test costs approximately $40 |

| Test | Publisher/Contact | Level/Age | Measures | Features |
|---|---|---|---|---|
| Student Oral Language Observation Matrix (SOLOM) | San Jose Unified School San Jose, CA or Office of Bilingual/Bicultural Education California State Dept. of Education 721 Capitol Mall Sacramento, CA 95814 916-657-3011 http://www.cde.ca.gov/cilbranch/bien/bien.htm | Middle/ Secondary Levels | English fluency: comprehension, vocabulary, pronunciation, and grammar skills | • Developed in 1978<br>• Rates students according to the second language used in academic settings<br>• Takes 20 minutes per child to administer this 5-scale test<br>• Rating is immediately available<br>• Popular throughout California<br>• 1-hour training for its use is recommended<br>• Examiner must speak native language of the student<br>• Test is free of charge |
| Woodcock-Muñoz Language Survey (LS-E) | Riverside Publishing Co. 425 Spring Lake Drive Itasca, IL 60143 800-323-9540 | Age 4–Adult | Cognitive academic language proficiency for Spanish and/or English | • Developed in 1993<br>• The four subtest battery takes 20 minutes per child to administer<br>• Picture vocabulary, verbal analogies, and letter-word dictation comprise the subtests<br>• Publisher boasts very high validity<br>• Full battery costs $147 |

* Detailed information on the validity, reliability, and theoretical foundations for many of these tests are available through Del Vecchio and Guerro's (1995) Handbook for English Language Proficiency Tests.

read or write; in some cases, the test may not even cover the more complex listening and speaking skills necessary for school learning. The results of oral language proficiency tests should not be used as the sole criterion for determining whether a student needs services or is ready to move into a mainstream classroom setting.

## Step 2: Monitor the LEP Student's Progress

Once the student is identified as LEP and placed in an ESL support environment, program monitoring is essential. Monitoring takes into account such matters as the influence of language and culture in instruction and assessment as well as learning-style preferences. For example, productive planning for integrated learning for any student would include an exploitation of the student's multiple intelligences and perceptual learning modalities. The latter would include auditory, visual, tactile-kinesthetic, and field-sensitive/field-independent preferences for learning. Howard Gardner (1999), the pioneer in multiple intelligences, has demonstrated that multiple intelligences are a significant variable among human differences. Their implications for instruction, as illustrated in Figure 7.2, are remarkable.

Although learners from a specific culture may possess a variety of modality preferences, certain cultures may emphasize certain modality styles more than other cultures. Thus, a culture whose language has strong oral tradition may place emphasis on auditory learning. Other cultures may stress learning behavior at variance with what may be encountered in U.S. classrooms. North African cultures, for example, stress oral memorization, a form of auditory learning. Still other cultures may stress greater social interaction as a function of learning, which may vary with the style of more independent, competitive learning behavior often found in the United States. In Latin American cultures, for example, families tend to cultivate a greater field-sensitive learning approach that values the importance of personal interaction in the learning process. The implication of these examples for assessment is that a variety of observational protocols should be used to monitor learners with different sensory modalities.

A related factor to consider in assessing student progress is the student's personality and attitudinal behaviors (e.g., extroversion and introversion). The research literature popularly suggests that certain personality characteristics affect motivation and learning. There appears to be a link between an introvert's ability and an extrovert's ability to listen and read language comprehensively. Of course, no individual culture is inherently extroverted or in-

## Figure 7.2   Multiple Intelligences Capacities Wheel

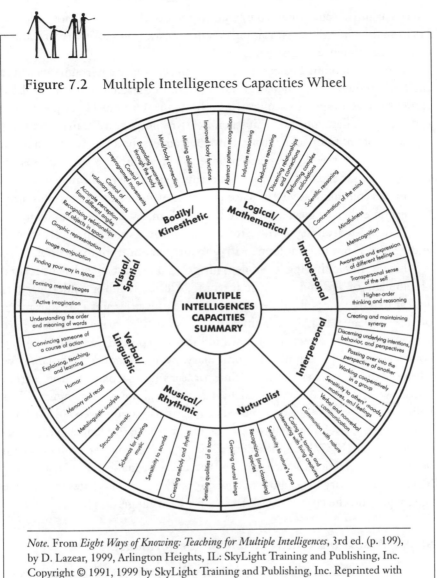

troverted; rather, individuals within that culture possess these characteristics. It is important to realize that the expressive style of one culture may be comparatively more extroverted or introverted in relation to another culture's style of expression. In this broad context, Asian learners, for example, are

viewed as introverted when compared to the extroverted behavior of learners from the United States. Valuing and demonstrating sensitivity to cultural
difference influences assessment.

Subtractive bilingualism can be found in schooling environments where
the LEP student's first language is not valued. In this environment, the LEP
student is encouraged to acquire English language as quickly as possible in
order to assimilate into the mainstream classroom. The ESL manager must
be aware of subtractive environments that adversely influence the normal
development of second language progress. For example, a student's loss of
proficiency in the native language can create a risk if he or she may be misdi-
agnosed as communicatively impaired because of an inability to manifest proficiency in either language. Additive bilingualism, by contrast, can be found
in schooling environments where the first language is valued in the classroom,
and its use is continued at home with encouragement from the school.

Finally, in monitoring for student progress, one must consider the related
phenomena of age and language learning. Unlike children, older learners
appear to have more fully developed cognitive capacities and a broader range
of life experiences to assist them in learning a second language. They also have
a greater ability to direct communication through posing questions, slowing
conversation, and manipulating vocabulary. Several language scholars have
advanced the theory that the prime time for learning a second language is from
8 to 12 years of age, once the student has mastered the native language. It is
believed that, prior to age 8, a student's capacity to acquire a second language
is impeded by developmental issues in acquiring the native language. According to Collier (1987/1988), learners above age 12 encounter problems with
peer group interactions, which may lead to a decrease in the normal risk-taking
behaviors necessary for language acquisition. Table 7.4 illustrates the relative
age ranges and the cognitive risk factors for each range.

## Step 3: Assess Integrative Academic Performance

Authentic assessment of the LEP student will provide sufficient data, in conjunction with information gathered from parents, to evaluate progress and
improve teaching. In addition to a more valid and reliable measure of learner
progress, a comprehensive approach of conducting informal as well as formal
assessment measures, as illustrated in Figure 7.3, will lessen the possibility of
misdiagnosing an LEP student's performance. Informal and formal assessments
are useful tools in this process.

## Table 7.4  Cognitive Risk Factors for Limited English Proficient Students at Different Ages

| Entry Age for Schooling | Risk Factor | Reason | Instructional Intervention |
|---|---|---|---|
| 4–7 | Moderate | Development of the first language (L1) is interrupted before transfer to learning the second language (L2) | Continued holistic language input integrating all language domains—listening, speaking, reading, and writing |
| 8–12 | Low | L1 has been adequately learned; enough time in school to achieve native-speaker peer proficiency in all content areas | Normal instructional provisions for English language learners (i.e., strategies for comprehensible input using contextualized language in all content areas) |
| 13–18 | High | Insufficient time to achieve grade-level parity with native peers; risk taking for language use is lowered due to embarrassment in producing language | Emphasis on metacognitive, cognitive, and socioaffective strategies to enable learners to process and contextualize language in content areas |

*Note.* From *What Matters in Building an Effective ESL Program: A Guide for ESL Program Evaluation* (p. 68), by D. L. Bouchard, 1995, Augusta, ME: Maine Department of Education. Adapted with permission from the ESL/Bilingual Education Office of the Maine Department of Education.

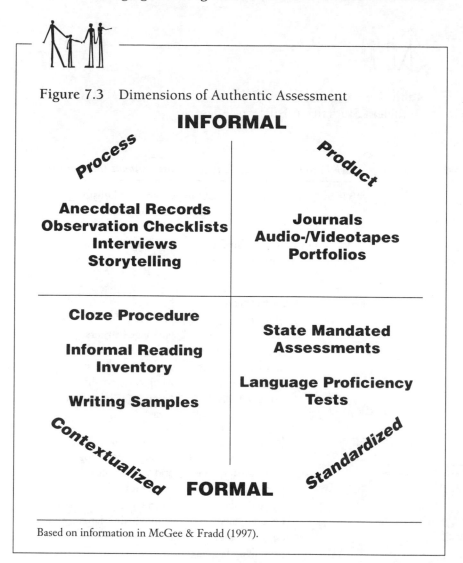

Figure 7.3    Dimensions of Authentic Assessment

**INFORMAL**

*Process*

**Anecdotal Records
Observation Checklists
Interviews
Storytelling**

*Product*

**Journals
Audio-/Videotapes
Portfolios**

**Cloze Procedure**

**Informal Reading
Inventory**

**Writing Samples**

**State Mandated
Assessments**

**Language Proficiency
Tests**

*Contextualized*    **FORMAL**    *Standardized*

Based on information in McGee & Fradd (1997).

Formal measures are commonly associated with tests in regimented set-tings, such as state required assessments and standardized achievement tests that all students at a given grade level are required to take. The ESL manager will be asked to include these measures in defending continued ESL services for LEP students. The ESL manager should use data from those sources cau-tiously, as they may serve only to measure English dysfluency though they purport to measure other skills in aptitude. They are also far more culturally biased than informal measures. Some standardized tests do make provisions for modifications when LEP students are required to participate in those test formats.

Informal measures are varied—from anecdotal records to rubrics to portfolios to cloze procedures, among many others. Anecdotal records are observations of daily student behavior that occurs through learning activities. They typically include social interaction, learning styles, work habits, and observation of communicative skills. Observations of social and academic performance in the classroom are provided through informal record formats called rubrics, which describe comprehensively what the LEP student can do. Rubrics generally consist of a continuum of four benchmarks that provides the teacher with information on ways to give meaningful instruction based on the data gathered in the observation.

Comprehensive assessment would, by definition, suggest a multidimensional interpretation of a student's performance over time. Enter portfolio assessments. The topic of portfolio assessment warrants a volume by itself, and many articles are available in the professional literature; this discussion will note some rudimentary features of portfolios. Portfolios typically include a wide range of samples of student work collected over time. Those samples may include student-generated selection of material as well as teacher-generated material to ascertain through measures or benchmarks that particular teaching or learning objectives have been met. In so doing, portfolios serve to help teachers improve instruction and, consequently, to help students see how they are progressing over time. Portfolios may also include work students have done in collaboration with classmates.

Portfolios are not simply a collection of tests, quizzes, essays, or reports, though any of these could appropriately find their way in a portfolio of student work. Neither are portfolios simply folders containing checklists or grading lists of each measured item. Portfolios are indeed far more comprehensive and more integral to teaching than that. A wide range of rubric formats for each of the communicative skills areas are detailed in O'Malley and Valdez-Pierce's (1996) *Authentic Assessments for English Language Learners: Practical Approaches for Teachers*. Included in that volume are several reproducible classroom guides, scales, and sample rubrics for use in portfolio applications of authentic assessment.

Contextualized indicators are valuable tools used in formal assessments. Cloze procedures are an example. Developed in the early 1960s from Gestalt psychology, the cloze procedure has proved helpful in providing useful information concerning a learner's ability to use context to infer meaning. As the sample cloze exercise in Figure 7.4 illustrates, cloze exercises consist of passages from which words are omitted at regular intervals, usually every fifth, sixth, or seventh word. Cloze passages may include 50–100 blanks, though the example in Figure 7.4 is an abbreviated one. The parenthetical words used to fill cloze blanks are provided here only for illustration of acceptable fill-ins. The cloze procedure can be used to assess learners' listening or reading ability. A modified cloze may use blanks, articles, or other syntactic structures to enhance instructional assessments. A variety of sources can be used; most common are stories.

No one word in a cloze is correct or incorrect; context is more important. Pace is irrelevant because this is not a timed test. Adequate measurement using a cloze can be made with the selection of a complete story of 250–350 words. Of those, 50 words can be removed, but the first and last sentences are always kept intact. Students should practice with the cloze procedure before it is used as an assessment tool.

Scoring a cloze is easy. To score a cloze, the teacher counts the number of correct words (those that make sense in the context given) and then calculates the percent of correct answers against the number of blanks in the passage. The teacher then compares those percentages against the percentages found in Table 7.5 to see if the reading level of the text selected is appropriate. Canales (1992) suggests using the following scale, ranging from non-English proficient student to fully English proficient student, based on the percentage of correct responses on the cloze test: 0–20, 21–30, 31–40, 41–49, 50.

**Figure 7.4    A Sample Cloze**

The sun is very important to us. The sun gives us light ____(and)____ warmth. Without the sun, the ____(earth)____ would be a very dark ____(and)____ cold place. Most things would ____(not)____ be able to live on ____(earth)____. The earth's plants would die. ____(They)____ would not have the light ____(they)____ need to produce food. There ____(would)____ be no food for the ____(plant)____ eaters. And how would the ____(animal)____ eaters feed themselves? Most life on earth depends on energy from the sun.

Interpreting the cloze varies widely. Hughes (1989) suggests that scoring is not directly interpretable and does not offer a scoring rubic. Some ESL practitioners make subjective judgments from a cloze such that they compare one LEP student to a non-LEP student at a given grade level for placement purposes. Hamayan and Perlman (1990) suggest that the LEP student would fall 10 points below the average score of other language minority students.

Another diagnostic assessment tool among individually administered informal tests is the informal reading inventory. This reading inventory is constructed by selecting a short passage among passages that increase in reading difficulty. These passages range from 60 to 200 words from a content-area text. Learners read from a prepared word list and, depending on the success in reading, then read the passage, either orally or silently, from which the list was taken. The teacher interprets strengths, weaknesses, and miscues on the basis of the student's performance in recognizing words in isolation. Other informal measures include student observation checklists, interviews, story retelling, journals, audio-/videotapes, and portfolios. The O'Malley and Valdez-Pierce (1996) text is a particularly good resource in developing informal tests.

## When all Students Take the Same Tests

A major goal in ESL program management is, of course, to ensure that LEP students are prepared to compete with their peers in English-only classrooms. One of the major goals of programs serving LEP students is to prepare them for academic work in fully English proficient classrooms. One indication that

Table 7.5   How to Determine the Appropriate Reading Level of Text Using a Cloze

| % Correct Responses | Comprehension Level | Appropriate for This Student |
|---|---|---|
| Between 50%–60% | Independent | Easy reading |
| Between 35%–50% | Instructional | Challenging reading |
| Below 35% | Frustration | Too difficult |

Based on information in O'Malley & Valdez-Pierce (1996).

LEP students are ready to be placed in mainstream classes without language support services is their ability to demonstrate requisite skills in English. In this case, the appropriate comparison group to use for assessing LEP students' performance would be their monolingual English-speaking peers. This will give an indication of whether or not the LEP student has the English language skills necessary to benefit from an education conducted in English.

Persistent correction of errors reaches a saturation point for some LEP students. A well-trained ESL teacher will know some of the nuances that are normal for bilingual students to demonstrate, even when assessments suggest they are fluent in English. A common tendency for those students is their fossilization of accent, vocabulary, and usage. Fossilization and change occur with *interlanguage*: the natural consequence of the bilingual interaction between languages developing simultaneously. Over time, LEP students internalize their ongoing use of sometimes incorrect forms in the new language. They do this through overgeneralizations of how the new language's syntax interacts with the native language. The gamble is that some forms may be naturally transferred from the native language; some do not. A balanced practice of noting errors would reduce the likelihood of fossilization gone awry. In testing, language use characterized by fossilization behavior may suggest deceptively that the student is nonfluent. There are, however, extenuating circumstances, such as a non-English accent, the use of words or phrases from the native language that are not literally translated to English, or the failure to use English words or phrases that do not exist in the native language. Indeed, the natural effects of interlanguage on test situations are a reasonable concern for fair appraisal of language minority performance on assessments.

With so much attention given to high-stake assessment standards for all students, without exceptions, one is tempted to ask, "Can LEP students take tests that non-LEP students take?" According to Rivera et al. (2000), 36 state-administered tests provide for accommodations for LEP students (and special needs students). Accommodations may include assistance with directions, translations, alternative methods of responding to test items, use of bilingual dictionaries, adjusting test settings, extending time, providing for independent testing, or combinations of these. Forty-three states allow exemptions for LEP students from taking those tests. Alternate tests (i.e., a replacement test or assessment tool) are permitted in 11 states.

All states require some kind of standardized test that each school district must administer. Many LEP children are, as a result, participants in such large-scale testing. Do those state-mandated tests measure what they seek to measure of LEP students (e.g., social studies, science, humanities)? It is the student's level of English proficiency that is the greatest factor in knowing the extent to which measures of achievement performance on a state test or on one developed by a school district will reliably and validly measure this special population. Another factor, particularly for LEP students performing at the basic interpersonal cognitive skills level (i.e., everyday, basic nonacademic conversational language skill), is culture. LEP students may have difficulty in verbalizing their knowledge and school achievement skills partly because they do not yet possess cognitive academic language proficiency (i.e., complex, higher level academic language skills). They are unfamiliar with the terminology, format, and procedures that are essential features of most tests.

Unlike LEP students, most monolingual students, throughout the course of their schooling, take many standardized tests and, over time, learn a variety of test-taking skills. LEP students often come from a different kind of school system and may not be familiar with some types of standardized tests. These students, even at the cognitive academic language proficiency level, have acquired enough English to take standardized tests but can be at a disadvantage simply because of their lack of experience in testing. The best way to help these students is to systematically teach them test-taking skills throughout the school year. This does not mean teaching to the test but rather teaching the student specific test-taking skills (e.g., how to fill out a computer answer sheet, the meanings of test-specific vocabulary, ways to allocate time). Students who have learned important test-taking skills are better able to demonstrate their actual level of learning on standardized tests.

A test-taking awareness workshop for all school personnel is advisable. A university instructor or a state department of education consultant should be well positioned to assist teachers in increasing their awareness of the effect that test-taking skills, or the lack thereof, can have on the assessment process; the consultant can provide a means for increasing the accuracy and usefulness of test scores. Basic test-taking skills and how they differ from teaching to the test can be part of that training. Specific activities that prepare the student to feel comfortable with testing situations should be presented.

As schools conduct assessments for their general population, consideration should be given to LEP students' unique experiences that their language and culture may bring to that testing environment. Although LEP students may have been taught the subject content in one language, this should not imply that testing should occur in that language; furthermore, assessment should be in the language and form most likely to yield accurate and reliable information on what the LEP student knows and can do. This may require significant modification in test administration, including testing in English, the native language, or both. In addition, a wide range of culture-related conventions may affect the testing environment. For example, some cultures may consider that showcasing achievement is arrogant and ought not to be displayed. In addition, some culture groups are unaccustomed to timed tests.

By providing LEP students with comprehensible test taking, the barrier that is set up when students are unaware of a few strategies to use in testing situations is eliminated. The ESL manager, as well as other school personnel, can help ensure that the information provided from tests will meaningfully reveal what an LEP student actually knows and can do.

## Summative Guidance for the ESL Program Manager

In this chapter, the ESL manager is confronted with the sometimes intimidating responsibilities associated with student assessment. This chapter attempts to shatter the conventional mode of assessment from one of pre- and posttesting to more comprehensive, authentic assessments and offers a step-by-step procedure for carrying the academic and language proficiency assessment cycle forward, taking into account issues of policy unique to each state and issues tailored to the particular needs of the LEP student (e.g., culture, age, multiple intelligences, test-taking skills, learning styles).

The selection of a test should be viewed as an integral part of the overall testing program. As part of a system of a comprehensive, authentic assessment, such selection must be approached thoughtfully. One of the major ways of examining ESL program effectiveness is its approach to testing. Selecting appropriate instruments to use in language proficiency testing is not a simple task, but it is necessary and extremely important. The information provided by carefully chosen tests can give project personnel valuable insight into how the program is functioning and how well LEP students are on their way to full fluency in English.

A range of common questions undoubtedly persists. ESL managers are not all as well versed in the assessment arena as some might wish. In addressing that need, this author offers answers to the following common questions. These are questions the author has encountered many times in working with rural schools and university campuses that serve these schools.

1.　Should a student be tested in the native language or in English?

Clarifying the purpose for conducting the testing activities and how the results will be used can help answer this question. For example, if one wants to determine if a student has learned certain skills, such as in math or science, then the testing should be conducted in the language that will not interfere with the student's ability to demonstrate his or her present level of learning. In most cases, this means testing the student in the same language in which he or she receives instruction. However, if the purpose of the testing is to establish the student's level of proficiency in English, then testing activities should be conducted in English. Similarly, if the purpose is to establish the level of proficiency in another language, then the testing should be done in that language. On the other hand, if the purpose of the testing is to help determine if the student has the skills necessary to move into the fully English proficient classroom, then the testing should be conducted in the language in which instruction is provided in that classroom.

Bilingual services are required to evaluate LEP students who are in special education to ensure nondiscriminatory assessment. The examiner should know the language of the child being tested and should be qualified in the area of special education in which the evaluation is being conducted. For special languages where no bilingual specialist is available, a translator who is fluent in the primary language of the child may be used along with a qualified special education evaluator. However, the district is cautioned to consider this alternative only when the search for a native language specialist has been futile.

2. What steps should we take to determine whether a student's lack of English may make him or her a candidate for special services?

This is a special situation that should be approached with care. In this situation, the following steps should be taken:

- Review the screening data collected when the student entered school. Note that all children (including transfer students) must be screened within 30 days of entry into school. The screening involves checking hearing, vision, and health records to identify any potentially handicapping condition that would require referral to a pupil evaluation team (PET) for further evaluation.
- Collect background information about the student (e.g., educational experiences; descriptive information about the student; descriptive information about the home, community, and native country). This may explain why a student is having problems in

school and is also critical for correctly interpreting test and other performance data.

- Establish the student's oral language proficiency in English to determine whether the present placement is the concern (e.g., the student simply does not have the English skills necessary to succeed in the present situation) and whether additional assessment activities can be conducted in English.
- Determine the student's dominant language in order to conduct further testing in the most appropriate language.
- Determine the student's level of functioning in the dominant language, including both oral (listening/speaking) and written (reading/writing) skills, as appropriate.

If a student's dominant language functioning is low, and background information indicates that the student has had suitable educational opportunities for development, recommendation for further evaluation procedures would be appropriate. Notices to parents or guardians, under special education procedures, should be in a language that LEP parents or guardians can understand so that they might be able to give their informed consent for program changes affecting their child.

If the student's stronger language appears adequate, it is advisable to test that student in academic areas using tests administered in that language. If the student's score falls within a range close to what would be expected, given the student's level of schooling and other background information, then the student is probably not in need of special services. The student's lack of English is most likely the barrier.

3.  We wish to use multiple criteria to ensure a comprehensive evaluation of our LEP students. What types of measures should we include?

The most commonly used evaluation criteria are test scores, which are a critical component for conducting authentic assessments. Scores from a variety of instruments should be considered, including standardized achievement tests, placement/diagnostic tests, language proficiency measures, and informal assessment tools. However, test scores alone cannot provide a complete picture of a student's instructional needs; it is necessary to collect various types of descriptive information as well. Existing records including student grades, teacher comments, attendance rates, referrals for discipline problems, parental attendance at school activities, participation in extracurricular or community activities, school health screening activities, and any other existing documentation that can help round out or complete an appraisal on a student. Other types of measures to consider as criteria for a comprehensive evaluation include questionnaires, oral interviews, and observations. By using a variety of criteria and multiple sources of data, a more comprehensive and accurate evaluation can be ensured.

4.  Why is it important to use multiple criteria for making decisions about exiting/reclassifying LEP students?

The decision to exit or reclassify an LEP student can have tremendous impact on that student's educational and personal future. If a student is misclassified or exited from a program prematurely and without the English language skills necessary to benefit from an education conducted in English, he or she is likely to encounter difficulties in the fully English proficient classroom. Test scores alone should not be used to make such an important decision, especially given the current state-of-the-art resources available for assessing LEP students. Therefore, in addition to standardized test scores, it is necessary to use a variety of other data sources (e.g., grades in other classes if the student is partially mainstreamed, opinions of other teachers, observations of the student in various learning situations, interviews with the student) to help ensure that the decision will accurately predict a student's ability to benefit from an education conducted in English.

5.  What information should be used when deciding whether a student is ready to move from a special language services (e.g., ESL program) classroom into a classroom with a fully English proficient population?

Deciding whether or not a student is ready to move into the mainstream is a critical decision and one that must be made with care. It is important to take into consideration a variety of information including:

- performance on standardized tests, including reading, language arts, and appropriate content areas (e.g., mathematics, science, social studies)

- grades in other classes, especially those courses in which the student is taking with a fully English proficient population
- teacher ratings of the student's skills necessary to benefit from an education conducted in English
- interviews with the student, covering academic, affective, and communication skills necessary to benefit from an education conducted in English

If there is some doubt about whether the LEP student has the skills necessary to benefit from an education conducted in English, it can be helpful to observe the student in a variety of academic settings to ensure that key skills have been mastered. Observations may also be necessary with younger students to determine whether they can, in fact, interact successfully in the classroom with a fully English fluent population.

Regardless of the criteria used to decide whether to mainstream a student, keep in mind that multiple criteria should always be used. Decisions to mainstream a student should not be made on a single criterion, such as the results of an oral language proficiency test. Exit criteria should include a variety of information to ensure that the student has developed the language skills necessary to use English for school learning.

Note that LEP students may be mainstreamed with monolingual English peers in nonacademic situations (e.g., physical education, music, art) earlier than in academic ones. LEP students should not be isolated or segregated any more than is necessary to ensure their ability to benefit quickly from an education conducted in English. Separation of LEP students from their mainstream peers should obviously meet a valid educational purpose.

6.   Can we use an interpreter to administer a standardized test to a student who does not speak English?

Yes. There are, however, some guidelines to follow when doing so. First, the interpreter must be trained for that role and for test administration procedures. Second, the interpreter and the test administrator should be given background information about the student and attempt to establish a comfort level for the testing relationship. Third, both the interpreter and the test administrator should review the student's response to the test items and the notes about the student after the testing session. Incorrect responses to items that were clearly cultural or national origin-bound should be disregarded. Fourth, the test norms should not be used when interpreting the student's scores. Instead, raw scores and percent correct for various skill areas should be interpreted. Finally, if interpreters are used on a regular basis, systematic training should be provided and observations made of the interpreters as a quality control check.

## Suggested Resources on the Web

For an overview of English language proficiency measures, including special education:
> *Assessment in ESL and Bilingual Education: A Hot Topics Paper* (Hargett, 1998, http://www.nwrac.org/pub/hot/assessment.html)

For research on the time it takes students to develop oral and academic English proficiency:
> *University of California Linguistic Minority Research Institute* (http://lmrinet.ucsb.edu/)

For the Office for Civil Rights (OCR) guidelines on legal principles justifying standardized testing:
> "OCR Issues Revised Guidance on High-Stakes Testing" (Blair, 1999, http://www.edweek.com/ew/ewstory.cfm?slug=17ocr.h19)

For a checklist on selecting appropriate tests:
> *Handbook of English Language Proficiency Tests* (Del Vecchio & Guerrero, 1995, http://www.ncbe.gwu.edu/miscpubs/eacwest/elptests.htm)

For a handout on identifying, transitioning, and exiting LEP students:
> *Identifying Limited English Proficient Students* (Evaluation Assistance Center-Western Region, 1996, http://www.ncbe.gwu.edu/miscpubs/eacwest/handouts/id-lep/backgrnd.htm)

For guidelines on evaluating assessments and a list of standardized tests used in ESL programs:
> "Guidelines: Evaluating Assessment" (Burkhart & Sheppard, n.d., http://www.ncbe.gwu.edu/miscpubs/cal/contentesl/c-esl8.htm)

For the current state of fossilization and interlanguage:
> *Papers in Interlanguage and Interdialect Linguistics* (http://www.bbk.ac.uk/llc/al/Larry.html)

For a description of current language testing tools and publications:

*Language Testing: Current Center for Applied Linguistics (CAL) Projects* (http://www.cal.org/public/topics/tests.htm)

For updated state-by-state data on LEP student assessments:

*Summary Report of the Survey of States' Limited English Proficient Students and Available Education Programs and Services, 1996–1997* (Macías, 1998b, http://www.ncbe.gwu.edu/ncbepubs/seareports/96-97 /index.htm)

To find out how to purchase *Ensuring Accuracy in Testing for English Language Learners: A Practical Guide for Assessment* (Council of Chief State School Officers, 2000), contact the Council of Chief State School Officers: (http://www.ccsso.org/news/pr060900.html)

# Chapter 8
# ESL Program Evaluation

*Evaluation is a determination of the worth of a thing.*

—Wilde & Sockey, 1995, p. 7

Few ESL program managers are researchers by trade. Although they and their supervisors seek to document outcomes of their programs accurately, most are generally unprepared to develop a local, research-based evaluation. Frequently, managers who have overseen the implementation of the ESL program they have designed may find it difficult to waver from their sincere positions of certainty that the program they are overseeing is working well. In addition, there is the potential politicization that comes from a schoolwide evaluation of a process that is viewed as marginal to the total operation. Enter the dilemma for developing fair and practical evaluations used to consider ESL program accountability.

One must begin, therefore, with a review of local policy and program direction (goals) as intended by the school board and its administration. A coherent, well-developed *Lau* plan (as outlined in chapter 3) is a good place to start. The following objectives might appear self-evident (at least as intended) in a school district's *Lau* plan:

- LEP students must master English.
- LEP students must master grade-level appropriate skills.
- The regular education curriculum must be equitably accessible to LEP students.
- LEP students must be taught by appropriately credentialed staff.

- ESL instruction must emphasize content learning as well as English where ESL/mainstream collaboration is essential.
- ESL methodologies should vary widely to match teaching style to student learning style in all learning modes.
- Ongoing staff development should be encouraged.

However, to ensure effective and appropriate ESL interventions for LEP children, a model for overall ESL program evaluation and subsequent decision making must be developed and implemented. The *Lau* plan, such as the sample Heartland Valley *Lau* plan in Appendix A, will outline a program plan—steps that are measurable in four critical areas as noted in Figure 8.1.

Ongoing program evaluation will typically illustrate the following:

- attainment of program outcomes
- attainment of learner outcomes
- a visible climate of support for the ESL program
- high-quality instructional materials
- instruction matched to student needs
- authentic assessments
- effective staff development
- ongoing and effective mainstream/ESL collaboration
- ongoing and effective communication with parents
- full implementation of the district's *Lau* plan as approved by its school committee

In rural and small urban schools, comprehensive and analytical research-based evaluations, such as those required under large bilingual education grants

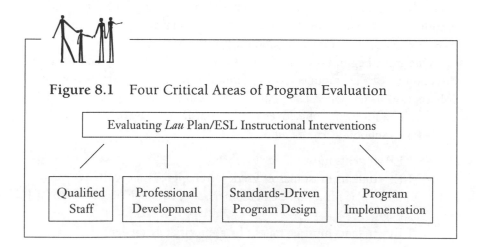

**Figure 8.1**    Four Critical Areas of Program Evaluation

Evaluating *Lau* Plan/ESL Instructional Interventions

| Qualified Staff | Professional Development | Standards-Driven Program Design | Program Implementation |

or substantive state grants, are not generally feasible. It is more common to review outcome data grounded on local goals, which are then reported to the administration and the school committee. For those seeking to broaden the scope of such an evaluation, August and Hakuta (1998) report lessons that can be learned from their 25 years of program evaluation, which was national in scope. Among those lessons:

- High-quality database evaluations should include these features: sound program design; full program implementation; creation of a control group (e.g., a group of LEP children without an intervention or without the ESL intervention approach used) and a comparison group (e.g., the performance of LEP students before and after the ESL intervention approach or comparable LEP students from another school district); analysis of the pre-post ESL program student measurement; establishment of analysis of students, classrooms, or district for part of an evaluation; and minimization of missing data (e.g., due to LEP student mobility).
- To be useful, local evaluations must be tools for program improvement—not merely administrative documents.
- The instructional approach should be grounded in sound theory connected to student achievement.

Local evaluations can meet those criteria when a district has a living, viable *Lau* plan. The first step in reviewing that plan in practice is to collect data.

## What Kinds of Data Should Be Collected?

ESL program accountability and demonstration of outcomes will ostensibly enhance the program's legitimacy in the school and will help the ESL manager achieve the ultimate goal of continually improving instruction that meets the needs of LEP children. To do this, comprehensive record keeping must be implemented for the identification and assessment of LEP students as well as the provision of and exit from ESL services. Such record keeping is necessary to keep track of the components of the student's learning plan and his or her progress within it; the language progress file (LPF), as described in the *Lau* plan, is a valuable source of evaluative information. If the student's family moves to a different school, the information in that file can help the new teacher set up a language support program more expeditiously. The LPF serves, in essence, to illustrate a school's commitment to quality services for LEP children. An LPF should be maintained by a member of the district's language assessment committee (LAC). Such a file should typically consist of the following three kinds of data:

1. demographic information (e.g., statistics about the students served)
2. outcome information that illuminates data descriptive of student academic performance
3. process variables over which the school has management authority (e.g., policy regarding standards and assessments)

Collection of those data types should include (as a minimum):

- language usage at home, vis-à-vis home language surveys and questionnaires
- all test scores pertaining to program decisions
- recommendations for the individual child's program
- portfolio of literacy work done by the student
- individual learning plans with program goals, objectives, and outcomes
- parent/guardian interviews or questionnaire notes
- time line of the LAC's quarterly meetings for carrying out its responsibilities as outlined in chapter 3
- recommendations for reclassification or exit from the ESL program
- notes from observations by school staff
- copies of report cards
- recommendations for resubmission of a revised districtwide *Lau* plan for board action if appropriate

## Evaluation as a Tool for Instructional Improvement

Appendix C illustrates how the three categories of instructional improvement must be examined in supporting ESL manager program evaluation. These categories include

1. qualified staff and professional development
2. standards-driven program design
3. ESL program implementation

Data from these categories, in turn, may be sorted by variables according to demographics, outcomes, and processes. Such strategizing for instructional improvement was originally crafted by the Reading Success Network of the Southern California Comprehensive Assistance Center, an agency funded by the U.S. Department of Education.

Staffing the ESL program, the first category, was broadly discussed in chapter 5, along with professional development. Guskey (1998) suggests that there are three evaluation types useful in determining professional development effectiveness:

1. planning what is to be accomplished (another *Lau* plan marker)
2. formative evaluation to gauge progress from what was planned
3. summarizing the accomplishments

A review of curriculum driven by high standards is the second category, which was extensively considered in chapter 4. Program implementation guidance, although dispersed throughout this volume, warrants added attention specific to certain difficult situations ESL managers may find themselves in. These include determining if students are fluent in English, accounting for age as a variable in acquiring English, and finding reasonable ways for engaging content teachers. Added to these are still more variables to consider in evaluating the need for sustained ESL program support.

## Is Length of Student Time in the ESL Program an Indicator of Its Success?

To be sure, giving LEP students enough instructional time to acquire English is one of the keys to establishing an effective ESL program. But how much? The issue of time can be considered from two points of view:

1. For what time period do students need ESL services each day?
2. How long should students retain the LEP classification?

There are no easy answers to either question. Rather, several important variables related to both the student and the school must be considered. Because there is no formula describing the number of hours of ESL instruction that will lead to the success of LEP students, the person making the decision about time allotment must consider many factors. A less comforting but reasonable answer is that all day, every day, day after day, and year after year, these students should have access to meaningful, comprehensible instruction in the English language and in the content areas responsive to the demand for aligning ESL instruction to high academic standards. Within this overall goal, it is useful to have an understanding of the factors that may make an individual's progress relatively slower or faster as compared to his or her peers.

The sometimes seemingly interminable questions about "how long" do need to be understood by the ESL advisory board (see chapter 6) and the administration. The LAC, informed about recent research and current knowledge and practices in second language acquisition by the ESL teacher, can assist in advising the board and administration on matters about the length of time during which a student should receive ESL services and the duration of those services. As the LAC oversees placement of the LEP students in an ESL program, monitors the student's progress, and makes the decision about when the student is ready to be mainstreamed, it is well positioned to know how long is enough and to determine if the LEP student is ready to be reclassified as non-LEP. The decision to exit a student from ESL services must be considered carefully because premature exiting can create serious academic problems later on and compound existing language acquisition needs. That sets the stage for all stakeholders to grasp the two most often misunderstood dimensions of addressing English fluency: duration of daily ESL support and duration of the ESL program from entry to exit.

## English Language Proficiency: Is the Student BICS or CALPS?

Moving the LEP student to full English language proficiency is usually the first and clearly the most obvious factor many would consider in evaluating the impact an ESL program is having. It is at the core of ESL programming decisions. That is why a school's *Lau* plan is critically important: because it will stipulate that multiple criteria be used to assess proficiency in speaking, listening, reading, and writing in order to get a complete picture of a student's English proficiency. As noted in chapter 7, ESL professionals assess students according to two broad levels of language fluency. These are basic interpersonal communication skills (BICS), which refer to face-to-face conversational proficiency, and cognitive academic language proficiency skills (CALPS), which refer to context-reduced, cognitively demanding aspects of language proficiency. The latter takes considerably longer to develop. Although some newcomers clearly do not speak or understand any English, the level of language proficiency of other students may be less apparent. Although some students appear to be bilingual or "sound about right," they are not approaching academic success. Students with fluency in interpersonal communication may still require support for CALPS. Language that is appropriate in a conversation is context embedded and allows the limited language speaker to negotiate meaning and avoid or circumvent difficulties. A context-reduced situation, such as listening to a teacher or reading a text, does not demonstrate that degree of flexibility. It is necessary for all LEP students to develop CALPS if they are to succeed in school. Authentic assessment of BICS and CALPS, both at the time of program entry and on a continuing basis, is the foundation upon which sound decisions about student programming can be built.

In shifting from the oral medium suggested by BICS to writing suggested by CALPS, the following sample may offer the reader an opportunity to sort BICS from CALPS. Illustrated in Figure 8.2 is a passage written by a Vietnamese newcomer student after 5 years of ESL-pullout instruction from Grades 8–12.

Can this student succeed in a full mainstream class functioning at the CALPS level? Evident in this passage is the student's considerable borrowing of features from her heritage language in composing English. A seasoned ESL manager will readily recognize from this passage that more time is needed to help this student in separating the syntactical differences between the two languages. It is a given premise: The less English a student knows, the more ESL support he or she will probably need. With that is a rule of thumb: Students with beginning-level English proficiency should have at least 3 hours of ESL instruction a day; an intermediate-level student might have 2 hours daily, and advanced ESL students only 1. However, one must remember that the

**Figure 8.2**    A High Honors Graduating Senior Writes Home From Camp

Hi, how's everybody doing? I'm doing o.k. I can't wait until camp it over. I'm looking foward to go to Canada, with you, mom, Kysa and Santhal my two baby sister. How's mam doing, I hope it wonderful. Duc come down to visit me today. Duc, ellse, Bobby Joe and Allison went to a beach today. We haved alot of fun. He go home around seven o'clock. I'm glass he coming down to visit me. He's very nice.

overall goal in educating LEP students is that they have access to comprehensible age- and grade-level appropriate instruction every day. In rural schools where low-incidence LEP student populations are common, ESL students are often placed in mainstream classrooms for a significant part of the day. It is imperative that ongoing consultation and mutual planning take place between the ESL teacher and the mainstream teacher. These are matters important to setting the stage for fair program evaluation.

An example of an effective, well-coordinated ESL/content teacher program comes from a small town in Maine. When one Russian newcomer entered the middle school, five content-area teachers, an ESL tutor, an ESL teacher under contract, an occasional interpreter/translator, and the special services coordinator developed a plan for how best this student might acquire English and content subjects without sacrificing elements from either. The plan was congruent with the elements of the school's *Lau* plan developed long before this child arrived. The student was held accountable for achieving the state's standards and, as specified by the plan, the school was accountable to provide comprehensible instruction. Nearly each day, most of the team members worked together to develop a joint plan and portfolio by subject area for this student. In-class specially designed academic instruction in English (SDAIE) (no pullout) was implemented by the ESL tutor with coaching from the supervising ESL teacher and overall supervision by the special services coordinator. In addition, there was a lot of support from the child's monolingual English peers. Full integration of this student in the student program from the first day made this model work. The student progressed remarkably well in her acquisition of English and in her content subjects.

A mainstream teacher who is provided with appropriate information and support can make the time an ESL student spends in the classroom effective learning time. For LEP students entering kindergarten, this kind of support enables them to stay on grade level. LEP students who enter at a later age may need some work to catch up before they can do grade-level work. However, it is important that students be engaged in content-area development immediately and not wait to pursue seemingly more difficult content work until they have gained some English language proficiency. See the introduction to SDAIE in chapter 4 to review why content support is so crucial to ESL instruction. Falling behind can lead to problems that intensify with every successive year. Students face more involved cognitive and literacy tasks as they move on to higher grade levels, and a gap between LEP students and their peers in second grade, for example, can grow into a chasm in middle school.

# What Difference Does Age Make?

Students of different ages tend to acquire a second language at differing rates. Responsible program evaluation assumes at the outset an awareness of these differing rates. Knowing those variables well will help in anticipating the length of a student's stay in a sound ESL program. It is a popular and persistent myth that young children innately acquire a new language quickly and easily. The reality is presented in well-respected research undertaken by Collier (1995a, 1995b) that sheds a light on how long it may in fact take LEP students to score at the 50th norm curved equivalent (NCE) on an academic achievement test when measured in their first language as they entered school in the United States and were from middle- or upper-middle-class backgrounds. Results showed that students under age 12 who had at least 2 years of schooling in the home country were the fastest learners: They took 5–7 years to reach the 50th NCE in reading, language arts, science, and social studies; in math they took only 2 years to reach the 50th NCE. Students who entered a U.S. school between ages 4 and 6 and who had no schooling in the first language reached the 50th NCE after 6 years and were projected to take 7–10 or more years based on their current rate of progress. Newcomer students entering school between ages 12 and 16 showed much slower progress than the 8- to 11-year-olds. After 6 years in a U.S. school, they had reached the 50th NCE only in math. At their rate of progress, they would be unable to reach the 50th NCE in the other content areas before graduating from high school.

The issue of time and rate of second language acquisition is especially critical in making placement decisions for older, newly arrived students. For younger children, an appropriate placement in a grade may often be based on age. For older students, however, considering age alone might make placement, say, as a senior appear to be appropriate, but would only give that student one year to fulfill requirements for high school graduation. Allowing LEP students who enter in their high school years a reasonable amount of time to achieve proficiency in English and to prepare for higher education or employment becomes an essential consideration when making grade placement. Providing a postgraduate study program is another way of giving LEP students the time they need to become competitive candidates for higher education or for postsecondary workforce experiences.

# Other Considerations for Evaluating Need for Sustained ESL Support

## Length of Time in the United States

Newly arrived students are likely to need survival and cultural information as well as longer periods of instruction on a daily basis in comparison to students who have been in the United States longer than they have. Survival skills, such as how to get the school bus, how to order lunch in the cafeteria, where to buy school supplies, or what to do on snow days, must all be taught.

## Circumstances of Immigration

Immigrants come to the United States from a wide range of circumstances. Some come to the United States as refugees, often under traumatic and stressful conditions. Some students come against their will. Others who come without their families face more intense culture shock and adjustment difficulties. Such students frequently have primary personal issues to address before they can consider language acquisition or a focus on academics.

## Fluency and Literacy in the First Language

Newcomer students from other countries acquire a new language at varying rates. A solid foundation in the first language is a predictor of student success. In his threshold hypothesis, Cummins (1994) postulates that children who have not had time to achieve fluency in their first language will have a harder time learning a second. Thus, pupils whose first language learning is interrupted may have difficulty in achieving competence in English. Some students may not readily produce spoken English; they are said to be in their silent period, which could last from several weeks to several months. In addition, if they have no instruction in literacy skills in the first language, reading in English may be delayed. Such children may be those whose non-English speaking or LEP parents believe that they must speak to their children in English, children whose parents do not regularly communicate with their children, or children who have entered an English-dominant household. Such situations may result in limited bilingualism, which means that the student may not have age-appropriate, nativelike competence in either his or her first language or in English.

    The language minority family can often avoid limited or subtractive bilingualism. Students whose parents read and talk to them in their heritage language, who nurture both first and second language acquisition, and who are able to share their cross-cultural perspectives and resources with teachers are at a relative advantage. Parental involvement within the school setting has also been shown to be a source of considerable motivation for students. In fact, Bérubé (1998) notes that the more bilingual families resist assimilation and maintain their heritage languages, the more intellectually successful their children will become. Outreach to and information for parents can help them understand the benefits of communicating with their children in their first or heritage language.

Several languages such as Khmer, Cantonese, Mandarin, Arabic, Hebrew, Russian, Greek, Japanese, Pashto, and many more do not use a Latin alphabet. Students literate in these languages must learn a writing system entirely different from their own. For example, Khmer does not use Arabic numerals, so number symbols must be learned. Some writing systems, such as Chinese, may not employ tonal sound-letter correspondences.

Speakers of other languages will have varying degrees of difficulty achieving comprehensible pronunciation in English. Vietnamese speakers, for instance, may have difficulty in distinguishing and pronouncing a number of tones, including word endings. Khmer students may have difficulty hearing and pronouncing [s] endings. Students from many Asian countries, among others whose languages are characteristically tonal, will need explicit instruction in English pronunciation.

First languages of still other newly arrived students may also differ from English syntactically. Word order and inflections may vary. Khmer, for instance, does not indicate plurals with noun endings and does not inflect verbs to indicate tense. Russian does not use articles and does not always require a sentence subject. Radical differences in syntax make the job of learning English more demanding for the student.

## Cultural Influences

Language proficiency alone is not enough to ensure that a language minority student can reach the same high academic standards as his or her English-only peers in the mainstream classroom across the hall. A student coming from a country with different cultural assumptions and values may require additional information and support to reach those performance standards. Expectations in social situations, school situations, and everyday interactions must often be explained by the ESL teacher and his or her collaborators.

Differences in values, attitudes, and experience are one of the main sources of social barriers incidental to second language acquisition. The widely accepted schema theory of reading, that the reader constructs meaning by storing background knowledge in memory (Carrell & Eisterhold, 1988; O'Donnell & Wood, 1992), provides insight into the comprehension challenges some second language readers experience. Because much background knowledge is culture-specific, it can be a significant factor in identifying reading comprehension problems. When an LEP student applies incorrect frameworks from background knowledge to information provided by a text, then the material read is in some measure incomprehensible. Culture-connected variables such as this can obviously play a critical role in assessments. Although no test is absolutely culture-fair, accommodations must be pursued to minimize this testing nuance.

## Previous School Experience in the Native Country

Children who have not been in school, or whose schooling has been interrupted, may not have acquired seemingly basic school skills. They may not have learned how to use scissors, hold a pencil, sit at a desk, modulate their voices, or attend to a teacher. They may not have experience doing homework, studying, using resources, or analyzing and applying knowledge. On the other hand, students with strong academic backgrounds in their native countries already have metacognitive skills to help them cope with both concrete and abstract classroom-connected skills. The extent of a student's school experience in the home country should be determined upon entry into a U.S. school so that an evaluation of instructional programs can be planned accordingly.

## Previous School Experience in the United States

If a student is transferring from another U.S. school, records from previous schools can give vital assessment information. Whether students received ESL services in their previous school must be considered, even if they have been in the country for some time. LEP students who have been submerged in an all-English environment (i.e., not provided with ESL instruction and support) will likely need additional services and probably more time in the ESL program.

## Quality Instruction

A program that is maximally effective and provides high-quality, content-rich holistic instruction at all times for all students will achieve results more quickly than a program that takes a fragmented or isolated approach to service delivery. Schools should continually strive to identify and take steps toward the improvement of student learning for all students, with no exceptions.

## Preferred Subject Area

Program evaluation of a school's application of high, challenging standards for LEP students may reveal a good deal about the opportunities those students are given to learn in all their subject areas. In keeping with holding LEP students to no lesser standard than those of their peers, modifications or alternative modes of testing should be available to them, rather than exempting them as most states regrettably still do (Wagoner, 1999). Standards, when applied from any subject area to a given LEP student, should include authentic assessments of that student's demonstrable performance and fulfillment of the opportunities for learning. In conducting such assessments, one may indeed discover that some LEP students do score competitively with their English-speaking peers and appear to learn more rapidly in some subjects than in others. The more language intensive and context reduced (lacking paralinguistic cues) the subject, the more time a student will need either a sheltered English classroom or SDAIE (as detailed in chapter 4). Math is typically the subject in which some LEP students might be more quickly successful; reading is typically the subject requiring the most time. Such preferences, however, are not universal among language minority students.

## Affective Environment

Student self-esteem and self-confidence are popularly linked with effective learning. Classrooms and communities in which LEP students are considered a resource, and not a deficit, encourage social and psychological proximity, hence language acquisition. Lowered anxiety appears to be related to successful second language acquisition (Krashen, 1982). Students, when given appropriate academic, social, and emotional support, tend to be more able to pursue demanding challenges.

In evaluating ESL program effectiveness, the ESL manager must recognize the flexibility that time accords for English language acquisition to occur for the school's LEP student enrollees. Decisions regarding time allotment may make the difference between a program that considers the needs of students and one that only purports to meet minimal requirements. The factors addressed above will affect these as well as other programming decisions. They should be weighed carefully when making scheduling and staffing decisions based on the students' needs and the ESL program design responsive to those needs.

## Benchmarking Integrative Language Assessment

The ESL manager's role in evaluating ESL program effectiveness for LEP students in the context of graduation requirements or for achievement to state and local standards is limited by local and state policy. There are volumes of literature and sources in cyberspace that focus on these broad areas of measurement and the LEP student. More germane to the experience of ESL managers, however, is in guiding the procedures by which LEP students are identified, provided ancillary language and content support, and continuously assessed for eventual mainstream placement (as discussed in chapter 3). Such integrative approaches to language assessment warrant administrative review to ensure program accountability.

As discussed previously in this volume, successful high-quality ESL management is comparable to successful standard non-ESL curriculum management. Benchmarks for high-quality ESL program evaluation were noted in previous chapters, such as:

- documented program goals consistent with the district's *Lau* policy and shared vision (chapter 3)
- inclusive, holistic program design and resources appropriate to student need, aligned to level of proficiency (chapter 4)
- collaborative schoolwide practices aligned with the district's challenging standards for all students (chapter 4)
- documentable compliance on the identification and placement and provision of services to the target population (chapter 4)
- ongoing staff development for all stakeholders in the education arena, including visible curriculum support at all levels of the school hierarchy (chapter 5)
- vigorous pursuit of parental and community engagement (chapter 6)
- specification of learning results (standards, outcomes) taught through a wide range of innovative alternative teaching mechanisms (e.g., SDAIE, CALLA) with corresponding authentic assessments (chapters 4 and 7)

Standardized placement/diagnostic tests are developed to identify a student's strengths and weaknesses in order to determine what the student needs to learn. Because the intent is to pinpoint instructional needs, placement/diagnostic tests typically cover a narrow range of content in depth. Most placement/diagnostic tests also provide norms that indicate how students at a similar grade- or age-level performed on the test. This information can be helpful when making decisions regarding which skills should be taught and improving instruction as a result of program evaluation data.

The results of a placement/diagnostic test can be used to help identify a student's instructional needs and to place the student in the most appropriate setting for instruction. As with other testing activities, it is important to ensure that the testing is conducted in a language that does not interfere with securing an accurate measure of the student's actual level of knowledge. The ESL manager is advised to consider how the results will be used before deciding how to test the student.

Standardized achievement tests are used to sample a student's current level of learning across a range of general skill areas. The content is typically related to formal school learning experiences. Because the intent is to sort and rank students, these tests cover a wide range of topical areas. The norms for a standardized achievement test show how the "typical" mainstream students performed. Hence, those norms can be used in program evaluation as a basis for determining how LEP students are progressing in relation to their fully English proficient peers. A caveat is in order: No standardized test should stand alone in assessing student learning, much less English language proficiency. This is a point currently hurled at colleges and the Educational Testing Service at Princeton, New Jersey, by the Office for Civil Rights (1999). In 1999, the OCR found that high-stakes testing, such as the SATs, might not stand alone in determining a student's entry into college. A year later, the OCR issued guidance on the use of tests to award diplomas, grade promotions, and college admission. The OCR presented the educational justifications for such tests as a planning tool for school districts rather than policy (Blair, 1999).

Because standardized achievement tests measure school learning, they can provide useful data in ESL program evaluation. The results of standardized achievement tests can, as a minimum, provide a picture of overall progress over time, identify skills that LEP students have learned and those that still need to be taught, and help determine whether LEP students are ready to move into the mainstream classroom. Once students have the language skills necessary to take a standardized achievement test, the results can be used to ensure that students in an ESL program are helped to develop the skills that would allow them to benefit from an education conducted in English. Through out-of-level testing, it is relatively easy to determine whether a LEP student is taking the appropriate level of a standardized test. If a student, for example, gets one third or fewer of the items on average correct on a test, she or he is probably guessing and should be given the next lower level of that test. Similarly, if a student on the average gets 75% or more of the items correct, she or he should probably be given the next higher level of the test. When unsure as to which level of a standardized test to administer, one should check to see whether there is a locator test available. Many test publishers have locator tests, which are short tests designed to help determine the appropriate test level for students.

# Summative Guidance for the ESL Program Manager

What is the worth of an ESL program? When can it end? Those are among the questions that the ESL manager is likely to struggle with, armed with a wealth of program evaluation data. The ESL manager faces substantial challenges for documenting accountability: He or she must weigh the usefulness of sometimes limited data in gauging the effectiveness of standards-driven program design, oversee comprehensive staff development, and balance as many assessment variables as are possible in describing the varied paths to success offered to the school district's LEP students.

Demographic, outcome, and process data were presented in this chapter as critical sources to be examined. These become archival data that serve as the foundation for making comparative judgments about the ESL program implementation, whether that data be within the institution or about student progress over time. Disaggregation of that data is suggested for planning program improvements, including continual review of the school district's *Lau* plan.

The role of the ESL manager in documenting LEP student achievement for high, challenging standards is indeed pivotal. The manager must

- document the identification of all LEP students (names of such students by language, grade, and method by which LEP status was determined)
- participate with administrators and teachers and others on the LAC in designing an ESL program that meets the needs of eligible students consistent with the district's *Lau* plan

- collaborate with teachers in planning for the teaching of the ESL program student in the English-only classroom
- manage the program consistent with the current knowledge base on ESL instruction
- support English as the principal medium of instruction in the areas of pronunciation, listening comprehension, speaking, structure, reading, and writing
- oversee activities and materials for ESL use that indicate an understanding of the language proficiency level of the students
- express interest in, and have an understanding for, the native cultures of the students
- provide experiences that encourage positive student self-concept
- promote and understand the supportive roles and responsibilities of parents/guardians
- remain vigilant in ensuring the district's compliance with its *Lau* plan and ongoing review for periodic update and presentation to the school committee for its action

Attending to these details should keep the OCR at bay with regard to the ESL manager's concern for defending a sound, effective ESL program. Federal laws do not include ESL program prescription unless those programs have been found to be unsuccessful in accessing LEP children to education in their new language. Effective ESL programs will ostensibly vary from school to school. The OCR (1999) has issued the following seven components as key guiding elements in program evaluation:

1. Goals: The intent is for the LEP student to acquire English and comprehensible academic instruction.
2. Scope: Program implementation practices and student performance are key.
3. Data Collection: Student outcomes over time, including LEP student exit from ESL support, must be appraised.
4. Appraisal of Results: Identification of concerns for follow-through should be made as a result of program evaluation.
5. Commitment: A commitment to implementing program changes as a result of evaluation should occur.
6. Time Line: A firm schedule for program improvement milestones as a result of evaluation should be set.
7. Follow-Up: Evaluation is ongoing. (pp. 25–26)

## Suggested Resources on the Web

For an ongoing perspective on language program administration:
"So You Are a Language Program Administrator?" (Smith, 1999,
http://www.tesol.org/isaffil/intsec/columns/199906-pa.html)

To conduct searches on ESL program evaluation:
*AskERIC* (http://ericir.syr.edu/ [search for ESL program evaluation])

For information about what ESL program directors should know:
"School-Based Management: What Bilingual and ESL Program
Directors Should Know" (McKeon & Malarz, 1991,
http://www.ncbe.gwu.edu/ncbepubs/pigs/pig5.htm)

For a look at an evaluation report on successful ESL/bilingual education
programs:
*Success Stories: A Case Study of Bilingual/ESL Education* (ERIC, 1990,
http://ericae.net/ericdb/ED333746.htm)

For ESL testing and evaluation Web sites:
*Kristin's ESL Page* (http://grove.ufl.edu/~klilj/#testeval)

# Chapter 9
# Professional Resources: From People to Print to Pixels

*If you want to become an expert in geopolitics, become an ESL teacher.*
—Flemming, Germer, & Kelley, 1993, p. 32

## Alone No More: A Community for ESL Teachers in Rural Areas

Rural and small urban schools are uniquely challenged in accessing the kinds of ESL resources larger urban schools typically enjoy. It is common for schools with low-incidence LEP enrollments, for example, to employ perhaps only one ESL teacher, if even that, to serve the entire district. As such, ESL teachers in rural schools have few colleagues with whom to initiate collaboratives and are frequently removed from state or local resources specific to their profession. Despite these challenges, the ESL teacher in the rural school can, in fact, access substantial resources, much of them free of charge, through the telephone or a computer modem. Prominent among them are state departments of education, regional education equity centers, regional educational laboratories, the National Clearinghouse for Bilingual Education, and the Center for Applied Linguistics. Each is detailed below.

## State Departments of Education

The ESL manager can benefit considerably by consulting the state department of education. Despite its value as a resource, its very being can present a stigma to the uninitiated. Sometimes school districts distance themselves from state departments of education and federal agencies because those agencies often earned the reputation of primary overseer and compliance officer for statutory enforcement. On the other hand, their value as a resource to schools, often overlooked, has been around for a long time. Not much, in fact, has changed in that regard since the context of government in this field was described in a bilingual education manager's field book in 1985 (Bérubé & Delgado). The resourcefulness of state departments of education to ESL managers include accessibility to publicly funded grants, staff training, technical assistance, and program advisement for school personnel and parents. Their function does generally include interpretation of federal and state statute and a degree of program compliance with statute. Any state government agency can be accessed on the Web at http://www.statescape.com.

## Regional Education Equity Centers

Other than state education departments, there are agencies that are publicly funded to support professional development for ESL teachers and other staff who serve LEP students. For example, in each region of the United States, there is an equity center funded by the U.S. Department of Education (USDE) under Title IV of the Civil Rights Act to support training that assures LEP children equal access to the full range of services available to all other children. To achieve this, such centers may undertake the following kinds of initiatives:

- preparation, adoption, and implementation of plans for the desegregation of public schools and the development of effective methods of addressing special educational problems occasioned by desegregation
- establishment of model school-based, on-site, train-the-trainer teams in states to assist school districts in ensuring equity and in developing effective approaches for improving the quality of education for all minority students
- creation of equity leadership teams of superintendents and school boards through specialized training designed to prepare team members to serve as regional troubleshooters and mentors in the dissemi-

nation of successful equity practices and creative solutions to compliance problems

- organization of community awareness focus groups through collaboratives with targeted grassroots organizations in the delivery of equity seminars
- support for educational researchers and practitioners through seminars and colloquiums that engage educators from institutes of higher education and school districts in joint classroom-based research focusing on the needs of language minority students

The following list includes contact information for the 10 equity centers across the United States. Phone numbers listed were operational as this volume went to press.

1. New England Equity Center (service to Maine, New Hampshire, Vermont, Connecticut, and Rhode Island) Telephone: 800-521-9550
2. Metro Equity Center (service to New Jersey, New York, Puerto Rico, and Virgin Islands) Telephone: 212-998-5100
3. Mid-Atlantic Equity Center (service to Delaware, District of Columbia, Maryland, Pennsylvania, Virginia, and West Virginia) Telephone: 301-657-7741
4. Southeast Equity Center (service to Alabama, Florida, Georgia, Kentucky, Mississippi, South Carolina, Tennessee, and North Carolina) Telephone: 305-669-0114
5. Great Lakes Equity Center (service to Illinois, Indiana, Michigan, Minnesota, Ohio, and Wisconsin) Telephone: 734-763-9910
6. South Central Equity Center (service to Arkansas, Louisiana, New Mexico, Oklahoma, and Texas) Telephone: 210-444-1710
7. Midwest Region Equity Center (service to Iowa, Kansas, Missouri, and Nebraska) Telephone: 785-532-6408
8. Mountain Region Equity Center (service to Colorado, Montana, North Dakota, South Dakota, Utah, and Wyoming) Telephone: 503-275-9604
9. Southwest Region Equity Center (service to Arizona, California, and Nevada) Telephone: 562-598-7661
10. Northwest Region Equity Center (service to Alaska, Hawaii, Idaho, Oregon, Washington, American Samoa, Guam, Northern Mariana Islands, and Trust Territory of the Pacific Islands) Telephone: 503-275-9604

## Regional Educational Laboratories

Like the equity centers, there are 10 regional educational laboratories located across the United States. These laboratories are educational research and development organizations supported by contracts with the USDE. Organized regionally, these laboratory centers help schools with all phases of systemic school improvement at no cost to schools. Fundamental to their mission is making the latest action research meaningful to school staff through training, publications, and direct involvement in laboratory activities. Each laboratory has a unique specialty area in systemic reform that it shares with the other laboratories throughout the United States. For ESL teachers, the expertise generally needed focuses on language and cultural diversity as well as rural education and assessment. Laboratories that support those areas nationally may be accessed as follows:

*Specialty: Language and Culture Diversity*

- The LAB at Brown University, 222 Richmond Street, Providence, RI USA 02903; Telephone: 800-521-9550; Web site: http://www.lab .brown.edu/public/index.
- Pacific Resources for Education & Learning, Ali'i Place, 25th Floor, 1099 Alakea Street, Honolulu, HI USA 96813-4513; Telephone: 808-441-1300; Web site: http://www.prel.hawaii.edu/.
- Southwest Educational Development Laboratory, 211 East Seventh Street, Austin, TX USA 78701-3281; Telephone 512-476-6861; Web site: http://www.sedl.org.

*Specialty: Rural Education*

- Appalachia Educational Lab, Inc., 1031 Quarrier Street, Charleston, WV USA 25301; Telephone: 800-624-9120; E-mail: aelinfo@ael.org; Web site: http://www.ael.org.

*Specialty: Assessment and Accountability*

- West Education Laboratory, 730 Harrison Street, San Francisco, CA USA 94107; Telephone: 415-565-3000; Web site: http://www.wested .org.

## The National Clearinghouse for Bilingual Education

Another federally supported organization, national in scope, is the popular National Clearinghouse for Bilingual Education (NCBE). NCBE is funded by the USDE's Office of Bilingual Education and Minority Languages Affairs (OBEMLA) to collect, analyze, and disseminate information on effective educational practices for linguistically and culturally diverse learners in the United States. NCBE provides information on-line; produces a biweekly news bulletin, *Newsline*; and manages a topical electronic discussion group called the *NCBE Roundtable*. As part of the USDE's technical assistance and information network, NCBE works with other service providers to provide access to high-quality information to help states and local school districts develop ESL and bilingual education programs and implement strategies for helping all students work toward high academic standards. The clearinghouse does this by:

- addressing critical issues that support the education of linguistically and culturally diverse students in the United States
- serving as a broker for exemplary practices and research as they relate to the education of LEP students
- serving as an informational clearinghouse for individuals working in foreign language programs, ESL programs, Head Start, Title I, migrant education, and adult education programs
- operating its biweekly *Newsline* newsletter made available free to anyone wishing to subscribe on-line
- announcing grant opportunities that support LEP students (although rural school districts frequently do not seek federal grant funds administered under IASA Title VII, they can form consortia with other schools to enhance their LEP enrollment numbers, which may help defend their collective need for such grants)

NCBE also operates an active on-line library. Current research resources about issues affecting language minority education are circulated via *Outreach News*. Federal grant and fellowship information and applications are announced in NCBE's *Funding Facts* on-line. A page on-line is devoted to publications that link to the USDE's network for special education as well as scores of articles relating to bilingual special education. The only site that permits access at large to state-by-state practices and resources for meeting the needs of language minority children is NCBE's *State Education Resources* Web page. In addition, there is the NCBE Roundtable Discussion Group, which is a forum where professionals can exchange information in virtually all areas of the language minority student schooling experience. All of these services are free and can be accessed from NCBE at http://www.ncbe.gwu.edu or 202-467-0867.

## The Center for Applied Linguistics

The Center for Applied Linguistics (CAL) is another prominent national organization that is both a contract and grant firm. Established in 1959, CAL continues to pursue its three objectives:

1. to promote and improve the teaching and learning of languages
2. to identify and solve problems related to language and culture
3. to serve as a resource for information about language and culture (Center for Applied Linguistics, 2000)

CAL assists international corporations, school systems, government agencies, social service providers, and private businesses in solving the language barriers that may impede their work. By conducting in-depth research, developing innovative training materials and language teaching programs, designing instruments, and actively participating in language policy formulation, CAL has become known as a leading resource on communication issues. CAL can be reached at 202-362-0700. Its Web site address is http://www.cal.org.

# Professional Organizations

Networking is soul food for ESL teachers in rural and small urban schools—particularly ones more typically isolated from others in their profession. There are, of course, state, regional, and national organizations whose function, at least in part, is to make the ESL classroom a less lonely place. Preeminent among these organizations is Teachers of English to Speakers of Other Languages, more popularly referred to as TESOL; the National Association for Bilingual Education (NABE); and the National Association for Multicultural Education (NAME). Each is detailed below.

## Teachers of English to Speakers of Other Languages (TESOL)

TESOL's mission is to develop the expertise of its members and others involved in teaching English to speakers of other languages. TESOL helps educators foster effective communication in diverse settings while respecting individuals' language rights. To this end, TESOL articulates and advances standards for professional preparation and employment, continuing education, and student programs. It links groups worldwide to enhance communication among language specialists. It produces high-quality institutes, a national conference, and instructional products, and it promotes advocacy to further the profession. TESOL publishes the research journal *TESOL Quarterly* as well as *TESOL Matters* and other serial publications containing articles of interest to the ESL profession. There are 43 TESOL affiliates across the United States. To reach TESOL or to find out about TESOL's nearest affiliate organization, call 703-836-0774. TESOL is also accessible at http://www.tesol.org.

## The National Association for Bilingual Education (NABE)

Another national professional and advocacy organization whose mission compares with that of TESOL is NABE. NABE appears to court bilingual educators in larger communities more than it does ESL teachers in rural areas. Nevertheless, its focus includes positive attention given to ESL concerns. NABE pursues research, professional development (i.e., a national convention), public education, and legislative advocacy on behalf of diverse populations in the United States, from preschool through adult. NABE publishes its *Bilingual Research Journal* quarterly and serial publications, such as *NABE News*, periodically. Based in Washington, DC, its headquarters can be reached at 202-898-1829. More information including affiliates to NABE can be accessed at its Web site at http://www.nabe.org.

## The National Association for Multicultural Education (NAME)

NAME is a professional organization that embraces the basic tenets of cultural pluralism. NAME hosts an annual national conference on diversity and multiculturalism for educators and advocates of diversity. Based in Washington, DC, NAME publishes the quarterly publication, *Multicultural Perspectives*. Its Web site, http://www.inform.umd.edu/NAME, hosts teacher education programs, a chat room, and an electronic discussion list among other resources. Its national headquarters may be reached at 202-NAT-NAME or 202-628-6263.

# Community Resources

Often overlooked, the rural and small urban school community can be a rich source of easily accessible and often free resources. There may be local clubs whose thematic orientation or whose membership is ethnic group-specific such as French, Italian, Cambodian, or Polish. If the ESL teacher can seek out such a group in the area whose direction coincides with the ethnicity of one or all of the children, it potentially becomes a valuable resource. From the members of such a club, the teacher can access authentic information about an LEP student's heritage culture. This information may assist the ESL teacher, for example, in organizing or participating in local cultural exchange programs. The more the community knows about the language minority students' cultures and vice versa, the more quickly those students become integrated into the school and community. The ethnic club can also serve as a resource. Such a club may have, for example, a pool of translators/interpreters for the parents of the LEP students, if they, too, are LEP. An ethnic club or organization may also serve as a sponsor organization for a family in the community. The sponsorship may serve to identify the club as a liaison between the family and the community. Such clubs often serve as the family's advocate at the school and other public settings beyond the home. The ESL teacher is advised to check with the local chamber of commerce to secure information about ethnic groups in the area. Small urban communities will more likely have more of such organizations than rural communities.

As described in chapter 6, parents and the local community are a potential source of support for the children the ESL manager oversees. Because they possess considerable information about their own children and culture, parents should be encouraged to share that information in some capacity for the benefit of all students. In doing so, parents of LEP children can assist the ESL teachers in helping their students become a part of the new culture as they sustain pride in their first culture. Parents as well as the broader community (which includes sponsors of refugee families such as charities, churches, and individuals) can become especially helpful with families that have little skill in reaching out to the community. Through the sponsors, a teacher can become enriched by learning the history and education of the family, as well as addressing ongoing concerns and needs. At the outset, they may, in fact, be a teacher's only means of communicating.

Local adult education, as well as literacy volunteers, should serve as another rich access to resources. The ESL manager is advised to connect with them to find helpful suggestions and materials to get started with students. The Literacy Volunteers (LITVOL) organization, in particular, offers programs that may help teachers feel more comfortable as they first begin to teach ESL. LITVOL provides training sessions that ESL teachers may find well worth pursuing. ESL managers and teachers later reveal that when they were less seasoned in the profession, they found programs established through areas such as adult education and LITVOL to be sources for securing "survival" materials and teaching ideas that were the genesis of their own programs.

In surrounding cities, counties, regions, or school districts, there may be other ESL personnel who may generously offer help in getting a new ESL teacher started. The ESL manager might visit with them, observe sessions, ask about their district's *Lau* plan, and look at their materials; in this way, the ESL teacher can be advised by the ESL manager on what is locally in place as a potential model. Much unneeded labor can be saved by listening to some of the experiences of neighbors. The ESL manager may also opt to establish an informal regional network of ESL teachers with a directory of names and telephone numbers.

Connecting with sponsors of new Americans such as refugees is sometimes the teacher's closest access to the home of the newly arrived student. Sponsoring agencies such as churches, synagogues, and the state's Roman Catholic diocese can help in accessing culture-related resources as well as seeking qualified interpreters. Town libraries, too, may offer suggestions on how they can assist the new student in acclimating to the new culture. In addition, there are organizations that can provide recreation and other richly informed sources to help the newly arrived student in building or renewing self-confidence and trust. These include the YMCA/YWCA, 4-H clubs, Boys & Girls' clubs, scouts, camps, and sports teams. By becoming aware and informed of what others are doing, proactive and geopolitically assertive ESL teachers will be helping their students to succeed in their new language and culture. Teachers will be minimizing their students' chance of failure as well as encouraging their success.

In many states, there are organizations of Returned Peace Corps Volunteers (RPCV). The members of these organizations have had extended experience working for the Peace Corps in countries all over the world. The ESL teacher may encounter in the membership people who have been to the country of origin of his or her students and who are bilingual in the students' native language and knowledgeable about the culture. These people could be a significant resource to an ESL teacher as linguistic and cultural translators/interpreters and as people who can share their own experiences as sojourners.

Religious groups can be significant resources for the ESL teacher as well. Their potential roles of sponsorship and advocacy are important strengths that can support a beginning ESL program. A liaison with sectarian groups can facilitate the integration of the students into the community and help increase sensitivity about the new culture to the students in the community. Yet another contact point is with local networks of professional educators. Consider foreign language associations, as well as reading and language arts associations, to learn more about how they may be interested in supporting ESL networking.

## Resources at the School

As noted in chapter 5, the password to a harmoniously engaging ESL program is *collaboration*. That is, of course, available closer to home. The ESL manager can solicit support from individuals and groups within the school district. Beyond the rhetoric, all school personnel and administrators should be there to support all children. Table 9.1 outlines typical roles that those colleagues may play in networking to support LEP student instruction. Most well-seasoned content-area teachers who have had LEP students in their classrooms frequently wish to support these students and track their progress. They may be coming to the ESL teacher for suggestions and as a resource. Many non-ESL teachers have been in their positions for several years and can help with or alleviate some of the problems the new ESL teacher may be experiencing.

In encouraging collaboration among school personnel, administrators should facilitate problem solving around ESL issues. The ESL manager may need to be assertive. Inform colleagues about what the ESL students' needs are, and offer some suggestions about how they can be met. It is helpful to get to know school board members and make them aware of ESL concerns. The more people that are aware of ESL needs, the more support ESL will probably receive. If there are issues that need to be presented for discussion, the ESL manager should be given the opportunity of being placed on the agenda of the school board meeting. When the ESL manager attends such a meeting, she or he should be accompanied by supportive people such as other teachers, parents, paraprofessionals, community members, and the district's or school's language assessment committee members.

With occasional cajoling, a supervisor can be nurtured along as a powerful advocate. A common error is to characterize supervisors as adversaries. Indeed, it can take time for some people to become aware of the special needs and concerns of the second language student. The ESL manager can present them with credible literature that may help to resolve issues that may be challenging them.

**Table 9.1** Help Is Just Down the Hall

| *Who?* | *To Do What?* |
| --- | --- |
| School administrators | • assist in negotiating student scheduling with ESL teacher<br>• secure volunteers<br>• connect to outside agencies |
| Counselors | • same as administrators above<br>• student transfers; transcript analysis<br>• assistance with modification of a test that may be used for placement; assistance in providing alternative student documents for those destroyed |
| Non-ESL teachers | • Use as resource, especially if bilingual, if they have traveled to countries known to the language minority student, if a former ESL teacher or ESL aide, if credentialed in speech pathology or special education; a collaborator; a friend |
| Librarians | • same as some of the above attributes<br>• provide stimulating, appropriate reading resources |
| School nurses | • same as some of the above attributes<br>• intervention on health concerns |
| Non-LEP student peers | • buddy<br>• peer tutor<br>• mediator during times of peer conflict |
| Support staff | • the welcoming gatekeeper<br>• one-on-one contact on getting around the school |
| In-school volunteers, parents, foster grandparents, and retired teachers | • classroom aides<br>• tutors<br>• featured guest speakers<br>• translators<br>• chaperones<br>• advisors |

# Cyberspace

Software, electronic discussion lists, and Web sites are all available in cyberspace. The richness, as well as the occasional risks, is the ESL manager's, via multimedia opportunities. The 21st century has arrived with so much continually evolving technology: animation, video, buoyant graphics, voice recording, and even voice and eyeball recognition. With all of this, however, is the uncertainty that comes with trial and error, short of endorsements of commercial products from well-respected ESL professionals. An ongoing hurdle to overcome is having quality ESL software, despite some lack of understanding among some entrepreneurs on the richness of the ESL market as well as the research base for what works best in second language acquisition instruction.

Given the inundation of the market with ESL software (and ESL print), the ESL manager is best advised to follow the professional literature and to network with colleagues to determine which materials are suitable for them. Software and print materials are routinely reviewed in publications such as *TESOL Matters, NABE News*, and *ESL Magazine*, to name only the more popular outlets. Attendance at professional ESL organizations' annual conferences and conventions affords the manager an opportunity to browse through a wide range of published material on exhibit. Most publishers will also permit use of obligation-free examination of their materials. Finally, state education ESL offices may also serve as useful advisors concerning materials currently on the market.

ESL professionals need to, and most of them like to, network. They also need the satisfying or even sometimes therapeutic resolution that may come from talking with their colleagues. Meloni (1998), for example, offers many opportunities for the ESL teacher to subscribe (and unsubscribe) to electronic discussion groups, popularly referred to as electronic discussion lists. Meloni recommends two electronic fora worthy of ESL teacher/manager energy. One is *TESL-L*, maintained at Hunter College, which focuses on computer-assisted language acquisition, holistic intensive English, and administrative issues. *TESL-L* also has an on-line journal as well as archival material connected to computer-assisted learning. Subscribe to *TESL-L* to receive articles, research documents, lesson plans, classroom handouts, teaching ideas, and Web links. To subscribe, send the message "sub TESL-L yourfirstname yourlastname" to listserv@cunyvm.cuny.edu. Example: sub TESL-L John Wayne. (Information is available by e-mail to teslhelp@cunyvm.cuny.edu.) The other list Meloni recommends is *Neteach-L*. Members of this electronic discussion list share ideas on how to use technology and the Internet in the ESL classroom. The list is hosted at the University of Kansas. The subscription process is similar to that for *TESL-L*. To subscribe, send the message "sub NETEACH-L yourfirstname yourlastname" to listproc@ukans.edu. (Available from http://www.ilc.cuhk.edu.hk/english/neteach/main.html.)

For ESL teachers seeking collegial assistance with curriculum and particularly with TESOL's ESL standards, CAL offers an active and worthy list, the *ESL Standards Implementation Electronic Discussion List*. To subscribe, send a message to request-eslstds@caltalk.cal.org. In the subject line, type: subscribe. Leave the rest of the message blank.

Cyberspace is replete with sites for ESL educators. Sites carry a very wide range of information, commercial pitches, more list opportunities, electronic mail, and linkages to related Web sites. Table 9.2 displays a sampling of some of the more common Web locations ESL professionals and those interested in the broader area of education tend to exploit. The sites expand to hundreds of other sites that serve as linkages.

## Summative Guidance for the ESL Program Manager

Although some ESL program managers may feel alone in low-incidence LEP school districts, this chapter has directed them to boundless resources that should assuage that discouragement. Upon arrival to a new school, the manager's first call for technical support should perhaps be to the state department of education. Depending on the area of need, a call to the regional education equity center may occur next for cost-free technical assistance. A database that few seasoned ESL managers could not survive without is that of NCBE.

Armed with those and other resources noted in this chapter, the manager can proceed to build an impressive network—a team of professionals prepared to help build a nascent ESL program into a mature model for others. Invitation to partake in such a network should occur with professional and advocacy organizations, community resources, ethnic clubs, parents, sponsoring agencies, adult education programs, and, above all, caring colleagues within the school district. Sometimes the only help not forthcoming is that which the manager has failed to request.

## Suggested Resources on the Web

The importance of exploring cyberspace would seem too elementary to mention here. However, the ESL manager may not be yet acquainted with competent on-line professionals who operate electronic discussion groups germane to ESL. Add to that electronic mail and the limitless opportunities for access to ESL-related Web sites and their universally available linkages. There is more activity available for the Web wanderer who may want to be updated on ESL activities going on in cyberspace. For that explorer, Meloni's (2000) column in *TESOL Matters*, "Wandering the Web Dot.com," is a fine resource. It is accessible at http://www.tesol.org/pubs/magz/wanweb/wanweb0002.html.

Several sites have been suggested throughout this volume, particularly those listed at the end of each chapter. All sites cited were in operation as this volume went to press. Should difficulties surface, the reader is advised to conduct a search using language in the Uniform Resource Locator (URL) given or in a description of that URL. Table 9.2 presents recommended sites for bookmarking. These are a sampling of useful ESL sites, though not an exhaustive list. Travel the Web, discover, explore, and have fun!

**Table 9.2   Some ESL Sites to Bookmark**

| Description or Title and Web Address | News and General Information | Curriculum | Research | Assessment | Policy and Statute | Materials | Methods | Grants |
|---|---|---|---|---|---|---|---|---|
| Center for Applied Linguistics http://www.cal.org | | | X | | | | | |
| *Dave's ESL Cafe on the Web* http://www.eslcafe.com | X | X | | X | | X | X | |
| Educators' Web sites http://www.mainecenter.org /seed/sites | X | X | X | X | X | X | X | X |

*Continued on p. 199*

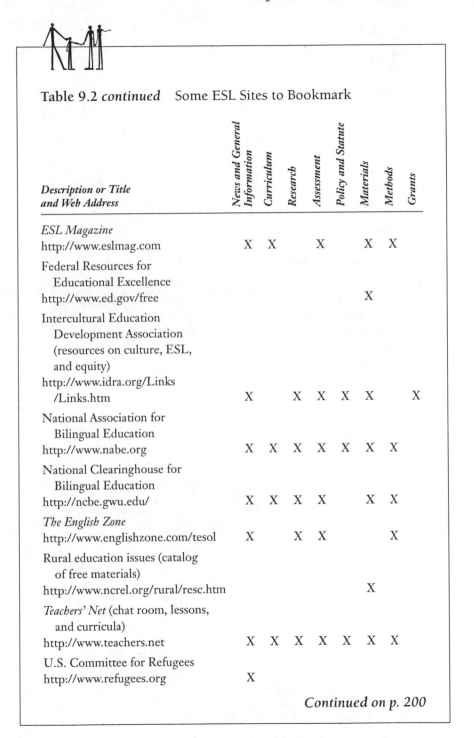

Table 9.2 *continued*    Some ESL Sites to Bookmark

| Description or Title and Web Address | News and General Information | Curriculum | Research | Assessment | Policy and Statute | Materials | Methods | Grants |
|---|---|---|---|---|---|---|---|---|
| *ESL Magazine* http://www.eslmag.com | X | X | | X | | X | X | |
| Federal Resources for Educational Excellence http://www.ed.gov/free | | | | | | X | | |
| Intercultural Education Development Association (resources on culture, ESL, and equity) http://www.idra.org/Links /Links.htm | X | | X | X | X | X | | X |
| National Association for Bilingual Education http://www.nabe.org | X | X | X | X | X | X | X | |
| National Clearinghouse for Bilingual Education http://ncbe.gwu.edu/ | X | X | X | X | | X | X | |
| *The English Zone* http://www.englishzone.com/tesol | X | | X | X | | | X | |
| Rural education issues (catalog of free materials) http://www.ncrel.org/rural/resc.htm | | | | | | X | | |
| *Teachers' Net* (chat room, lessons, and curricula) http://www.teachers.net | X | X | X | X | X | X | X | |
| U.S. Committee for Refugees http://www.refugees.org | X | | | | | | | |

*Continued on p. 200*

**Table 9.2 *continued***   Some ESL Sites to Bookmark

| Description or Title and Web Address | News and General Information | Curriculum | Research | Assessment | Policy and Statute | Materials | Methods | Grants |
|---|---|---|---|---|---|---|---|---|
| U.S. Dept. of Education grant announcements http://www.ed.gov/funding.html | X | | | | | | | X |
| U.S. Dept. of Education publications http://www.ed.gov/pubs /edpubs.html | X | X | X | | | X | | |
| U.S. Office of Bilingual Education and Minority Languages Affairs http://www.ncbe.gwu.edu/obemla /index.htm | X | | | | X | | | X |
| World Languages Resources (multiple languages) http://www.worldlanguage.com | | | | | | X | | |

# Chapter 10
# A Postscript

ESL managers and ESL teachers have a heightened appreciation of the world through their interactions with the nearly 3 million youngsters in U.S. schools for whom English is their new or developing language. Their heritage language could be one of any of the world's languages, and these students reside in every state and in every U.S. territory. Some of these youngsters come to the United States with traumatic experiences that often come from being a refugee; others come voluntarily, whereas others may be U.S.-born children whose non-English heritage language pervades their home life.

In the previous nine chapters, this volume has presented some of the challenges that the manager of an English-support system for LEP students must assume. The matter of establishing a quality program of services to students identified as LEP students is not grounded in the size of the program or even the number served. It is grounded in excellence only. However, the most accessible guidance for the uninitiated manager still appears to come largely from urban schools. This volume focused on rural and small urban U.S. schools. In invoking much about statutory guidance, this volume placed its emphasis on the 44% of LEP students in the United States who may be loosely referred to as low-density or low-incidence enrollees acquiring an education conducted in their new language.

In chapter 1, the ESL manager acquired a working understanding of the concept of limited English proficiency. Given the demographics of the past decade and projections for the next decade and beyond, it is plausible to assume that virtually anyone entering the teaching profession can expect to teach at least one LEP student in his or her career.

As this volume goes to press, it is worth noting the recent passing of the 25th anniversary of the most famous U.S. Supreme Court decision since the Brown decision of 1954: the *Lau v. Nichols* decision of 1974. Most famous, that is, from the perspective of advocates of the diverse youth in U.S. schools— and of language minority students in particular. In this unanimous ruling, all schools were compelled to take steps in ensuring that the intent of Title VI of the Civil Rights Act of 1964 was scrupulously followed. That decision and many others discussed in chapter 2 became the overarching legal rationale for the ESL manager's work: to participate in ensuring that LEP children are provided free and equitable access for education, both in theory and in subsequent practice.

Chapter 3 targeted both rural and small urban school boards and the ESL manager they employ. The school boards and the administrators who serve at their pleasure must provide their LEP enrollees with a staff employed to provide them with instruction modeled on sound research and housed in well-lighted, well-ventilated, and clean classrooms that maintain current equipment and supplies suitable for quality instruction. Such a model of instruction is described in a school district's *Lau* plan. The model *Lau* plan from the Heartland Valley Schools in Appendix A was presented as a way of assisting the manager in developing a local plan in accommodating his or her own circumstances with that of a prototype.

Enter the standards debate. Should any child be denied access to standards otherwise open to all other students? Should the bar be lowered for the LEP student? The operative answer suggested in chapter 4 is a resounding no. The transition from adherence to statutes, case law, and policy to the development of standards-driven curriculum is the prologue to high, challenging standards that LEP students should and must reach. Program models and strategies were presented in this chapter to assist the manager in developing curriculum that incorporates both content and English fluency requirements. Yes, the LEP student is held accountable to the same challenging standards expected of non-LEP students. The ESL teacher and colleagues share that accountability.

The revelation of data may have brought somewhat embarrassing news to the schools and universities across the United States. U.S. schools have a poor record regarding the credentials expected of their ESL staff—and a more dismal record for their content-area teachers who serve LEP children. Chapter 5 raised questions about ESL staff positions and the duties associated with those positions and offered guidance in the recruitment of qualified ESL teachers and ancillary personnel. Everyone is a stakeholder, especially in collaborative teaching environments. Balkanized, truncated ESL programs are doomed to fail. Continuous professional development helps avoid the temptation of pursuing the quick fix. Personnel who are well qualified and credentialed for the work they do demonstrate that they like their work and their LEP students and continuously work toward professional improvement on behalf of all students.

Chapter 6 reinforced much of what is well known in education circles: Connecting with parents and the communities works at all levels of the school organization. Language barriers must not result in covertly excluding the parents of LEP students; reaching them simply requires effort. A dedicated ESL manager and the entire school staff demonstrably respect the parents as the LEP student's first teachers and value the parents' rights and responsibilities; they welcome their advisement for the best possible education affordable to their children. Several tools and resources for meeting this challenge were provided in that chapter.

Students of limited English proficiency deserve multiple authentic, unbiased assessments that are valid, reliable, and usable for instruction in their new language and that are appropriate to their performance in content subjects. The shortcomings of traditional testing versus authentic assessments for the LEP student were reviewed in chapter 7. The chapter presented detailed procedures for conducting authentic assessments as they relate to English language acquisition. The ESL manager, in designing and selecting assessments, must remain mindful of the variables the LEP student brings to the testing environment. Culture, learning styles, and multiple intelligences surface as critical considerations.

Does the ESL program work? Is the investment from a small rural school for this new population worth it? Addressing the complex aspects of program evaluation framed the discussion for chapter 8. The ESL program manager must continually review the school district's ESL program as presented in its *Lau* plan. Data connected to demographics, outcomes, and instructional procedures guide program evaluation. Utilization of a wide range of criteria is essential in determining that the instructional approaches of the ESL program used remain worthy of continued implementation. Failing that, a revised *Lau* plan may be in order.

Chapter 9 presented the ESL manager with sources of access to nearly all the human, material, and electronic resources as are needed to ensure that a wide range of appropriate tools supports the ESL program. Departments of education, regional education equity centers, regional educational laboratories, and NCBE were presented as examples of technical assistance outlets that are free of cost to schools limited only by the capacity and jurisdictions of those state or federally supported agencies. The ESL manager was also directed to the wealth of resources accessible via professional organizations, local communities, and the school itself. The Web and several useful sites were offered as incredibly valuable tools to the ESL profession, all of which are easily accessible to the ESL teacher through a telephone modem.

# Acronyms Commonly Used in the ESL Profession

Like most other professions, ESL instruction is engulfed in acronyms as part of its argot. These are listed below.

BINL:      Basic Inventory of Natural Language

BSM:       Bilingual Syntax Measure

BVAT:      Bilingual Verbal Ability Test

CAL:       Center for Applied Linguistics

EEOA:      Equal Educational Opportunities Act (1974)

IASA:      Improving America's Schools Act (1994)

IHE:       institution of higher education (college or university)

IPT:       IDEA Language Proficiency Test

L1:        first language (the first language a student has acquired)

L2:        second language (the second language a student has acquired)

LAB:       Language Assessment Battery

LAS:       Language Assessment Scales

LAS-O:     Language Assessment Scales-Oral

| | |
|---|---|
| LEA: | local education agency (any school district) |
| LITVOL: | Literacy Volunteers |
| MAC: | Maculaitis English Language Proficiency Test |
| NABE: | National Association for Bilingual Education |
| NAME: | National Association for Multicultural Education |
| NCBE: | National Clearinghouse for Bilingual Education |
| OBEMLA: | Office of Bilingual Education and Minority Languages Affairs of the U.S. Department of Education |
| OCR: | Office for Civil Rights of the U.S. Department of Education |
| PET: | pupil evaluation team (specific to special education referrals) |
| PTA: | parent teacher association |
| SEA: | state education agency (a state department of education) |
| SOLOM: | Student Oral Language Observation Matrix |
| TEFL: | teaching English as a foreign language |
| TESL: | teaching English as a second language |
| TESOL: | Teachers of English to Speakers of Other Languages |
| USDE: | U.S. Department of Education |

# Glossary

*Additive bilingualism:* Process by which a student's native language is nurtured to permit the student to acquire English as a second language without losing the native language. Subtractive bilingualism, on the other hand, attempts to phase out the heritage language completely to provide the student with English only. Examples of additive bilingual programs are two-way or developmental bilingual education programs.

*Anecdotal records:* Used as a component of authentic assessments, these are observations of a student's behavior through learning activities, social interaction, and work habits.

*Authentic assessment:* An integrative and comprehensive approach for collecting demographic, outcome, and process data on LEP student learning, particularly as the information relates to the student's acquisition of English and academic subject mastery.

*Basic interpersonal communication skills (BICS):* A component of second language proficiency that usually occurs on an informal level that precedes the more complex skills of cognitive academic language proficiency. If only an oral assessment of a student's skills is taken, the student may appear proficient according to BICS. BICS are less abstract and more concrete than the more demanding cognitive academic language proficiency skills. (See Cognitive academic language proficiency skills [CALPS].) BICS can be acquired in less than 2 years; CALPS require 4–10 years.

*Bilingual education:* A program of instruction that uses more than one language as the medium of instruction.

*Bilingualism:* The ability to communicate in two languages. A balanced bilingual is one who can use both languages equally well. Most bilingual persons prefer one language to the other, depending on the context of the communication.

*Chronic orientation:* Behaviors that are culturally determined that may affect learning, such as attention individuals may display toward the use of time or their management of simultaneous pursuits of activity.

*Cloze procedure:* In this tool used for authentic assessments in reading and writing, the LEP student is given passages from which words have been omitted at regular intervals (i.e., every fifth or sixth or seventh) word, leaving the opening and the last sentences intact. The student's ability to fill in the blanks of omitted words with logical, meaningful terms provides information on the student's ability to use context to infer meaning.

*Cognitive academic language learning approach (CALLA):* Developed by Chamot and O'Malley (1987), CALLA is an intermediate and advanced transition program that permits post-elementary LEP students to acquire greater English fluency and content-area mastery by teaching them unique learning strategies.

*Cognitive academic language proficiency skills (CALPS):* A component of second language proficiency that occurs at the complex higher language acquisition level after the simpler, basic interpersonal communication skills (BICS). According to Collier (1995b), it may take at least 4 and as many as 10 years for an LEP student to reach national grade-level norms of native English speakers in all subject areas of language and academic achievement as measured on standardized tests. The span of time for acquiring CALPS is directly influenced by factors such as (a) age at arrival in a second language culture, (b) amount of uninterrupted schooling in the heritage language, and (c) length of residence. (See Basic interpersonal communication skills [BICS]).

*Comprehensible input:* Understandable messages through which young students acquire the second language as they learn other academic subjects. According to Krashen (1982), such input ensures that the learner understands the communication.

*Content ESL:* An approach to second language teaching that utilizes content-area subject matter to teach language. With contextualized and understandable concepts attached to content-area school subjects, the second language acquisition process is enhanced through content ESL. Concepts and vocabulary may be set at a lower academic level to target the student's level of English proficiency. This approach helps the second language learner maintain the cognitive structures that may have already been developed in the native language. The ESL teacher usually pursues this approach. (See also Specially designed academic instruction in English [SDAIE].)

*Culture-free tests:* Culture-free tests or assessment instruments purport not to discriminate on the basis of a student's non-American culture. Many will agree that culture-free tests do not exist. For example, asking a student who was raised in the rural heartland about skyscrapers may produce an inappropriate response. Testing should measure what is intended to be measured and not a culture-related perceived shortcoming.

*Developmental bilingual education:* See Two-way bilingual education.

*English as a foreign language (EFL):* English taught as a school subject only, usually in a non-English country.

*English as a second language (ESL):* An instructional approach whereby LEP students are placed in regular English-only instruction for most of the day. During part of the day, however, these students receive extra instruction in English. This extra help is based on a curriculum designed almost solely to teach English as a second language. The non-English home language may sometimes be used in conjunction with ESL instruction.

*English for speakers of other languages (ESOL):* Special English language instruction for non-English speakers.

*English for specific purposes (ESP):* Includes technical English for professions, science, or vocational needs.

*English language informants:* See Peer tutors.

*Entry and exit criteria:* Standards developed to define when an LEP student begins or has completed a language support program. Students are enrolled or removed from language support based on an evaluation of whether they will benefit (or are still benefiting) from the language support program to permit them entry in a mainstream program of education with English-only peers.

***ESL pullout:*** Through this kind of instruction, services to LEP children are provided in isolation from the regular curriculum and the mainstream classroom. Instruction is typically one-on-one or in very small groups offered for almost 40 minutes daily. It is the least effective approach short of submersion (which is illegal).

***Fossilization:*** The internalized practice of some bilingual students to continue to use vocabulary and usage incorrectly, even after they would otherwise appear fluent in English—even to themselves. Incorrect forms, as well as accent, are naturally transferred from the native language—a feature of interlanguage.

***Fully English proficient (FEP):*** A language proficiency category that refers to formerly LEP students who become capable of functioning in an English-only educational environment in the skills areas of comprehension, speaking, reading, and writing. FEP students perform at the cognitive academic language proficiency skills (CALPS) level.

***Heritage language:*** The student's native or primary language. See Primary or home language other than English (PHLOTE).

***Home language survey:*** A simple form, administered by school systems, to determine the language spoken at home by a student. Such surveys are often in English and another language. The survey, by itself, does not determine English proficiency.

***IASA Title VII:*** See Title VII of the Improving America's Schools Act.

***Individual learning plan (ILP):*** A process used to define the special language service needs of LEP students. Each student has such a plan developed for him or her. Such a process is analogous to the individual education plan (IEP) developed for students with disabilities.

***Informal reading inventory:*** Part of authentic assessment for reading, this is an individually administered test where the LEP student orally reads a passage from which a prepared word list is derived.

***Input hypothesis:*** A theory that states that language is acquired when the learner understands what he or she hears. According to Krashen (1982) and Cummins (1994), the more the student understands, the more language he or she acquires.

*Interlanguage:* The natural result of the simultaneous interaction of newly acquired language that bilingual individuals produce as they transition to the new language. Given a bilingual individual's two separate language systems, errors are transferred from the first language to the new language as a result of overgeneralizations about elements being transferred. Fossilization, inaccurate syntactic forms, and errors occur with interlanguage.

*I-17:* A form required by the Immigration and Naturalization Service (INS) by foreign nonimmigrants students used to petition that federal agency for approval of attending a U.S. high school.

*Itinerant ESL:* In this type of instruction, one or two periods of English language instruction is given on a "pull out" basis by a teacher who travels to more than one school each day.

*I-20:* The Immigration and Naturalization Service (INS) processes two kinds of I-20 forms for foreign nonimmigrant students wishing to study in U.S. high schools. Form I-20 A–B is a certificate for a student's eligibility to acquire student status to study academics or English in the United States. Form I-20 M–N provides a verification of eligibility for foreign nonimmigrant students seeking vocational student status.

*K-W-L chart:* A chart used to help students access prior knowledge about a particular topic (What I *K*now), ask questions about a topic (What I *W*ant to Know), and record what they learn (What I *L*earned). A K-W-L chart may be done by the class as a group, with the teacher recording the information on a large chart on the chalkboard or on poster paper. This technique is often used to record what students are learning throughout a unit.

*Language assessment committee (LAC):* A group of building or district-level educators whose responsibilities are outlined in the district's *Lau* plan. The committee is generally charged with the task of ensuring that all LEP students are served according to district policy consistent with state and federal statute.

*Language dominance:* The language in which a person is most fluent or most comfortable. Dominance can be determined through testing. It is not unusual to have one language dominant in certain situations and the other language dominant in other situations.

*Language laboratory:* A locale where students can work on individual language needs using specialized equipment, materials, or other technologies to strengthen their ESL skills.

*Language minority students:* Students whose primary or home language is other than English.

*Language process file (LPF):* A tool (e.g., a portfolio) for recording the progress an LEP student is making in academic performance as well as in acquisition of English. The ESL teacher maintains the LPF.

*Language proficiency:* Language fluency skills acquired in one or more languages.

**Lau** *plan:* An equal access plan and policy targeted for language minority youth of a given school district. The plan includes identification of LEP students, an academic program plan for them, and criteria for their ultimate exit from a language support program.

**Lau v. Nichols:** A 1974 U.S. Supreme Court unanimous decision, which upheld Title VI of the Civil Rights Act of 1964 for students of limited English proficiency. The *Lau v. Nichols* decision required school districts to take steps for providing special assistance to LEP students who were unable to benefit from an education conducted primarily in English.

*Limited bilingualism:* Lacking age-appropriate, nativelike competence in either the first or the new language.

*Limited English proficient (LEP):* A descriptor for one who comes from a non-English language background and whose language skills limit that person's ability to function successfully in an all-English classroom. An LEP student is not fluent in all communicative skill areas of English speaking, listening, writing, or reading and cannot compete with peers in an English-only academic setting.

*Limited English-speaking ability (LESA):* Students with a primary language other than English who have difficulty with speaking English.

*May 25th Memorandum:* Guidance issued by the Office for Civil Rights in 1970, which interpreted Title VI of the Civil Rights Act of 1964 to extend or include its protection on the basis of national origin nondiscrimination to students of limited English proficiency.

*Minority:* A mathematical reference to people who collectively make up less than 50% of an identified population. It is frequently cited that those in a minority do not have the same access to wellness and benefits in comparison to others more closely allied or aligned to the majority population.

*Multicultural:* Descriptive of the existence of diverse cultures of a society, region, community, or people.

*National origin:* The origin of a person rooted in a country other than the United States. Title VI of the Civil Rights Act of 1964 prohibits discrimination on the basis of a person's national origin in any program or activity that receives federal financial assistance. Such national origin protection includes limited English proficiency.

*Native language:* The language normally used by an individual, the family, or both at home. Also referred to as the heritage or first language.

*Non-English language background (NELB):* See Primary or home language other than English (PHLOTE).

*Non-English proficient (NEP):* An NEP student has virtually no command of English in the communicative skills areas of speaking, listening, reading, or writing.

*Normed curve equivalent (NCE):* A standard score that has 99 equal intervals. The 50th NCE always corresponds to the 50th percentile; the 1st and 99th NCEs correspond to the 1st and 99th percentile. Because NCEs are equal-interval scores and are the same across different tests, NCEs can be used as a basis for various computations across different tests, as well as within a test.

*Office for Civil Rights (OCR):* The civil rights enforcement arm of the U.S. Department of Education, which is charged with enforcing federal civil rights laws prohibiting discrimination on the basis of race, color, national origin, sex, handicap, and age in services, programs, or activities receiving federal assistance. Through complaint investigations, compliance reviews, and technical assistance, the OCR oversees the education of LEP students in public schools across the United States.

*Oral language proficiency tests:* Oral language proficiency tests measure how well a student is functioning specific to language. Measurement of oral proficiency ranges from informal measures to commercial tests that cover language acquisition skills, ranging from those necessary for conducting basic interpersonal communications to those required for conducting complex activities.

*Out-of-level testing:* Out-of-level testing involves administering a test that is either above or below the level of the test recommended by the publisher as appropriate for the student's age or grade level. Testing out of level allows the administration to give the student a functionally appropriate level of the test, rather than a test that is too hard or too easy. Out-of-level testing may be an appropriate way to use standardized tests with LEP students who may be behind their age/grade peers in order to establish skills already learned. Caution should be exercised in using a test normed in English with students whose home language is other than English. An instrument not designed to test language proficiency must measure only what it purports to measure, rather than the student's proficiency in English.

*Peer tutors:* Non-LEP students who help LEP students in class. This is generally performed by those students who can speak the same native language as the LEP students but who understand English better. Peer tutors are sometimes referred to as English language informants.

*Percentiles:* Percentiles range from 1 to 99 and indicate the percentage of students scoring at or lower than the test score in question. Percentiles describe a student's relative position in relation to the entire group of students who took the same test. For example, a score in the 75th percentile would mean that 75% of the students who took the test scored at or below that point. Percentiles are not equal-interval scales; that is, distance from one percentile to the next is not always the same size. In fact, the distance from one percentile point to the next is very large at the ends of the scale and very close toward the middle. For example, a student who moves from the 28th to the 63rd percentile cannot be compared to the student who moves from the 52nd to the 72nd percentile. Because percentiles are not equal-interval scales, they cannot be added, averaged, or used in other types of computations. See also Standard scores.

*Potentially English proficient (PEP):* This descriptor is a variant of limited English proficient (LEP).

*Primary language:* The first language the student acquired and which he or she normally uses; generally, but not always, the language usually used by the parents of the student. This is frequently referred to as the heritage language.

*Primary or home language other than English (PHLOTE):* This designation identifies a student who comes from a background or home environment where a language other than English is spoken. It does not necessarily mean that the student is limited in English proficiency but that the student is influenced by a language other than English in his or her home environment that may affect English proficiency. PHLOTE designations generally come from home language surveys.

*Proficiency:* Proficiency in conversational English is that which is well developed by native speakers by the time they reach school and is used informally for interpersonal relations. This level of proficiency may not be sufficient to allow LEP students to excel in school subjects. The kind of English proficiency that does relate with school achievement can be referred to as academic English. This is the kind of language skill required for literacy skills, such as decoding meaning from context, study skills, writing mechanics, and vocabulary development. This kind of proficiency is most often measured on norm or criterion-referenced tests of language, reading, writing, and mathematics. See also Cognitive academic language proficiency skills (CALPS).

*Pullout ESL:* See ESL pullout.

*Qualified ESL personnel:* Individuals who have received special training in English language methodology and linguistics with attention to all four communicative language skills—listening, speaking, reading, and writing. In many states, ESL licensures (certification and endorsements) determine such credentials.

*Rubrics:* Often used in conducting authentic assessments, these are fixed scales used to describe what an LEP student can or cannot do. A continuum of four benchmarks is commonly used as a checklist of data on student performance outcomes.

*Sheltered English:* See Content ESL and Specially designed academic instruction in English (SDAIE).

*Specially designed academic instruction in English (SDAIE):* An approach designed for LEP students at the intermediate or advanced level in English acquisition that may utilize some simplification of the English language for subject-area content at a higher academic level than occurs for less fluent students. It is used at the middle to secondary levels. Actual content is the same as that taught to non-LEP students. The content-area teacher, in collaboration with the ESL teacher, provides the instruction.

*Standard scores:* Standard scores are a way to describe the amount by which a student's test score departs from the average. Unlike percentiles, standard scores are equal-interval scores, so one standard score point always represents the same number of raw score points. Because standard scores are equal interval in nature, they can be added, subtracted, multiplied, or used in other types of computations. Not all test publishers use the same standard score system; therefore, they cannot be used to make comparisons across different tests. See also Normed curve equivalent (NCE).

*Structured immersion:* Comparable but dissimilar to sink or swim submersion for the learning of English, structured immersion instruction is also instruction conducted in English but with significant differences. The immersion teacher understands the non-English home language, and students can address the teacher in the non-English language; the submersion teacher, however, generally replies only in English. Furthermore, the curriculum is structured so that prior knowledge of English is not assumed as subjects are taught. Content is introduced in a way that can be understood by the student. The student, in effect, learns the second language and content simultaneously. Most immersion programs also teach the non-English language arts for 30–60 minutes a day. Submersion as an approach for teaching LEP students English is illegal. Structured immersion differs from the transitional bilingual instruction in that the non-English home language is rarely used by the teacher (except where it is a subject), and subject-area instruction is given in the second language from the beginning of the program. Emphasis is on contextual clues with syntax and vocabulary adjusted to a student's level of proficiency. See also Submersion.

*Submersion:* In this type of instruction, LEP students are placed in an ordinary classroom where English is the sole medium for all instruction. There is no supplemental program to help students overcome the barriers to understanding English. The minority home language is not used at all in the classroom. Submersion is aptly described as sink or swim and its approach is illegal.

*Subtractive bilingualism:* The attempt to replace a child's native language with English. By contrast, additive bilingualism describes the attempt to sustain and nurture the heritage language. ESL pullout programs as well as transitional bilingual education programs result in subtractive bilingualism. Two-way or developmental bilingual education programs result in additive bilingualism.

*Threshold hypothesis:* A concept developed by Cummins (1994) that posits that a student who has not had sufficient time to achieve fluency in the first or heritage language will find that learning a new language will be even more difficult.

*Title VI of the Civil Rights Act of 1964:* Passed by Congress, this law prohibits discrimination in education on the basis of race, color, sex, and national origin. The Office for Civil Rights of the U.S. Department of Education is the enforcement agency for implementation of this law that protects LEP students based on their national origin or race.

*Title VII of the Improving America's Schools Act (IASA):* The seventh major section of the Elementary and Secondary Education Act, passed by Congress in 1968 and amended through 1994 under IASA. This law enables bilingual education to be offered to LEP children when there are enough children of the same language background attending the same school. IASA is a federal funding act, not a civil rights enforcement act.

*Transitional bilingual education (TBE):* In TBE, instruction is provided in both the non-English home language and English until the students' second language (English) is fluent enough for them to participate successfully in an English-only classroom. ESL is often used to help minimize the time needed to master English, particularly in the area of reading. Use of the non-English home language for instruction is phased out as English instruction is gradually phased in. TBE is differentiated from ESL by the use of the non-English home language for instruction in subject areas that are less English intensive and by teaching literacy in the non-English language as a school subject.

*Transitionally English proficient (TEP):* A classification reference for students of limited English proficiency indicating a level of English language acquisition that, though limited, is more proficient than that of the non-English proficient student. A TEP student is often in partially mainstreamed classes.

*Tutorial program:* Students in a tutorial program receive one-on-one and small group instruction in English and regular subjects, usually by a paraprofessional. A tutorial program may also be done bilingually. If conducted by unqualified staff, by student peers, or not done as part of an organized system of instruction, it may not pass legal sufficiency by the Office for Civil Rights.

*Two-way bilingual education:* Also called developmental bilingual education, this additive bilingual approach is a maintenance model in which speakers of two languages are placed together in a bilingual classroom to learn each other's language and work academically in both languages.

*Vocational English as a second language (VESL):* Similar to English for specific purposes, VESL targets workforce communication skills.

# Appendix A
# Sample *Lau* Plan From the Heartland Valley School Department

*POLICY:* ENGLISH AS A SECOND LANGUAGE
NEPN/NSBA CODE: XYZ (APPROVED 12-7-00)

It is the policy of the Heartland Valley School Department not to discriminate against limited English proficient (LEP) students. According the Equal Educational Opportunities Act (1974), this district must make an effort to do whatever is educationally appropriate to address the English and educational needs of the LEP student so that he/she can compete with his/her same-age English-background peers. Qualifying students will be identified and placed in programs and services in accordance with statutory guidelines. The Heartland Valley School Department will strive to provide a linguistically and culturally rich learning and teaching environment. It is the policy of the Heartland Valley School Department to comply with all federal and state laws prohibiting discrimination against students on the basis of all civil rights categories.

A language assessment committee (LAC) will be created to coordinate and oversee the educational program of LEP students enrolled in the Heartland Valley School Department. The LAC will be composed of the guidance counselor, building administrators, classroom teacher(s), parents when appropriate, an English as a second language (ESL) teacher, and other ESL consultants who may be involved with the committee on an as-needed basis. The LAC meetings will be scheduled and conducted by the director of school services or an administrator of the Heartland Valley School Department.

The LAC responsibilities will include the following:

- to review the home language surveys to identify potential LEP students who have not already been identified through mandatory special education screening, parent/teacher referral, or LAC surveys
- to annually administer multicriteria evaluations to potential LEP students
- to make decisions from multicriteria evaluations about placement, programming in regards to amount of services, time of delivery of services, and types of programs for LEP students
- to meet quarterly to monitor each student's language and academic progress
- to make recommendations for placement of students and program type for the next school year
- to recommend revisions and additions to the Heartland Valley School Department *Lau* plan for action by its board
- to recommend modification of ESL support services or reclassification of a student from limited English proficiency to full English proficiency
- to carry out annual monitoring for 3 years after an LEP student's reclassification to full English proficiency

To aid in the identification and classification of any student, the following information will be sought:

- student's level of functioning in
  — dominant language of both oral and written language
  — secondary language in both oral and written language
  — relevant subject matter areas in the native language and English
- baseline of student's oral language proficiency in English
- identification of the student's dominant language
- social and educational background information as appropriate

The following instruments may be used to identify LEP students:

- home language surveys
- a review of all relevant educational documents and student records
- standardized achievement or diagnostic test data

- Language Assessment Battery
- Bilingual Syntax Measure
- Basic Inventory of Natural Language
- IDEA Language Proficiency Test
- Language Assessment Scales (LAS and pre-LAS)
- Maculaitis English Language Proficiency Test
- oral language proficiency tests
- teacher observations
- teacher-developed devices (e.g., inventories, cloze tests)

The director of school services will be responsible for maintaining and updating LEP student files. Those files may include all or some of the following:

- results of the multicriteria evaluation
- LAC's placement recommendations
- samples of student's work
- copies of communication between home and school
- documentation of student's academic progress
- summary of program at the time the student exits the ESL program

Resources available to the Heartland Valley School Department and the ESL teacher include the following:

- ESL curriculum materials
- professional library available schoolwide
- library staff and resources
- computer technology
- curriculum materials consistent with state standards
- classroom material and programs consistent with state standards
- parent-teacher association
- publications and resources of the state's department of education
- consultation services from an endorsed ESL teacher
- instructional materials, technical assistance, and in-service training from the state department of education's ESL/BE office
- access to research data, workshops, and listings of local interpreters from the state's Library Information Exchange
- state's Refugee Resettlement Program
- U.S. Department of Education-funded resources (clearinghouse, regional center)
- university's College of Education

The definitions of classifications of proficiency levels for language minority students include

1. *Beginner*

   Through testing, this student would be characterized by being at a non-English proficiency level

   - having no basic (or minimal) interpersonal communication skills
   - having no cognitive academic language proficiency skills
   - beginning to associate sound and meaning, the way that spoken language relates to his or her environment
   - using nonverbal expressions, rather than words, to indicate comprehension
   - relying heavily on contextual clues
   - depending on key words, not the complete utterance, to comprehend the main idea
   - having little or no literacy skills in English (for students in the second grade or older)
   - having little or no receptive vocabulary
   - attempting speech (although elements may be missing and individual words may be mispronounced)
   - developing comprehensive skills
   - having some simultaneous development of literacy readiness skills
   - having oral language that is replete with errors

2. *Intermediate*

   Through testing, this student would be characterized by

   - having limited English proficiency
   - attempting more elaborate speech
   - continuing to make errors and at a greater rate because of more speech production
   - requiring extensive vocabulary development
   - increasing literacy skill development in English
   - developing basic interpersonal communication skills
   - having low cognitive academic language proficiency skills
   - understanding most of the everyday language he or she hears during a typical school day
   - continuing to develop comprehensive skills, especially in order to acquire higher level vocabulary

3. *Advanced*

Through testing, this student would be characterized by

- having a wide range of abilities in the instructional setting, both basic interpersonal communication skills and cognitive academic language proficiency skills (formally and informally)
- having a wide range of literacy skills (for students in the second grade and older)
- requiring further facilitation of vocabulary and development of higher level comprehension
- being almost mainstreamed and requiring less ESL support

4. *High Advanced*

The student would be totally mainstreamed, requiring little or no ESL assistance (except in specialized areas of academic study). The LAC will monitor this student's progress in mainstream classes for up to 3 years.

Time allocations for ESL services may include any of the following:

- Appropriate daily time allotment during school hours, dependent on English proficiency levels. Instruction during all or part of a language intensive class (reading, social studies, language arts) in collaboration with the regular content classroom teacher.
- Appropriate daily time allotment after school hours if requested by the student or parent/guardian. A document of consent signed by the parent/guardian for ESL services after school will be in the student's file and approval will be requested on an annual basis. After-school support is to supplement, not supplant, the language support program of the regular daytime schedule.

## Program Types

There are many types of structured language support programs that the Heartland Valley School Department believes can be beneficial to language minority-LEP children. This district's ability to provide some of these programs depends on both availability of native-language-speaking personnel and availability of instructional materials in students' native language for sheltered English. The keys to an effective and appropriate program choice will include careful consideration of the child's needs, full research into the resources available (personnel, materials), and a full understanding of the possible program configurations.

Some of the likely structured language support programs to be used in this district will include

*English as a second language:* A structured language learning program or curriculum designed to teach English to students whose native language is not English. In low-incidence situations, this instruction may occur through "pull out" from regular English literacy instruction, where students are supported in mainstream subject areas for most of the school day. Services are provided by or supervised by a state-certified teacher endorsed in ESL.

*Sheltered English:* An approach that utilizes the simplification of the English language to teach ESL and subject-area content simultaneously (sometimes called content ESL). Although the actual content is the same as that taught to non-LEP students, key concepts and vocabulary are targeted to fit the ESL student's proficiency level in English.

*Structured immersion:* Instruction for the LEP student is conducted in English in a setting where the teacher understands the student's non-English home language. The student uses the non-English native language with the teacher, who usually responds in English.

A structured language support program encompassing the above models will be provided in a time allocation that will most benefit the ESL learner. The consideration of many factors must take place when a program is being set up. However, the ultimate goal is to provide effective and appropriate services to the student so that he or she may benefit fully from and succeed in an education conducted in English.

The determination of a time allotment for structured language support program will be determined by the LAC with assessment information in hand. The long-term effects of the programmatic decisions must take precedence over the short-term effects (i.e., cost of the services); if a shorter time allotment or time span of services is opted for, it may result in greater difficulties for the child in the mainstream classroom and in his/her accomplishment of academic success. The investment in a quality-structured language support program will be obvious in the broad range of abilities that an ESL student will acquire.

## Grade-Level Placement

Before making a permanent grade-level placement decision for a language minority student, the LAC will need to have pertinent background information about the child. That information would include, as a minimum,

- the child's chronological age
- the child's educational background
- the child's English-language proficiency level
- the child's academic performance

With this information, which should have been collected as expeditiously as possible, the LAC will decide at which grade level the student should be placed. Under no circumstances will a student be placed in a grade level that is more than 1 year below his or her chronological age. Although it may seem logical to place a language minority child at a grade level that matches the kind of English skills he or she needs to acquire, it would be a great disservice to the child both socially and cognitively to do so. The school committee is obligated to provide a structured language support program that meets the ESL as well as content-area needs of the student.

If the student is at the low end of the English-language-proficiency spectrum, the necessary ESL services will probably focus on survival skills and basic communication regardless of the child's grade level. Even though the focus of the program at that time is on basic interpersonal cognitive skills, the school has the obligation to assist that child in learning the content-area information that has been taught in earlier grades.

Regarding the issue of grade-level retention, on the whole, retention is only advisable when a language minority student is lagging behind peers socially and emotionally (and even that may not be appropriate). It stands to reason that a language minority-LEP child will not be on grade level academically until he or she has had the opportunity to acquire the English skills and content necessary for academic success. It is not appropriate to retain an LEP child solely for the reason of limited English proficiency because the child has unique needs and must be given ample time from grade level to grade level to acquire English proficiency. The school committee accepts the research findings that the acquisition of a second language for cognitive/academic proficiency can take from 4 to 10 years under optimal circumstances.

The most advantageous way to avoid grade-level retention is to make accommodations for the LEP child in the mainstream classroom and to maintain a close collaborative relationship between the mainstream and ESL programs. If an LEP child is referred for retention, the LAC should be included in that process to ensure that language proficiency is not the sole reason for the referral.

## Teacher Skills

Just as with any other teaching field, ESL teachers in this district will require special training to provide the best services for our LEP students. Our state has an ESL endorsement for teachers. It requires 15 semester hours of course work in five cluster areas:

1.  ESL methods
2.  ESL curriculum
3.  ESL assessment
4.  language acquisition
5.  culture

Our structured language support services can be provided in two personnel staffing configurations:

1.  An ESL-endorsed teacher provides direct ESL instruction.
2.  A paraprofessional or non-ESL endorsed teacher provides direct ESL instruction and is supervised and guided by an ESL-endorsed teacher.

The presence of an ESL-endorsed professional is imperative for an effective and appropriate program to be implemented. In opting for the recommended configuration, one must realize that if a paraprofessional or non-ESL endorsed teacher is engaged to provide direct services, that person must still participate in training in ESL, though it might be less formal.

Acceptable and desirable qualifications for ESL tutors (education technicians) who do not possess an endorsement would be

- experience in a second language setting
- experience in a non-English speaking culture
- experience working effectively with children in an instructional setting
- a knowledge of instructional methods for communication skills and content areas
- a working knowledge of ESL, second language acquisition, and LEP students

## Exit and Reclassification Criteria

If a structured language support program is effective and appropriate and the ESL student is adequately receptive, there will come a time when the student is ready to be (a) reclassified at a higher level of proficiency or (b) exited from the structured language support program entirely. Any member of the LAC, the parents, or the child may recommend reclassification or exit.

Once the recommendation has been made for reclassification or exit, an evaluation process and a review of records will be undertaken. The evaluation criteria and review of records are similar to those implemented in the entry criteria with one very crucial exception: the comparability of the student to his or her mainstream peers and the likelihood/predictability of academic success in the totally mainstreamed instructional setting. This range of criteria will be identifiable in the student's scores on a standardized achievement test normed on fluent English-proficient children, a portfolio of the student's literacy work, observations of the student in both formal and informal settings, teacher observations, and interviews with the child and parent(s)/guardian(s). The compilation of this information would necessarily bear out the viability of a recommendation for reclassification or exit.

The criteria would include a cutoff score for the standardized achievement test to determine the child's ability to compete with monolingual English-speaking peers. If the child has difficulty taking standardized achievement tests, the LAC may set up an alternative test-taking situation.

When the student is found to be eligible for reclassification or exit, the LAC will monitor the child's academic performance and psychosocial well-being after the placement is made. In the case of a student who is reclassified, the decreased ESL instructional time should be monitored in terms of continued academic success, adjustment to a longer time period in the mainstream classroom, and instructional needs being met in the structured language support program. In the case of a student's exit from the program, the full mainstreaming should be monitored for academic success, adjustment to the full-time mainstream classroom, and any gaps in language skills that may appear after the mainstreaming.

After a student has been exited from a structured language support program, that child's language performance and growth must be monitored for 3 years (if the child is still in school). This could be done in the regularly scheduled LAC meetings. At any time during those 3 years, if the student experiences a pattern of difficulty with language or content skills, the LAC can re-enter the child into an appropriately structured language support program.

In the monitoring process, the LAC members would be considering criteria similar to those considered in the exit criteria.

## Program Evaluation

To ensure the most effective and appropriate programming of structured language support for LEP children, a model for overall program evaluation must be developed and utilized. An annual program evaluation will illustrate attainment of program outcomes, attainment of learner outcomes, school climate and support for the program and children, the quality of instructional materials, the maintenance of information about students, the effectiveness of staff development activities, the amount and effectiveness of mainstream-ESL collaboration, the effectiveness of school and program communication with parents, and the implementation of the *Lau* plan itself.

The program accountability and demonstration of outcomes will enhance the program's legitimacy in the school and will consummate the work and methods of the program toward the ultimate goal of continually improving instruction to meet learner instructional needs.

## Caveats

The three circumstances noted below could present themselves. The policy of the school committee is duly noted for each situation.

1.  Although language minority students may be eligible for Improving America's Schools Act (IASA) Title I services under the same criteria as other children, other students may receive those services as well. Title I services cannot supplant structured language support services (such as ESL).

2.  Limited English proficiency is not a disability as defined by the Americans With Disabilities Act of 1994 and state special education regulations. If a language minority child is referred for a special education evaluation, a culturally and linguistically nonbiased evaluation must comply with state and federal regulations. An assessment of the child's native language skills as soon as possible after the child is enrolled in school is advisable so that any significant problems can be identified and noted for future references.

3.  In the event that a parent/guardian refuses ESL services for his or her child, a signed letter of refusal will be placed in the student's file. These ESL services will be offered yearly, and a letter of refusal must be signed annually. The parent may withdraw refusal of services at any time.

# Heartland Valley *Lau* Plan

## *Parent Home Language Survey and Questionnaire\**

(available in languages other than English)

Parent/Guardian

Name: _____ Relationship: _____

Student's Name: _____

Grade: _____ Teachers: _____

SURVEY: Part I—Please circle your answers.

1. Is English the primary language of your child?                    Yes    No
2. Is English the primary language of the parents?               Yes    No
3. Is English the only language spoken in your home?         Yes    No
4. Has English been used exclusively by all caregivers
   of your child including grandparents, other relatives,
   and babysitters?                                                              Yes    No

Parent/Guardian

Signature _____ Date _____

**\*\*\*\*\*\*\*\*\*\*\*\*\*\*\*\*\*\*\*\*\*\*\*\*\*\*\*\*\*\*\*\*\*\*\*\*\*\*\*\*\*\*\*\*\*\*\*\*\*\*\*\*\*\*\*\*\*\*\*\*\*\*\*\*\*\*\*\*\*\*\*\*\*\*\*\*\*\*\*\***

If any answers for Part I were "No," please fill out the rest of the form, sign it, and return it to your child's teacher.

QUESTIONNAIRE: Part II

1. From what country or part of the United States did your family come?

   _____

2. What language(s) does the father speak?

   _____

3. What language(s) does he read or write?

   _____

4. What language(s) does the mother speak?

   _____

\*To be sent to the homes of all students newly entering Heartland Valley School District. A cover letter rendered in the parents' language and English will be attached.

5. What language(s) does she read or write?

   _____

6. When did the parents come to the United States?

   _____

7. How long have they lived and worked here?

   _____

8. In what country was the child born?

   _____

9. When did the child come to the United States?

   _____

10. How long has the child lived here?

   _____

11. If the child has traveled back and forth to the United States, please explain:

   _____

12. What language or languages do you speak to your child?

   _____

13. How frequently do you speak to your child?
    ____ a. Under 10 hours a week
    ____ b. 10–20 hours a week
    ____ c. 20–30 hours a week
    ____ d. 30–40 hours a week
    ____ e. More than 40 hours a week

14. What language or languages does the child speak to you?

   _____

15. What language or languages does the child speak with friends?

   _____

16. What language or languages does the child speak with brothers and sisters?

   _____

17. If there are grandparents in the home, what language do they use with your child?

   _____

18. Are there any other relatives or babysitters who speak a language other than English with your child?
    ____ Yes    ____ No
    What language do they use?_____

Thank you for taking the time to carefully complete this form. This information is useful to us in providing the best possible education for your child.

Parent/Guardian
Signature _____ Date _____

# Heartland Valley *Lau* Plan

## *English as a Second Language Student Plan*

*Identifying Information*

Student Name:_____School_____

Birthdate:_____School Year_____Grade_____

*Tests Administered:*

*Summary of Results:*

*Recommendations/Strategies:*

*Methods of Evaluation:*

*The Need for Continued Services Will Be Evaluated in the Month of*
_____

*Date of Program Review:*_____

*Participants in Plan Development*

| *Name* | *Role* |
| --- | --- |
| _____ | _____ |
| _____ | _____ |
| _____ | _____ |
| _____ | _____ |
| _____ | _____ |

This plan is developed for the purpose of ensuring continued student progress with English and content-area subjects. Its intent is to further ensure continuity in the programs of former LEP students who have previously received special services. The plan will be reviewed on the specified review date above or sooner if requested by the parents or school staff.

# Heartland Valley *Lau* Plan

*Request for Approval of District Funds for LEP Students*

Student's Name_____Date of Birth:_____

School:_____Grade:_____

Native Language:_____Home Language:_____

Mother/Stepmother/Guardian:_____

Address:_____Phone Number:_____

Father/Stepfather/Guardian:_____

Address:_____Phone Number:_____

Former Address of Student:_____

Service(s) Requested:_____

The above named ESL student was referred by the Language Assessment Committee as a result of a committee meeting, involving the parents, held on _____

(date)

The committee notified the superintendent of schools of its action on

_____

(date)

Comments (e.g., estimated cost, length of service, service provider and/or agency) _____

_____

Attachments: Copies of all test reports documenting student needs for ESL services.

_____

(Signature of Person Completing Form/Date)

_____

(Building Principal/Date)

_____

(Superintendent of Schools/Date)

cc:    (as necessary)
       Parent
       Cumulative Record
       Superintendent of Schools

# Appendix B
# CALLA Sample Lesson: Using Prepositions in Giving and Following Directions

*Language: ESL/Social Studies Content Area*

*Language Level: Intermediate*

*Grade Level: Middle School*

*Focus Language Learning Strategy: Elaboration; Making Inferences*

*Language Objective*

Use prepositions in giving and following directions; ask questions for clarification.

*Strategy Objective*

Use elaboration to expand on existing knowledge; identify resources.

## Strategy Rationale

The state standard at this level requires that the student can demonstrate giving and following directions. Elaboration will involve expanding on existing knowledge of cross-country travel; identification of resources will involve using items such as train and bus schedules and contacting travel agents.

## Materials

A U.S. geography text and a wall map of the United States will be needed to help students in giving directions. A flip chart or blackboard and markers are needed to chart students' responses from brainstorming and to note their use of prepositions. Blindfolds will be needed for one of the practice activities.

## Procedures

### Preparation

1. Brainstorm with the students places in the United States where they have traveled, and list these places on a flip chart or blackboard.
2. Ask the students, "Where would you like to travel in the United States and how would you get there?"
   (This two-part question goes on two columns.)

### Presentation

1. Highlight the prepositions used above in Column 2.
2. Present elaboration by asking for student responses to the highlighted words in the above presentation (e.g., to New York, to California).
3. Ask the students, "How would I find _____ ( e.g., New York, California)?" and steer the students toward prepositions (e.g., *west* to California, *near* Pennsylvania).
4. Present the strategy of a language rule (i.e., a rule of syntax as in preposition placement in sentences) to show the direction of something or somewhere; one cannot avoid prepositions. Demonstrate how prepositions are used in sentences. Solicit more examples of giving directions.

*Practice*

1. Have students repeat Question 3 in the presentation above in pairs, and ask them to record the prepositions used.
2. Have students use prepositions to direct each other to various points or objects in the room. They are to record the prepositions they use. They could be challenged with a blindfold, which would effectively force the use of more prepositions (e.g., proceed *near* the desk, go *around* the door, move *behind* the basket, you will find it *on* the other side).
3. Have one student record the prepositions and a language rule that was used to identify them.

*Evaluation*

Review students' lists of phrases and the rules suggested by their use from the practice above, noting correct identification of prepositions, and return the list with teacher comments to the students. Ask students if using these language rules helps them understand how to identify and use prepositions. Seek their feedback about the correctness of their work or their need to make changes to their work.

*Expansion*

1. Ask the students, "Did giving directions as you have done help you to understand prepositions? Did prepositions such as *near*, *behind*, and *on* help you understand directions more easily?"
2. Have students ask this question in pairs, "What are some of the ways I could travel there?" Or this variation, "If you have to travel far away, how you would get there?"

   This question is different in that it will seek more prepositions but in the context of resource usage (e.g., on a bus, with the help of a map, or through a travel agent). Seek elaboration on how the students identified the prepositions used.

# Appendix C
# Using Evaluation Data to Support Instructional Improvement

## 1. Qualified Staff and Professional Development

| Demographic Information | Outcome Information | Process Variables |
| --- | --- | --- |
| Identification of certified, endorsed ESL teachers | Teacher goals/expectations | Selection of staff for training (including paraprofessionals) |
| Identification of volunteers | Professional development aligned to need | Staff collaboration in professional development |
| ESL teacher experience (years; areas of study) | Level of implementation of staff training | Quality of staff training |
| Number of sessions attended by staff | Staff evaluation of training events | Preservice training design |
| Topics and agendas for staff training | Training implementation/ practice and follow-up | Staff development collaboratives |
| Documentation of frequency of volunteerism | | Curriculum development collaboratives |
| Identification of comprehensive training models (e.g., methods, culture, second language theory course work) | | |

## 2. Standards-Driven Program Design

| Demographic Information | Outcome Information | Process Variables |
|---|---|---|
| Up-to-date *Lau* plan in place | Identification and reporting of student completion rates (e.g., dropout, promotion, retention, graduation) | Curriculum aligned with state/local/TESOL standards |
| Comprehensive record keeping of referrals for discipline | Achievement data from multiple, authentic assessments and state assessment requirements | Curriculum aligned with authentic assessments |
| Roster of extracurricular activity participation | | Sound instruction grounded in respectable research and promising practices |
| Listing of accessible interpreters | Interpretation of LEP student performance after program exit | Content and ESL teacher collaboratives (minimal pullout for ESL) |
| Identification of coordinated LEP student services with gifted and talented, special needs, and migratory students | Documentation of process for reporting LEP student progress to parents | Informed LAC decision-making procedures consistent with district's *Lau* plan |

## 3. ESL Program Implementation

| *Demographic Information* | *Outcome Information* | *Process Variables* |
|---|---|---|
| Collection of socioeconomic data of LEP students served | Monitoring of student activities provided by paraprofessionals, peer, and cross-age tutors | Classroom coteaching and peer coaching |
| Identification of language proficiency level for student progression from LEP to FEP | Multiple, authentic assessments used to improve instruction | Ongoing LAC reviews of student's LPF |
| | | Evidence of *Lau* plan criteria for student exit from ESL program |
| Accessibility of job and skill descriptions of volunteers and ancillary staff | Differentiation of BICS and CALPS assessments | Comparability of LEP students to non-LEP students for accessibility to special services, applied technologies, migratory programs, gifted and talented, and Title I |
| | Determination of student fluency in native language and in English | |
| Adequacy of record keeping of assessment results (formal/informal) for accountability | Determination of impact of student's previous education background on current progress | |
| Learning progress (i.e., monitoring) report to continue for 2 years following exit from ESL program services | Student admission to postsecondary education (e.g., college, workforce training, military) | Team-based referrals (including LAC) of LEP students to special services (if applicable) |
| | | Using culture-fair testing in the student's stronger language |
| Additional factors contributing to decision making | Communication with stakeholders of degree to which LEP student has attained achievement outcomes | Other efforts the school may use to promote high levels of student performance |

# References

Adger, C. T., & Peyton, J. K. (1999). Enhancing the education of immigrant students in secondary school: Structural challenges and directions. In C. Faltis & P. Wolfe (Eds.), *So much to say: Adolescents, bilingualism, and ESL in secondary school* (pp. 205–224). New York: Teachers College Press.

Arlington Public Schools. (1992). *ESOL high-intensity language training.* Arlington, VA: Author.

August, D., & Hakuta, K. (Eds.). (1998). *Educating language minority children.* Washington, DC: National Academy Press.

August, D., Hakuta, K., Olguin, F., & Pompa, D. (1995). *LEP students and Title I: A guidebook for educators* (NCBE Resource Collection Series). Washington, DC: National Clearinghouse for Bilingual Education.

August, D., & Pease-Alvarez, L. (1996). *Attributes of effective programs and classrooms serving English language learners.* Santa Cruz, CA: National Center for Research on Cultural Diversity and Second Language Learning.

Bennett, B. (1995). *Pen 102: Why don't they understand?* Newtown, Canada: Primary English Teaching Association.

Bérubé, B. (1992). An invitation to the dance: From dragons to wolves. *Community Education Journal, 19*(4), 20–21.

Bérubé, B. (1998). Two polyglots, three languages. *The Bilingual Family Newsletter, 15*(2), 20–21.

Bérubé, B., & Delgado, M. (1985). Government context of the bilingual program: National and state. In G. P. De George (Ed.), *Bilingual program management: A problem-solving approach* (pp. 127–149). Cambridge, MA: Lesley College Evaluation, Dissemination, and Assistance Center.

Bialystok, E. (1997). Effects of bilingualism and biliteracy on children's emerging concepts of print. *Developmental Psychology, 33*(3), 429–440.

Blair, J. (1999, May 26). OCR issues revised guidance on high-stakes testing. *Education Week*, p. 5.

Bouchard, D. L. (1995). *What matters in building an effective ESL program: A guide for ESL program evaluation.* Unpublished manuscript, Maine Department of Education.

Brown, H. D. (1994). *Principles of language learning and teaching.* Englewood Cliffs, NJ: Prentice-Hall Regents.

Burkhart, G. S., & Sheppard, K. (n.d.). Guidelines: Evaluating assessment. In *A descriptive study of content ESL practices.* Retrieved August 3, 2000, from the World Wide Web: http://www.ncbe.gwu.edu/miscpubs/cal/contentesl /c-esl8.htm.

Canales, J. (1992). Innovative practices in the identification of LEP students. In *Proceedings of the Second National Research Symposium on LEP Student Issues: Focus on evaluation and measurement.* Washington, DC: U.S. Department of Education.

Cantoni-Harvey, G. (1987). *Content-area instruction: Approaches and strategies.* Reading, MA: Addison-Wesley.

Carrell, P., & Eisterhold, J. (1988). Schema theory and ESL reading pedagogy. In P. Carrell, J. Devine, & D. Eskey (Eds.), *Interactive approaches to second language reading* (pp. 73–99). New York: Cambridge.

Casteñada v. Pickard, 648 F.2d 989 (5th Cir. 1981).

Center for Applied Linguistics (CAL). (2000). *Mission statement.* Retrieved August 3, 2000, from the World Wide Web: http://www.cal.org/public /about.htm.

Center for Equity and Excellence in Education. (1996). *Promoting excellence: Ensuring academic success for limited English proficient students.* Arlington, VA: Author.

Center for Research on Education, Diversity & Excellence (CREDE) Registrar. (1997). *Mission statement.* Retrieved July 11, 2000, from the World Wide Web: http://lmrinet.gse.ucsb.edu/crede/crede.htm.

Chamot, A. U. (1992, November). *Changing instruction for language minority students to achieve national goals.* Paper presented at the Third National Symposium on Limited English Proficient Student Issues, Washington, DC. Retrieved July 10, 2000, from the World Wide Web: http://www .ncbe.gwu.edu/ncbepubs/symposia/third/chamot.htm.

Chamot, A. U., Barnhardt, S., El-Dinary, P. B., & Robbins, J. (1999). *The learning strategies handbook.* New York: Addison-Wesley.

Chamot, A. U., & O'Malley, J. M. (1987). The cognitive academic language learning approach: A bridge to the mainstream. *TESOL Quarterly, 21,* 227–233.

Cintron v. Brentwood Union Free School District, 455 F. Supp. 57 (E.D. N.Y. 1978).

Civil Rights Act of 1964, Title VI, 42 U.S.C. § 2000d; 34 C.F.R. Part 100 §§ 100.3, 100.7.

Collier, V. P. (1987/1988, Winter). The effect of age on acquisition of a second language for school. *New Focus: Occasional Papers in Bilingual Education* (No. 2). Retrieved July 11, 2000, from the World Wide Web: http://www.ncbe.gwu.edu/ncbepubs/classics/focus/02aage.htm.

Collier, V. P. (1995a). Acquiring a second language for school. *Directions in Language and Education, 1*(4). Retrieved October 20, 2000, from the World Wide Web: http://www.ncbe.gwu.edu/ncbepubs/directions/04.htm.

Collier, V. P. (1995b). *Promoting academic success for ESL students: Understanding second language acquisition for school.* Alexandria, VA: TESOL.

Collier, V. P., & Thomas, W. P. (1999, October/November). Making schools effective for English language learners, part 2. *TESOL Matters*, p. 1.

Cornell, C. (1995). Reducing failure of limited English proficient students in the mainstream classroom and why it is important. *Journal of Educational Issues of Language Minority Students, 15.* Retrieved July 31, 2000, from the World Wide Web: http://www.ncbe.gwu.edu/miscpubs/jeilms/vol15/reducing.htm.

Council of Chief State School Officers. (2000). *Ensuring accuracy in testing for English language learners: A practical guide for assessment.* Washington, DC: Author.

Crawford, J. (1997). *Best evidence: Research foundations of the Bilingual Education Act.* Washington, DC: National Clearinghouse for Bilingual Education.

Crookes, G., & Arakaki, L. (1999). Teaching idea sources and work conditions in an ESL program. *TESOL Journal, 8*(1), 15–19.

Cullum, A. (1971). *The geranium on the windowsill just died but teacher you went right on.* London, England: Harlin Quist.

Cummins, J. (1994). The acquisition of English as a second language. In K. Spangenberg-Urbschat & R. Pritchard (Eds.), *Kids come in all languages: Reading, instruction for ESL students* (pp. 36–62). Newark, DE: International Reading Association.

Cummins, J., & Swain, M. (1986). *Bilingualism in education: Aspects of theory, research, and practice.* Harlow, England: Longman.

Del Vecchio, A., & Guerrero, M. (1995). *Handbook of English language proficiency tests.* Albuquerque, NM: Evaluation Assistance Center-Western Region. Retrieved August 2, 2000, from the World Wide Web: http://www.ncbe.gwu.edu/miscpubs/eacwest/elptests.htm.

Enright, D. S., & McCloskey, M. (1988). *Integrating English*. Reading, MA: Addison-Wesley.

Equal Educational Opportunities Act, 20 U.S.C. § 1703(a)–(f) (1974).

ERIC. (1990). *Success stories: A case study of bilingual/ESL evaluation*. Retrieved August 3, 2000, from the World Wide Web: http://ericae.net/ericdb /ED333746.htm.

Evaluation Assistance Center-Western Region. (1996). *Identifying limited English proficient students*. Albuquerque, NM: Author. Retrieved August 2, 2000, from the World Wide Web: http://www.ncbe.gwu.edu/miscpubs /eacwest/handouts/id-lep/backgrnd.htm.

Fadiman, A. (1999). *The spirit catches you and you fall down*. New York: Noonday Press.

Finn, C. E., Jr., Petrilli, M., & Vanourek, G. (1998). *The state of state standards*. Washington, DC: Thomas Ford Foundation. Retrieved August 7, 2000, from the World Wide Web: http://www.edexcellence.net/standards /summary.html.

Fleischman, H. L., & Hopstock, P. J. (1993). *Descriptive study of services to limited English proficient students: Volume 1, summary of findings and conclusions*. Arlington, VA: Development Associates, Inc.

Flemming, D., Germer, L., & Kelley, C. (1993). *All things to all people*. Alexandria, VA: TESOL.

Forgione, P.D. (1999). *Teacher quality: A report on the preparation and qualifications of public school teachers*. Speech at the U.S. Department of Education, Washington, DC.

Freeman, Y. S., & Freeman, D. E. (1992). *Whole language for second language learners*. Portsmouth, NH: Heinemann.

Freeman, Y. S., & Freeman, D. E. (1998). *Teaching: Principles for success*. Portsmouth, NH: Heinemann.

Garcia, A., & Morgan, C. (1997). *A 50 state survey of requirements for the education of language minority children* [Abstract]. Washington, DC: READ Institute. Retrieved July 26, 2000, from the World Wide Web: http:// www.read-institute.org/50state.html.

Gardner, H. (1999). *Intelligence reframed: Multiple intelligences for the 21st century*. New York: Basic Books.

Golden, J. (1994). *Professional tutor's handbook for multilingual students*. Aurora: CO: Project TALK.

Grove City College v. Bell, 465 U.S. 555 (1984).

Guskey, T. R. (1998). The age of our accountability. *Journal of Staff Development, 19*(4), 36–44.

Haas, T., & Nachtigal, P. (1998). *Place value*. Charleston, WV: Clearinghouse on Rural Education and Small Schools.

Hakuta, K., Butler, Y., & Witt, D. (2000, January). *How long does it take English learners to attain proficiency?* (Policy Report 2000-1). Santa Barbara, CA: University of California Linguistic Minority Research Institute.

Hamayan, E. (1990). Preparing mainstream classroom teachers to teach potentially English proficient students. In *Proceedings of the First Research Symposium on Limited English Proficient Student Issues*. Retrieved July 31, 2000, from the World Wide Web: http://www.ncbe.gwu.edu/ncbepubs /symposia/first/preparing.htm.

Hamayan, E., & Perlman, R. (1990). Helping language minority students after they exit from bilingual/ESL programs: A handbook for teachers. *NCBE Program Information Guide Series*, (No. 1). Retrieved August 7, 2000, from the World Wide Web: http://www.ncbe.gwu.edu/ncbepubs/pigs /pig1.htm.

Hargett, G. (1998). *Assessment in ESL and bilingual education: A hot topics paper*. Portland, OR: Northwest Regional Educational Laboratory. Retrieved August 2, 2000, from the World Wide Web: http://www.nwrac.org/pub /hot/assessment.html.

Haynes, J., & O'Loughlin, J. (1999, June/July). Meeting the challenge of content instruction in K–8 classroom: Part 1 and part 2. *TESOL Matters*. Retrieved July 31, 2000, from the World Wide Web: http://www.tesol.org /isaffil/intsec/columns/199904-ee.html (Part 1) and http://www.tesol.org /isaffil/intsec/columns/199906-ee.html (Part 2).

*Helping parents and children understand each other in their new life in the United States*. (2000). New York: International Catholic Child Bureau. Retrieved August 1, 2000, from the World Wide Web: http://www.eric-web.tc .columbia.edu/families/refugees/tacoma.html.

Hughes, A. (1989). *Testing for language teachers*. New York: Cambridge University Press.

Idaho Migrant Council v. Board of Education. 647 F.2d 69 (9th Cir. 1981).

Igoa, C. (1995). *The inner world of the immigrant child*. Mahurah, NJ: Lawrence Erlbaum Associates.

Improving America's Schools Act of 1994, 20 U.S.C. § 7501.

Intercultural Development Research Association. (1998). *Resource links: Parent, family, and community involvement*. San Antonio, TX: Author. Retrieved June 13, 2000, from the World Wide Web: http://www.idra.org/Links .Links.htm.

Jerald, C. D. (2000). *Quality counts 2000: Who shall teach*. Retrieved June 8,

2000, from the World Wide Web: http://edweek.com/sreports/qc00/tables/gradesum-t1b.htm.

Jolly, E., Hampton, E., & Guzman, W. (1999). *Bridging homes and schools: Tools for family involvement in multilingual communities.* Dubuque, IA: Kendall/Hunt.

Kagan, S. (1985). *Cooperative learning resources for teachers.* San Juan Capistrano, CA: Resources for Teachers.

Keller, B. (1999, February 24). Report calls for more minority superintendents. *Education Week on the Web.* Retrieved July 27, 2000, from the World Wide Web: http://www.edweek.org/ew/1999/24iel.h18.

Krashen, S. D. (1982). *Principles and practice in second language acquisition.* New York: Pergamon Press.

Krashen, S. D. (1999). *Three arguments against whole language and why they are wrong.* Portsmouth, NH: Heinemann.

Lachat, M. (1997). *What policymakers and school administrators need to know about assessment reform and English language learners.* Providence, RI: Northeast and Islands Regional Educational Laboratory at Brown University.

Lau v. Nichols, 414 U.S. 566 (1974).

Lazear, D. (1999). *Eight ways of knowing: Teaching for multiple intelligences* (3rd ed.). Arlington Heights, IL: Skylight Training and Publishing.

Macías, R. (1996). *Summary report of the survey of the states' limited English proficient students and available educational programs and services, 1994–95.* Washington, DC: National Clearinghouse for Bilingual Education.

Macías, R. (1998a). *Summary report of the survey of the states' limited English proficient students and available educational programs and services, 1995–96.* Washington, DC: National Clearinghouse for Bilingual Education.

Macías, R. (1998b). *Summary report of the survey of the states' limited English proficient students and available educational programs and services, 1996–97.* Washington, DC: National Clearinghouse for Bilingual Education.

McCollum, H., & Russo, A. (1993a). Introduction to model strategies in bilingual education. In *Model strategies in bilingual education: Family literacy and parental involvement.* Washington, DC: U.S. Department of Education. Retrieved August 1, 2000, from the World Wide Web: http://www.ncbe.gwu.edu/miscpubs/used/familylit/approach.htm.

McCollum, H., & Russo, A. (1993b). Profile 8: Florida International University Family Literacy Project. In *Model strategies in bilingual education: Family literacy and parental involvement.* Washington, DC: U.S. Department of Education. Retrieved August 1, 2000, from the World Wide Web: http://www.ncbe.gwu.edu/miscpubs/used/familylit/profile8.htm.

McGee, P., & Fradd, S. (1997). *Instructional assessment: An integrative approach to evaluating student performance.* Reading, MA: Addison-Wesley.

McKeon, D., & Malarz, L. (1991). School-based management: What bilingual and ESL program directors should know. *NCBE Program Information Guide Series,* (No. 5). Retrieved August 1, 2000, from the World Wide Web: http://www.ncbe.gwu.edu/ncbepubs/pigs/pig5.html.

McKnight, A., & Antunez, B. (1999). *State survey of legislative requirements for educating limited English proficient students.* Washington, DC: National Clearinghouse for Bilingual Education.

Meier, D. (1995). *The power of their ideas: Lessons from a small school in Harlem.* Boston, MA: Beacon Press.

Meloni, C. (1998, January/February). Listservs serve ESL/EFL professionals. *TESOL Matters,* p. 19.

Meloni, C. (2000). Wandering the Web dot.com. *TESOL Matters.* Retrieved August 17, 2000, from the World Wide Web: http://www.tesol.org/pubs /magz/wanweb/wanweb0002.html.

Merino, B., & Rumberger, R. (1999, Spring). Why ELD standards are needed for English learners. *University of California Linguistic Minority Institute Newsletter, 8,* 1.

Mingucci, M. (1999, April/May). Action research in ESL staff development. *TESOL Matters,* p. 60.

Mohan, B. A. 1986. *Language and content.* Reading, MA: Addison-Wesley.

National Center for Education Statistics. (1996). *Schools and staffing survey in the U.S.: A statistical profile, 1993–94.* Washington, DC: U.S. Department of Education.

National Center for Education Statistics. (1997a). *The condition of education 1997.* Washington, DC: U.S. Department of Education. Retrieved July 18, 2000, from the World Wide Web: http://www.nces.ed.gov/pubs/ce /c9745c01.html.

National Center for Education Statistics. (1997b). *Public and private school principals in the United States: A statistical profile, 1987–88 to 1993–94.* Washington, DC: U.S. Department of Education. Retrieved July 18, 2000, from the World Wide Web: http://www.nces.ed.gov/pubs/ppsp/97455-2.html.

National Center for Education Statistics. (1998). *The condition of education 1998.* Washington, DC: U.S. Department of Education. Retrieved July 18, 2000, from the World Wide Web: http://www.nces.ed.gov/pubs98/condition98.

National Clearinghouse for Bilingual Education. (1999). *United States data on the LEP student population.* Washington, DC: Office of Bilingual Education and Minority Languages Affairs.

National Clearinghouse for Bilingual Education. (2000). *Teacher education programs in the U.S.: Bilingual & ESL.* Washington, DC: National Clearinghouse for Bilingual Education. Retrieved July 31, 2000, from the World Wide Web: http://www.ncbe.gwu.edu/links/teachered/index.htm.

National Education Association. (1997). *Status of the American public school teacher, 1995–96 highlights.* Retrieved July 27, 2000, from the World Wide Web: http://www.nea.org/nr/nr970702.html.

National Education Goals Panel. (2000). *1999 key findings.* Retrieved July 26, 2000, from the World Wide Web: http://www.negp.gov/page7-9.htm.

North Central Regional Educational Laboratory. (2000). *Critical issues in parent and family involvement.* Oak Brook, IL: Author. Retrieved August 1, 2000, from the World Wide Web: http://www.ncrel.org/sdrs/areas/pa0cont.htm.

O'Donnell, M. P., & Wood, M. (1992). *Becoming a reader: A developmental approach to reading instruction.* Boston, MA: Allyn & Bacon.

Office for Civil Rights. (1991). *Provision of equal educational opportunities to national origin minority and Native American students who are limited English proficient.* Washington, DC: U.S. Department of Education.

Office for Civil Rights. (1999). *Programs for English language learners: Resource materials for planning and self-assessments.* Washington, DC: U.S. Department of Education. Retrieved July 31, 2000, from the World Wide Web: http://www.ed.gov/offices/OCR/ELL/index.html.

Office of Bilingual Education and Minority Languages Affairs. (1995). *Digest of education statistics for limited English proficient students.* Washington, DC: U.S. Department of Education.

O'Malley, J. M., & Valdez-Pierce, L. (1996). *Authentic assessment for English language learners: Practical approaches for teachers.* New York: Addison-Wesley.

Plyler v. Doe, 457 U.S. 202 (1982).

Pottinger, J. S. (1970, May 25). *Identification of discrimination and denial of services on the basis of national origin* [Memorandum]. Washington, DC: U.S. Department of Health, Education and Welfare. Retrieved August 1, 2000, from the World Wide Web: http://www.ed.gov/offices/OCR/ELL/may25.html.

Rennie, J. (1998, December). Education reform and language minority students. *ERIC/CLL Minibib.* Retrieved July 26, 2000, from the World Wide Web: http://www.cal.org/ericcll/minibibs/edreform.html.

Rios v. Read, 480 F. Supp. 14 (E.D. N.Y. 1978).

Rivera, C., Stansfield, C., Scialdone, L., & Sharkey, M. (2000). *An analysis of state policies for the inclusion and accommodation of English language learners in state assessment programs during 1998–1999 (executive summary).* Arlington, VA: George Washington University Center for Equity and Excellence in Education.

Rosado, A. (1994). Promoting partnerships with minority parents: A revolution in today's school restructuring efforts. *Journal of Educational Issues of Language Minority Students, 14,* 241–254.

Rosenberg, M. (1996). Raising bilingual children. *The Internet TESL Journal, 2.* Retrieved August 1, 2000, from the World Wide Web: http://www .aitech.ac.jp/~iteslj/Articles/Rosenberg-Bilingual.html.

Sakash, K., & Rodriguez-Brown, F. V. (1995). Teamworks: Mainstream and bilingual ESL teacher collaboration. *NCBE Program Information Guide Series,* (No. 24). Retrieved July 31, 2000, from the World Wide Web: http://www.ncbe.gwu.edu/ncbepubs/pigs/pig24.htm.

Sandel, M. J. (1996). *Democracy's discontent: America in search of a public philosophy.* Cambridge, MA: Belknap Press of Harvard University Press.

Smith, H. (1999, June/July). So you are a language program administrator? *TESOL Matters.* Retrieved August 3, 2000, from the World Wide Web: http://www.tesol.org/isaffil/intsec/columns/199906-pa.html.

Smith, W. L. (1985). *The Office for Civil Rights Title VI language minority compliance procedures* [Memorandum]. Washington, DC: U.S. Department of Education, Office for Civil Rights. Retrieved August 1, 2000, from the World Wide Web: http://www.ed.gov/offices/OCR/ELL/december3 .html.

Snow, M., Met, M., & Genesee. F. (1989). A conceptual framework for the integration of language and content in second/foreign language instruction. *TESOL Quarterly, 23,* 201–217.

Stowe, P. (1993). *New teachers in the job market, 1991 update* (NCES Publication No. 93392). Washington, DC: Government Printing Office.

TESOL. (1975). *Guidelines for the certification and preparation of TESOL in the United States.* Washington, DC: TESOL.

TESOL. (1996). *Promising futures: ESL standards for pre-K–12 students* (TESOL Professional Papers 1). Alexandria, VA: Author.

TESOL. (1997). *ESL standards for pre-K–12 students.* Alexandria, VA: Author.

Thomas, W. P., & Collier, V. P. (1997). *School effectiveness and language minority students.* (NCBE Resource Collection Series, No. 9). Washington, DC: National Clearinghouse for Bilingual Education.

University of Illinois at Chicago (UIC) Center for Literacy. (2000). *Bilingual brochures for parents.* Chicago: University of Illinois at Chicago.

U.S. Department of Commerce. (1990). *Census of population and housing summary tape file 3C.* Washington, DC: Bureau of the Census, Data Users Services Division.

U.S. Department of Education. (1994, May 11). *National Education Goals.* Washington, DC: Author.

U.S. Department of Education. (1998, April). *Teachers leading the way: Voices from the National Teachers' Forum.* Symposium at the National Teachers' Forum, Washington, DC.

Verplaetse, L. S. (1998). How content teachers interact with English language learners. *TESOL Journal, 7*(5), 24–28.

Violand-Sánchez, E. (1991). Fostering home-school cooperation: Involving language minority families as partners in education. *NCBE Program Information Guide Series,* (No. 6). Washington, DC: National Clearinghouse for Bilingual Education.

Vocational Education Programs Guidelines for Eliminating Discrimination and Denial of Services on the Basis of Race, Color, National Origin, Sex and Handicap, 44 Fed. Reg. 17166, 17167 (1979). Retrieved August 9, 2000, from the World Wide Web: http://www.ed.gov/offices/OCR /vocre.html.

Wagoner, D. (1999, March). States' report on exemptions from student assessments. *Numbers and Needs, 9,* 2.

Wilde, J., & S. Sockey. (1995). *Education handbook.* Albuquerque, NM: Evaluation Assistance Center.

# Index

251

of teachers and administrators, 5–7, 7t, 97

Web resources on, 13

Department of Commerce

on high-incidence LEP communities, 8

on limited English proficiency, 2

on minority enrollment, 1–2

Department of Education, United States (USDE)

contact information for, 133, 200t

Eight National Education Goals of, 64–65, 117

equity centers funded by, 186

on ESL student enrollment, 2

publications for parents by, 135t

on teachers and communities, 134

Development, professional. *See* Training

Development Associates, Inc., 2

Developmental bilingual education, 45

Direct instruction, effectiveness of, 47

Discussion lists, electronic. *See* Electronic discussion lists

Distance learning, for teachers, 109

Distribution, of LEP students, 8–12, 9t, 11t

District of Columbia

enrollment in, 9t

identification criteria in, 142t

standards in, performance on, 65, 66t

teacher credentials required by, 96t

teacher education programs offered in, 110t

*Doe, Plyler v.*, 23, 36

Duration of language support. *See also* Time, daily allotment

age and, 175

litigation on, 21

program evaluation and, 171–172

Educators' Web sites, 198t

EEOA. *See* Equal Educational Opportunities Act

Eisterhold, J., 178

El-Dinary, P. B., 47, 89, 90

Electronic discussion lists, 196–197

*ESL Standards Implementation*, 91, 197

*NCBE Roundtable*, 189–190

*Neteach-L*, 196–197

*TESL-L*, 196

Elementary school, schedule for sheltered English in, 81t

Endorsements, teacher, 95–96

Enforcement, of federal guidelines and requirements, 35–36

Enforcement Policy of 1991, Office for Civil Rights, 24–26

English language informants, 102–103

English language learners, 4

English-only rules, 31–32

English as second language. *See* ESL

English for speakers of other languages (ESOL). *See* Pullout instruction

English variants, litigation on, 29

The English Zone Web site, 199t

Enright, D. S., 78

Enrollment

by ESL students

growth in, 2

projections for, 2

among minorities, 1–2, 7t

Equal Educational Opportunities Act (EEOA), 19, 20

compliance with, measurement of, 22–23

on equal participation, 35

on role of states, 27, 28

Equal educational opportunities policy. *See* *Lau* plan

Equal opportunity

Civil Rights Act on, 36–37, 77, 119

Equal Educational Opportunities Act on, 19, 20, 22–23, 27, 28, 35

Equity centers, regional education, 186–187

contact information for, 187

services provided by, 186–187

ERIC, 184

*ESL Magazine*, 196, 199t

ESL speakers, prevalence of, projections for, 2

*ESL Standards Implementation* electronic discussion list, 91, 197

*ESL Standards for Pre-K–12 Students* (TESOL), 72

ESOL (English for speakers of other languages). *See* Pullout instruction

Ethnic clubs, as resource, 191–192

Evaluation. *See* Assessment

Evaluation Assistance Center-Western Region, 165

Exit criteria

assessments in, 140

in *Lau* plan, 51

sample of, 226–227

legislative provisions in, lack of, 16
requirements/restrictions on education in, 70*t*
standards in, performance on, 66*t*
teacher credentials required by, 96*t*
teacher education programs offered in, 110*t*
Haynes, J., 116
Head Start programs, 124
Heartland Valley School Department, *Lau* plan by, 219–232
*Heavy Runner v. Bremner,* 27
*Helping Parents and Children Understand Each Other in Their New Life in the United States: Tacoma Story,* 132
High-incidence LEP communities, 8
*vs.* low-incidence LEP communities, 11–13
Hispanic students. *See also* Latino(s)
litigation on bilingual education for, 29–30
Home, bilingualism at
practices to support, 131*t*
rationale for, 128–129, 176–177
Home language surveys
as identification criteria, 140, 141
prevalence of, 144*t*
sample of, 229–231
Homerooms, recommendations on use of, 55*t*
Hopstock, P. J., 3*t*
Hughes, A., 157

IASA. *See* Improving America's Schools Act
Idaho
identification criteria in, 142*t*
requirements/restrictions on education in, 70*t*
standards in, performance on, 67*t*
teacher education programs offered in, 110*t*
*Idaho Migrant Council v. Board of Education,* 28
IDEA Language Proficiency Test (IPT), 144*t*, 147*t*
IDEA Oral Language Program, prevalence of, 144*t*
Identification of LEP students
criteria for, 140–141, 142*t*–143*t*, 144*t*
immigration status in, 23
in *Lau* plans, 51
litigation on, 26–27

methods for, 5, 6*t*, 141–150, 146*t*–149*t*
prevalence of, 6*t*, 144*t*–145*t*
with tests, 140, 144*t*, 145*t*
Igoa, C., 117
Illinois
identification criteria in, 142*t*
requirements/restrictions on education in, 70*t*
standards in, performance on, 66*t*
teacher credentials required by, 96*t*
teacher education programs offered in, 110*t*
*Illinois State Board of Education, Gomez v.,* 27
Immersion
structured, 42*t*, 43, 44*f*
*vs.* submersion, 47
Immigrant(s)
circumstances of arrival, and ESL needs, 176
illegal, educational access for, 23, 36
parental involvement among, 119
*Immigrant Students: Their Legal Right of Access to Public Schools (A Guide for Advocates and Educators),* 38
Immigration laws, resources for information on, 38
Immigration and Naturalization Service (INS), contact information for, 38, 39
Implementation, program, 41–61
approaches to, 42–47, 42*t*, 44*f*
recommendations for, 46–47
research on, 45
constraints on, potential, 53–59
evaluation of, 239
*Lau* plan design in, 48–53
Improving America's Schools Act (IASA)
definition of LEP in, 3–4
in OCR Enforcement Policy, 25
Title I program, 32–33
Incidence of LEP student enrollment, by urbanicity, 8–12, 11*t*
Indiana
identification criteria in, 142*t*
requirements/restrictions on education in, 70*t*
standards in, performance on, 66*t*
teacher credentials required by, 96*t*
teacher education programs offered in, 110*t*
Informants, English language, 102–103

# Also Available From TESOL

*New Ways in Teaching Young Children*
Linda Schinke-Llano and Rebecca Rauff, Editors

*New Ways in Using Authentic Materials in the Classroom*
Ruth E. Larimer and Leigh Schleicher, Editors

*New Ways in Using Communicative Games in Language Teaching*
Nikhat Shameem and Makhan Tickoo, Editors

*New Ways of Classroom Assessment*
James Dean Brown, Editor

*Reading and Writing in More Than One Language: Lessons for Teachers*
Elizabeth Franklin, Editor

*Teacher Education*
Karen E. Johnson, Editor

*Teaching in Action: Case Studies From Second Language Classrooms*
Jack C. Richards, Editor

*Training Others to Use the ESL Standards:*
*A Professional Developmental Manual*
Deborah J. Short, Emily L. Gómez, Nancy Cloud, Anne Katz,
Margo Gottlieb, and Margaret Malone

For more information, contact
Teachers of English to Speakers of Other Languages, Inc.
700 South Washington Street, Suite 200
Alexandria, Virginia 22314 USA
Tel 703-836-0774 • Fax 703-836-6447 • publications@tesol.org •
http://www.tesol.org/